PHOTOGRAPHY:
BUYING · CHOOSING · USING

PHOTOGRAPHY: BUYING · CHOOSING · USING

Marc Levey, Margaret Irish & Samuel Kazdan

Amphoto
American Photographic Book Publishing Co., Inc.
New York, New York

Dedication

This book is dedicated to the students of Marc Levey whose questions and concerns about the tools of photography reinforce the authors' belief that this book was indeed necessary.

Published in New York, New York, by American Photographic Book Publishing Co., Inc.

Library of Congress Cataloging in Publication Data

Levey, Marc B
Photography, buying, choosing, using.

Includes index.
1. Photography—Apparatus and supplies. I. Irish, Margaret, joint author. II. Kazdan, Samuel, joint author. III. Title.
TR196.L48 771 79—483

ISBN: 0-8174-2459-8 (hardbound)
ISBN: 0-8174-2133-5 (softbound)

Manufactured in the United States of America

Acknowledgments

In writing a book dealing with photographic equipment, you quickly realize the major role experience plays in helping you through the maze of auto-thyristors, multicoated lenses, and the electronic wizardry that exemplifies modern photography. Experience also dictates that special acknowledgments should and must be paid to those in the industry and profession who have given us help in preparing this book. We are grateful to the following companies for their assistance: Vivitar, Inc., Santa Monica, California; Spiratone, Inc., Flushing, New York; EPOI (Ehrenreich Photo-Optical Industries, Inc.), Garden City, New York; Canon U.S.A., Inc., Lake Success, New York; Berkey Marketing Companies, Woodside, New York; the Bell & Howell-Mamiya Company, Chicago, Illinois; the Polaroid Corporation, Cambridge, Massachusetts; the Minolta Corporation, Ramsey, New Jersey; and the Eastman Kodak Company, Rochester, New York. Special thanks go to Celestron International, Torrance, California; Ultimate Experience, Santa Barbara, California; Braun North America, Cambridge, Massachusetts; Edmund Scientific Company, Barrington, New Jersey; and Yashica, Inc., Woodside, New York.

Beyond these companies there are literally scores of individuals who deserve mention. Among those who profoundly affected the creation of this work, we would like to thank Don Myrus of EPOI for his encouragement, Trigvie Duryea, whose backpacks are a photographer's dream come true, Herb Taylor of Amphoto, who has cooperated to the fullest, and finally the students of Marc Levey, past and present, who in a very substantial way made this book possible.

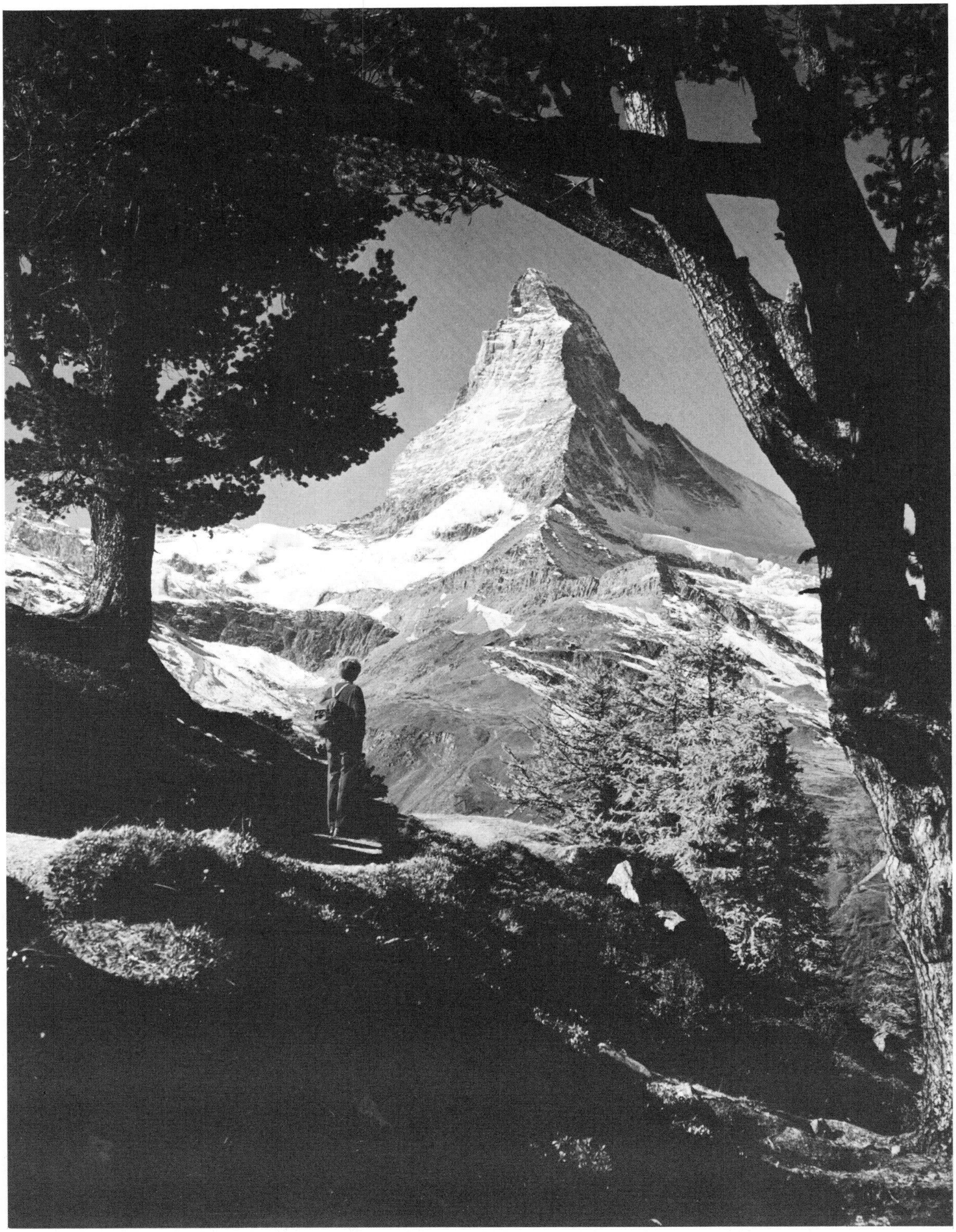

Photo by L. P. Greenhill, F.R.P.S.

Contents

Introduction

Today's photoequipment market could give any prospective buyer a thrashing migraine by sheer volume, if not only by variety. Look what's out there. Everywhere the photographer turns one manufacturer after another is touting his latest photographic achievement, whether it be film, cameras, lenses, or other accessories: "The electronic system camera that's changing the course of photography . . ." "The most versatile photographic flash system ever created . . ."

Who should you believe? How do you work your way through this ever-increasing jumble of hype to pick out the photographic equipment that suits your needs and, just as important, your pocketbook? These are the basic questions we pondered as we began to write this book.

Our orientation favors the consumer. However, this doesn't mean that we intend to portray the photo product manufacturers as the "bad guys" of the industry. They have every right to regain their research costs and to make a profit, too. However, you, the consumer, *do* have rights. Such rights start with educating yourself to the language of the photographic marketplace; in short, learning how to read between the lines and ask questions.

We have come a long way during the last year and a half in learning to practice what we are now preaching. Since the outset of this project, Marc, as the professional photographer, teacher, and general entrepreneur of the trio, has literally tried almost every major photographic device on the market today. His experience in attempting to answer his students' questions about photoequipment motivated the writing of this book. Sam, the amateur photo buff who has had an interest in photography for a number of years, has made the leap from his trusted rangefinder to a fine SLR system. Meg, with her outside interest in photography, finally knows where to begin her search for the right equipment. The fact that we as writers brought these three different perspectives of photography into this venture is not entirely coincidental. The point we are making is that all three of us often feel that inner urge to run out and buy a new piece of equipment, such as a Nikon FM (naturally, with a motor drive). But there are some basic steps we take that direct our buying activities within the photographic market *before* we take the plunge. They can be summarized as follows:

Be honest with yourself. Do you really need a sophisticated $700 camera with 1/2000 sec. shutter speed simply to snap Uncle Henry pulling in his prize-winning carp? If the answer is "Yes," then go ahead and buy it—but first read Chapter IV, "Photoequipment Buying." If after careful thought you find that you're not as interested as you first thought you were, don't be afraid to start off with a simpler piece of equipment, such as a meterless rangefinder or, if you feel a little more venturesome, a used SLR sans meter. There's no better way to learn the basics of composition and lighting than with a tool you must program yourself. This brings us to the next point.

Learn the potentialities and the limitations of your equipment. Asking yourself questions like, "What does my wide-angle lens do pictorially?" or, "Should I use black-and-white film instead of Kodachrome 25?" is essential in mastering the complexities of today's modern photographic systems. The unfortunate truth is that many photographers who invest hundreds and even thousands of dollars in equipment far too often never learn to use it to their best creative advantage. To quote ourselves at a later point in the book, in the final analysis *we* are the chief limiting factors in our creative quest for the ultimate photograph.

There are always trade-offs in photography. The longer your lens, the more likely it is to produce camera shake. The faster your film speed, the grainier your enlargements are likely to be. Gaining experience in shooting technique and in darkroom work will teach you some ways of compensating for such trade-offs; for instance, using a tripod with long lenses to counteract the camera shake or using a grainy film on purpose to produce a dramatic effect. However, nothing in photography is ever, if you'll pardon the expression, black and white. There will always be compromises in producing esthetically appealing photographic statements.

Try not to burden yourself with too many accessories. You will no doubt find that certain accessories, such as tripod and flash unit, are almost indispensable. With the tremendous variety in filters, carrying bags, and so forth, however, it is far too easy to find yourself lugging around 30 or 40 pounds of equipment that is euphemistically referred to as being "portable." The wise photographer does not weigh himself down with every instrument he owns each time he goes out to shoot. Instead, if he has a choice in equipment he thinks ahead to the type of shooting he wants to do that day or evening, whether it is macro work, photographing wildlife from a blind, or doing still lifes in a studio. Learn to travel light. In doing so you'll come to depend upon the spontaneity of your own creative senses. If you come to the point where you are totally dependent upon a soft lens to bring a sense of creativity to your photographs, in our opinion you are in trouble. Before you reach for that diffusion filter next time, ask yourself this question: Could this picture stand on its own *without* that filter?

Be assertive in finding information about a potential buy. Keep in mind that, just because someone claims that he is an expert in photography, he doesn't automatically have all the answers. Photography is an art, and as such is open to different interpretations. Read through some of the letters in Petersen's *PhotoGraphic, Modern Photography,* or *Popular Photography* magazines and you'll see how much agreement there is on performing a certain technique. Don't take one person's word as gospel. Further, do not believe everything you read. Once you are done reading the advertisement or test report, put it down for a while and return to it later, when you can look at it more objectively. Look for weak points in the arguments (surely there are some), so that you can balance your appraisal of the item. Talk to people who own the type of equipment you are interested in. See if you can handle the lens or camera, or even better, take some shots with it to get the feel of your potential tool. You may learn that people who are advising you, like the local dealer and your friends, are in very close agreement about the attributes of that lens. Their opinions may also be quite different, which calls for you to dig out a little more information before you are satisfied with your purchase. Bear in mind that there is little practical difference in performance between similarly priced equipment of major manufacturers, despite what advertising claims would have us believe.

In the following pages you are going to be exposed to information on: electronic camera systems, fisheye, macro, and zoom lenses; tripods, filters, and polarizers; electronic flash; the vast array of film types; and buying tips. It will be up to you to take advantage of this information. Ultimately, you are the one who will make the purchase, and no one will deny that it is a lonely, exasperating, exciting experience. Through this verbiage (not too excessive, we hope) we are saying: Choose wisely, and you should be satisfied with your new acquisition for many years to come.

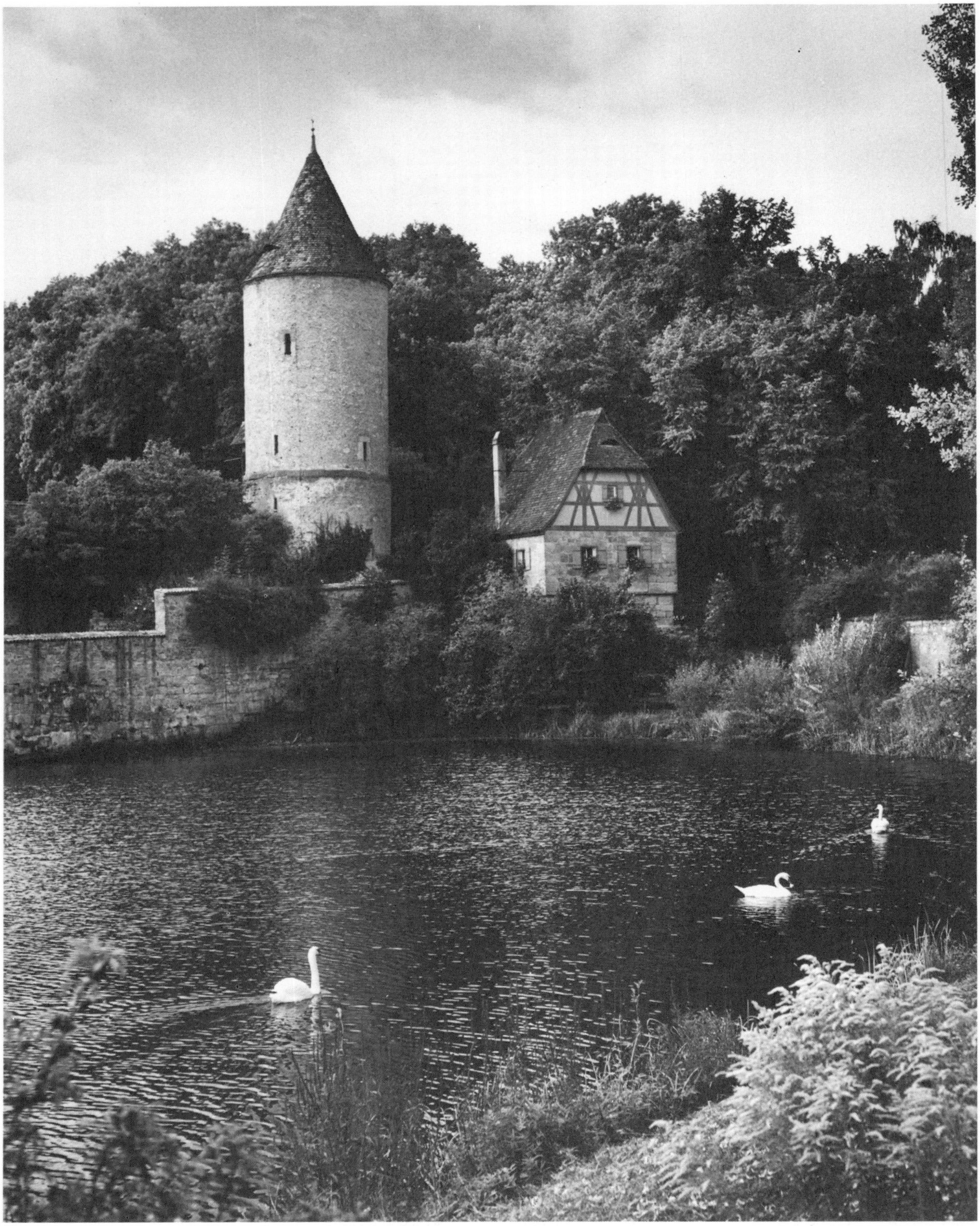

Photo by L. P. Greenhill, F.R.P.S.

I

Implements of the Craft

Someone, somewhere, once said that the best camera in the world is no better than the photographer using it. What this voice of photographic wisdom meant to imply is that it is the photographer that makes the picture—not the machine. But a full understanding of the proper use of your equipment is requisite to the creation of an enduring image on film. Just as a painter must learn to manipulate canvas, brushes, and pigment, so too must a photographer realize the *potentialities* and the *limitations* of his tools.

The sad truth is that few of us who own precision photographic equipment ever truly understand that equipment's potential. So in the final analysis *we* are the chief limiting factors in our creative quest. Our goal in this section, then, is to provide you with information gained from our own experiences (including our mistakes) in the selection of cameras, lenses, filters, and film so that you will be able to make proper equipment choices. In short, we'd like to prevent your equipment from becoming a burden.

CAMERAS

Before opening a discussion of different camera types, it would help if we quickly consider just how various classes of cameras get their names. Film size and, to a large extent, camera nomenclature come either from the width of the film or from the diagonal length of a single frame (the area of the actual image falling on the film through any lens on that camera). Thus, a 35 mm camera uses film measuring approximately 35 mm in width.

What photographic gear you buy and use largely depends on your picture needs. If you want a camera to snap pictures of the kids playing hopscotch to send Aunt Emma, a sophisticated 35 mm *single-lens reflex* (*SLR*) might become a financial burden where a less complex, cheaper camera would prove to be more satisfactory. If, on the other hand, you are pursuing photography as more than a hobby and are interested in nature panoramas or large display prints, a pocket instant-load camera would be next to useless.

Form follows function. Determine your purpose first and *then* you can make an equipment decision to suit your needs.

Instant-Loading and Pocket Cartridge-Film Cameras

By far the most popular cameras today in terms of sales are the small, pocket-sized

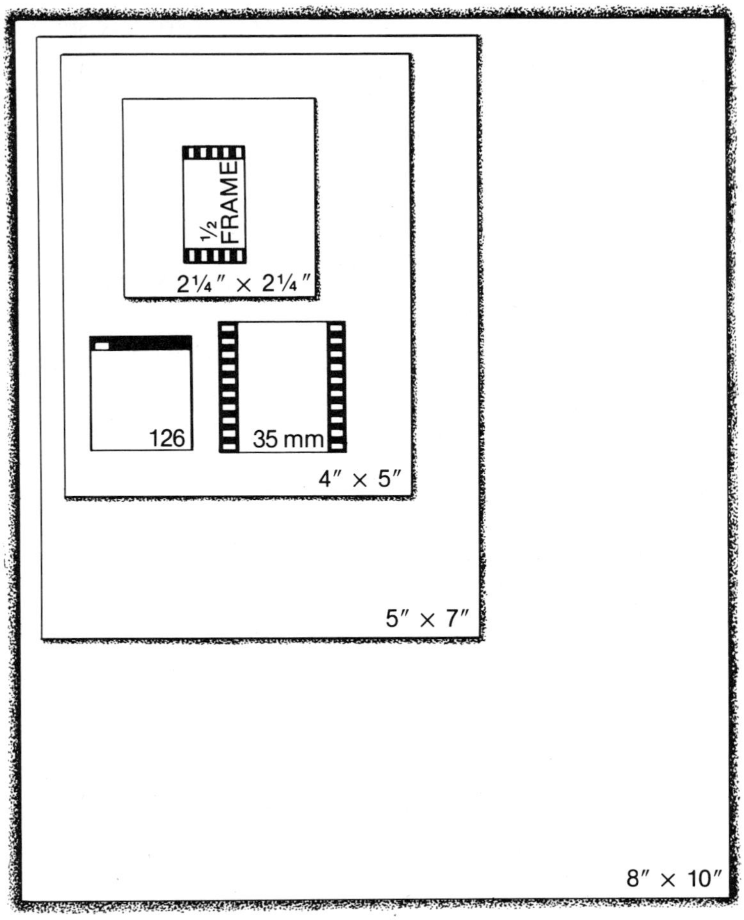

(Left) Film size chart. Note especially the difference in film areas of 110, 35 mm, and 2¼″ × 2¼″ films. (Below) The model for this typical camera schematic is the Leica R-3 Electronic. Photo courtesy E. Leitz.

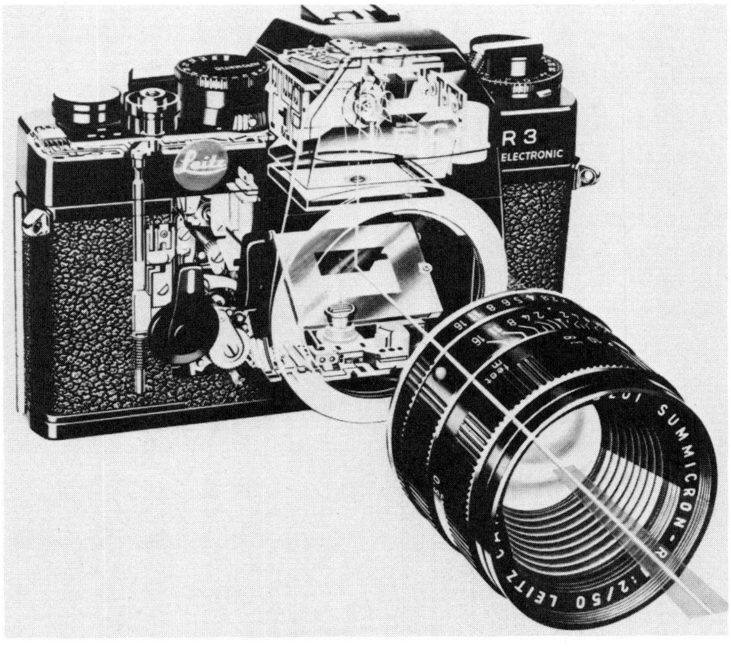

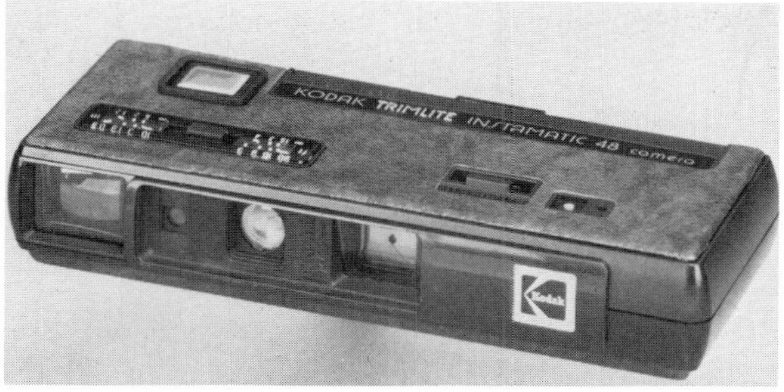

(Above) One of Kodak's Instamatic® line, this is the top of the line Kodak Trimline Instamatic® 48. Photo courtesy Eastman Kodak Co. (Right) This Canon 110 ED is a professional quality 110 pocket camera. Photo courtesy Canon U.S.A.

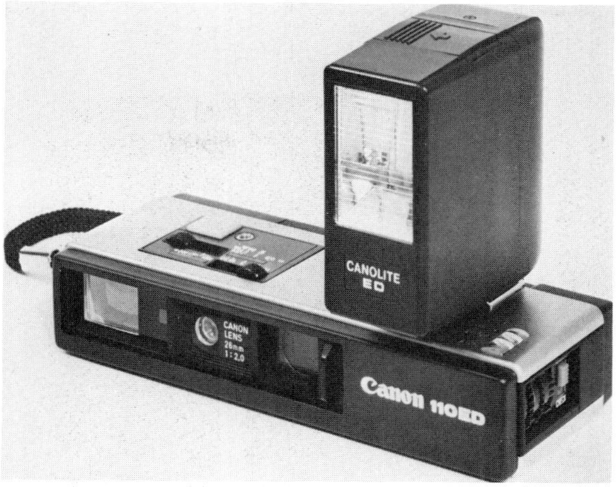

cameras that use film packaged for drop-in loading. They come in various shapes, degrees of sophistication, and prices. There are three basic small cameras: the *instant-loaders* that use 126 film (such as Kodak's Instamatic); the *pocket* models, using size 110 film; and the *subminiature* cameras, which use 16 mm film. Although the 110 format is pretty much replacing its 126-sized predecessor, 126 cameras are still available. The 110 yields a negative half the size or less of a 35 mm camera, thus limiting the size of an enlargement to about 20 × 25 cm (8 × 10 in.) for the most sophisticated of this type and about 13 × 18 cm (5 × 7 in.) for the simpler ones.

These cameras measure 10–13 cm (4–5 in.) in length, 5 cm (2 in.) in depth, and about 2.5 cm (1 in.) in thickness and weigh 198–340 g (7–12 oz). Some use the newly developed acrylic lens elements, while others have all-glass lenses.

All pocket instant-loaders currently available, excepting the latest from Fuji and from Minolta, carry fixed-focal-length lenses. But from information received, we will possibly be seeing increasing numbers of more sophisticated designs, with zooms and large-aperture lenses, on the market in the future. Only the limitations of the film size prevent the best of these cameras from seriously challenging larger-format cameras for dominance in the devoted amateur market and even in the professional market. In fact, many advanced amateurs and pros use pocket-sized cartridge-load back-up cameras because of their automatic metering, small size, and light weight. It seems logical to suppose that the pocket-110 will make great strides in the next five to ten years to approach, if not surpass, the prestige 35 mm SLR cameras now available.

The advantages of the 126 and 110 instant-load cameras are:

1. small size
2. light weight
3. great price range
4. drop-in cartridge for film loading
5. automatic function.

The disadvantages of the instant-loading cameras are:

1. limited film selection
2. limited enlargement potential, to 13 × 18 cm (5 × 7 in.) or 20 × 25 cm (8 × 10 in.) prints from the best of them
3. relatively few quality 110 cameras available

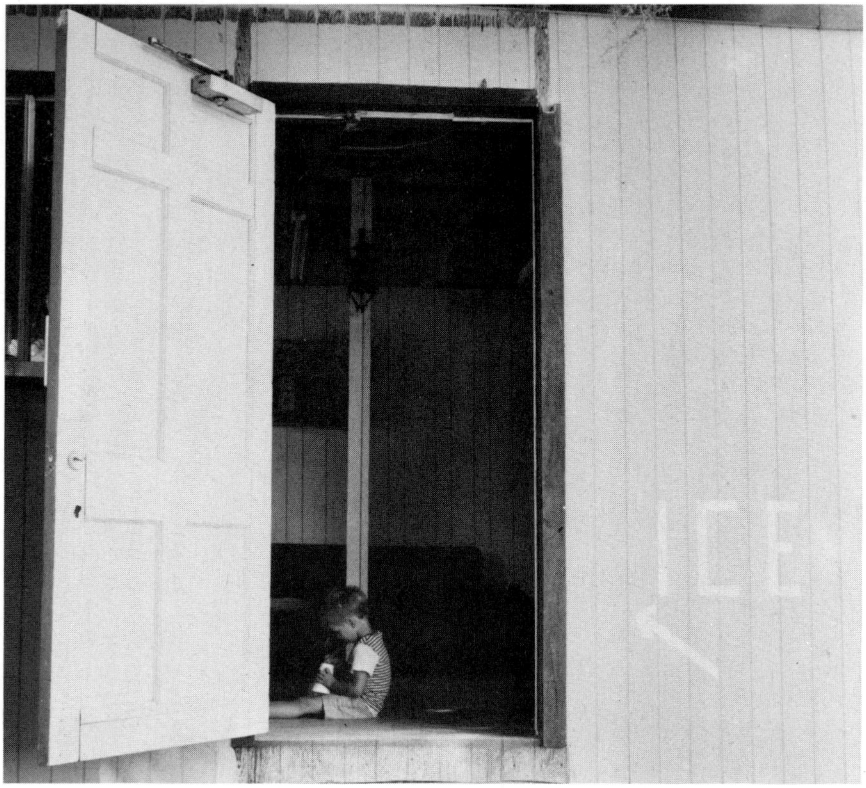

This photograph is a typical example of the quality possible with a good 110 pocket camera. Photo by James Forkner.

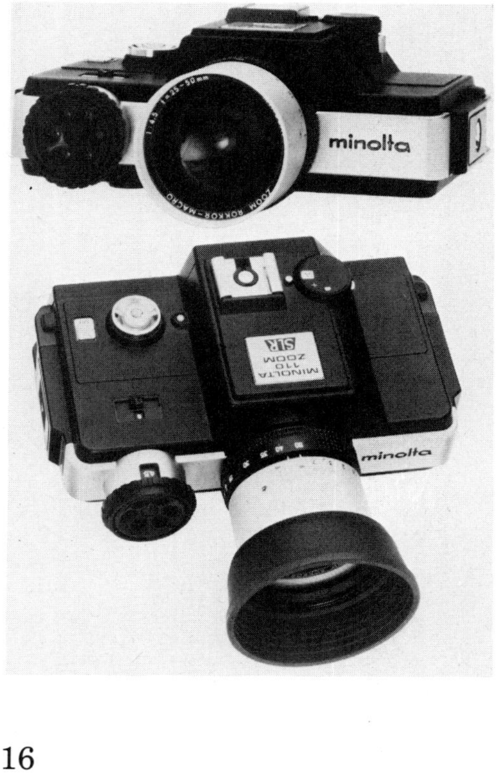

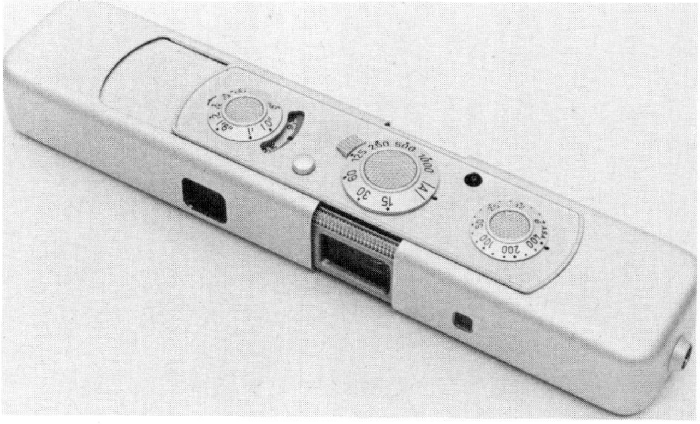

(Left) The Minolta 110 Zoom SLR is one of the most advanced and expensive of 110 pocket cameras. Photo courtesy Minolta, U.S.A. (Above) The Minox Subminiature camera produces a 16 mm negative—about ¼ the area of 35 mm film. Photo courtesy E. Leitz.

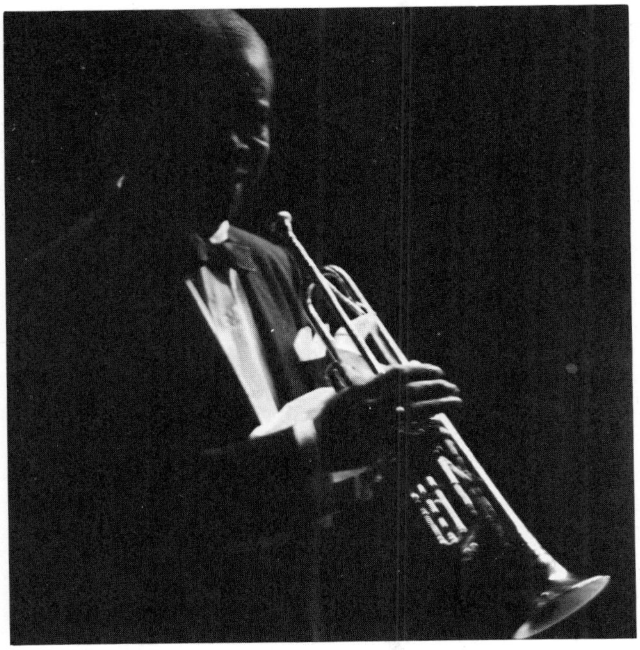

Young Louis Armstrong, as captured with a subminiature camera. Photo by John P. Mertz.

4. little control possible by photographer, since most are fully automatic
5. almost no lens interchangeability
6. limited lens apertures—only a few 110's are as fast as *f*/2.8, and only a few models sport *f*/2 or faster lenses
7. general lack of rangefinders—most models use "guesstimate" focusing.

There are 30 or more "instant" brands available at present. Some of the better-known are made by Eastman Kodak, Canon, Minolta, Fuji, Ricoh, Hanimex, Copal, and Rollei. Of these, the Canon 110ED, Kodak Trimline Pocket Instamatic 48, Minolta SR110, and Rollei A110 are the most advanced and possess the greatest flexibility. Just starting to reach the consumer as of this writing is a Minolta-designed SLR 110 boasting a built-in zoom lens. This camera is likely to point the way to future adaptations in the field, and other designs will no doubt appear with zooms and with interchangeable lenses. At press time Pentax introduced a 110 SLR with interchangeable lenses and motor drive.

Subminiatures

These so-called "spy cameras" produce a small negative, 16 mm (a bit over a half-inch) in width. Their usefulness is limited for most of us because of the very small film format and the limited availability and variety of film. Generally, the greatest enlargement you could hope for would be a 13 × 18 cm (5 × 7 in.). Only Minox and Minolta are now making 16 mm cameras.

The 35 mm-Format Camera

Two major types of 35 mm cameras are now available, the *35 mm rangefinder or viewfinder* and the *35 mm single-lens reflex (SLR)*. The difference between the two is in their focusing mechanisms. The rangefinder camera requires viewing through two windows, as it employs two prisms to focus the subject (find the range, or distance). The SLR has

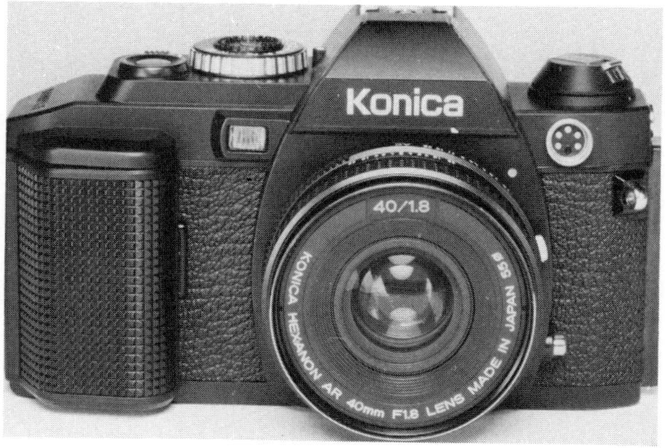

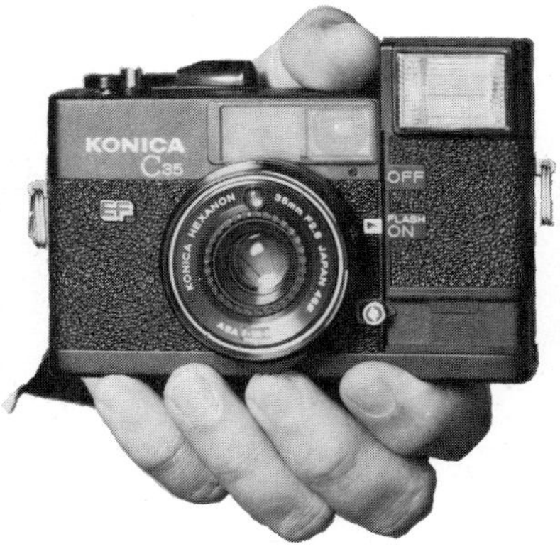

(Left) A typical compact 35 mm SLR, the Konica Autoreflex TC. (Right) The Konica C35EF is an example of the typical 35 mm rangefinder SLR. Note the small, built-in electronic flash. Photos courtesy Konica Camera Co.

only a single finder for viewing, and you actually view through the lens to see what will appear on the film.

Manufacturers of the moderate-priced 35 mm rangefinder and viewfinder cameras aim at the person who wants more operating flexibility (greater film choice, not totally automatic function) and a larger film format than the 110 user asks for. In other words, these cameras are a step up from the point-and-shoot pocket camera.

There are between 10 and 20 models currently available in this class. Most of them are about 13 cm (5 in.) long, 6.5 cm (2½ in.) high, and 7.5 cm (3 in.) deep. Most have built-in light meters, automatic (programed) light measurement, semiwide-angle lenses in the 35–45 mm range, and shutters calibrated from 1 second to 1/500 sec. They weigh anywhere between 397 g and 680g (14 oz and 1½ lb).

You will find that most of these are capable picture takers that provide reliable service. They are not designed to handle as broad a variety of applications as the 35 mm SLRs, however.

The advantages of 35 mm rangefinder cameras are:

1. relatively small size and light weight
2. standard 35 mm film format, which allows user a wide variety of film choices
3. relatively inexpensive ($79.95 to $139.95, discounted)
4. usually excellent lenses
5. more flexibility than with smaller film formats
6. greater enlargement possibilities from negatives and slides than

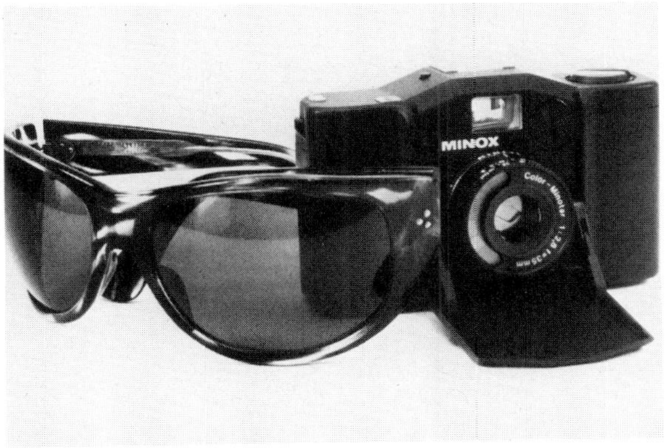

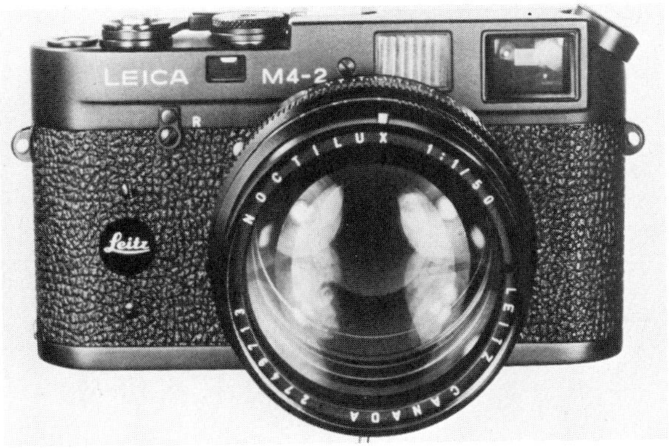

The Minox 35 BL is the smallest 35 mm rangefinder made. (Right) The Leica M4-2 precision rangefinder camera offers prestige and excellent quality, but at a considerable price. Photos courtesy E. Leitz.

those of smaller film formats—up to 28 × 36 cm (11 × 14 in.) at least.

The disadvantages of 35 mm rangefinders of low-to-middle cost are:

1. most do not have interchangeable lenses
2. construction quality is somewhat less than that of top-grade 35 mm SLRs, in most cases
3. close-focusing capability is limited—usually no closer than 1 m (about 3 ft).

Precision Rangefinder Cameras. Only one manufacturer, Leitz, continues to produce professional-quality 35 mm rangefinder cameras, the latest of which is the M4-2. Still available are the Leicas M4 and M5, and the CL, all of which have fully interchangeable lens systems. The M4-2 is a bit lighter and smaller than most current 35 mm SLRs, while the CL, a joint venture with Minolta, is a compact, lightweight (492 g [17 oz]) camera. All are unquestionably outstanding picture takers, but unfortunately they are out of most photographers' price range—particularly the M series, which starts at $900.

Top-quality rangefinder cameras have the advantages:

1. quiet, low-vibration operation (no moving mirror)
2. exceedingly fine construction and finish
3. bright viewfinder (compared to 35 mm SLRs)
4. extensive accessory line (especially the M series)

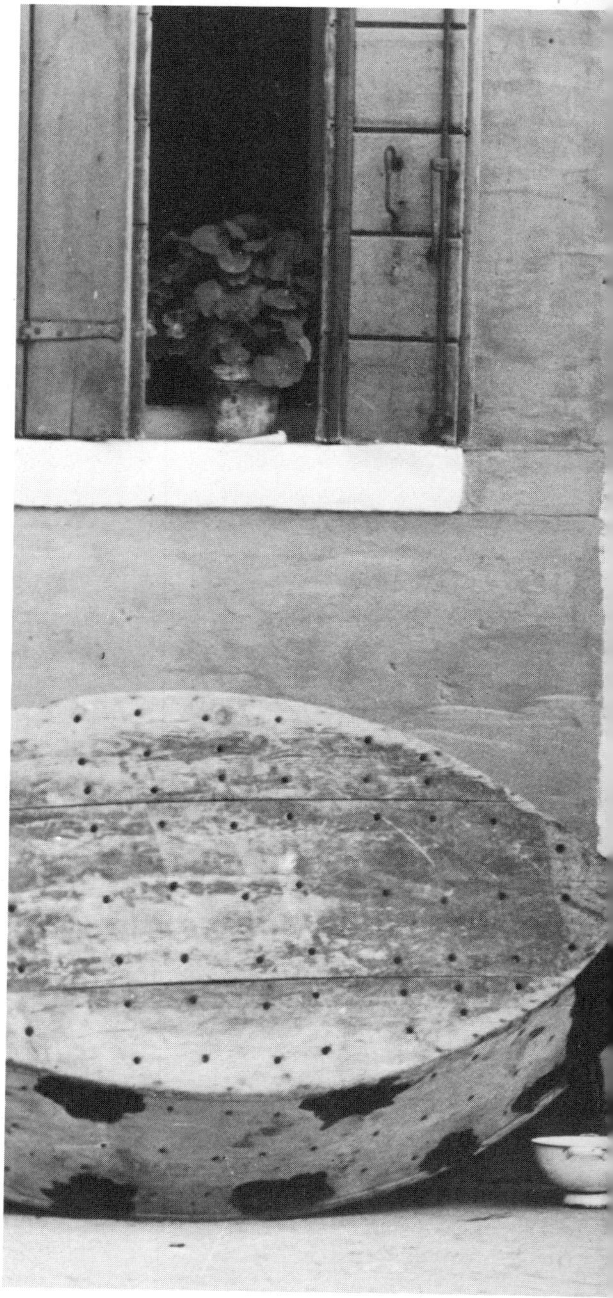

This photograph demonstrates the quality that can be achieved with a precision rangefinder camera. Photo by Bill Coleman.

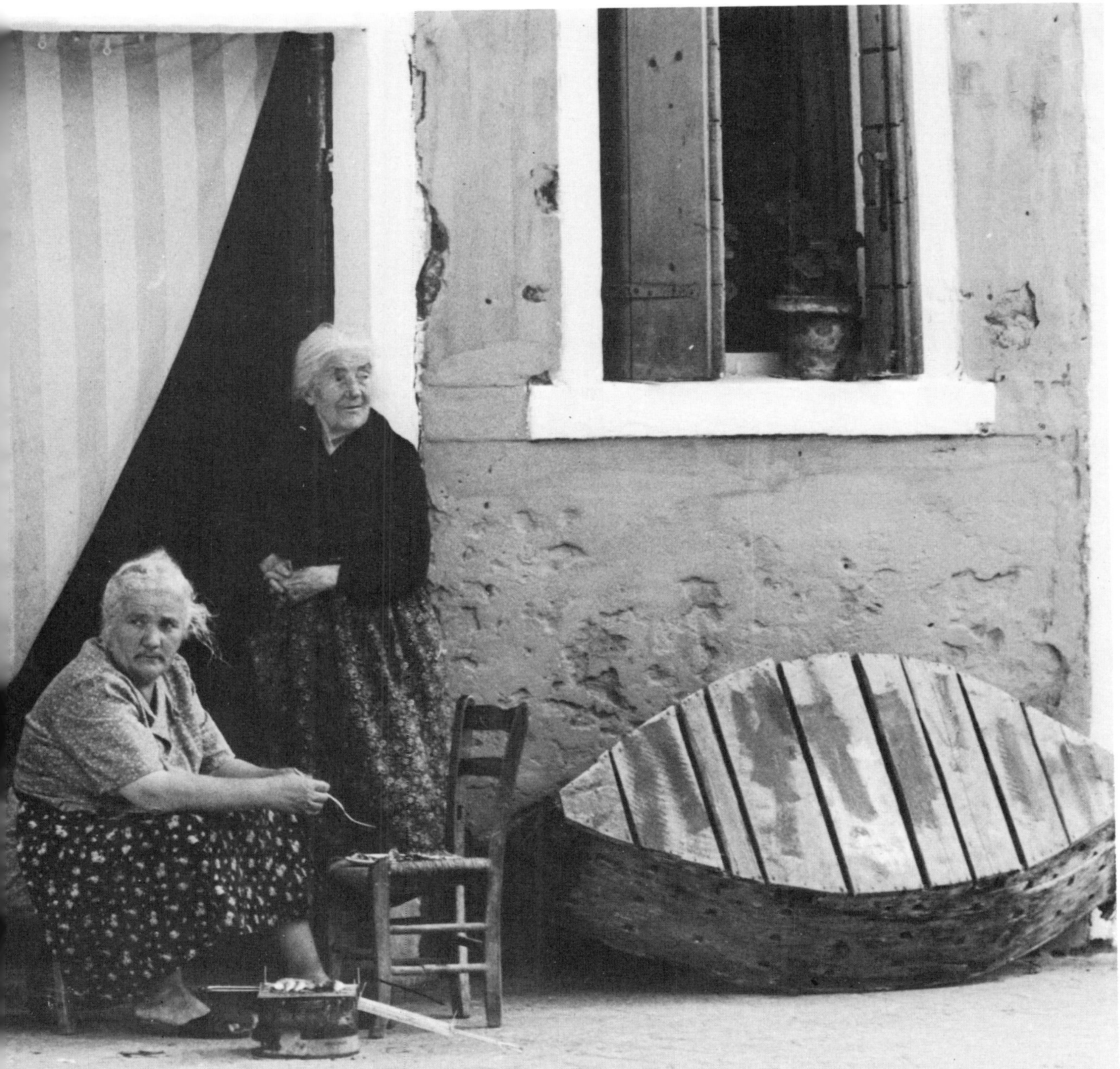

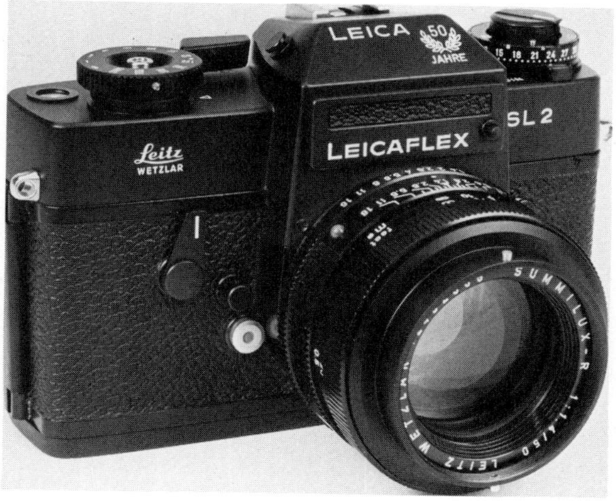

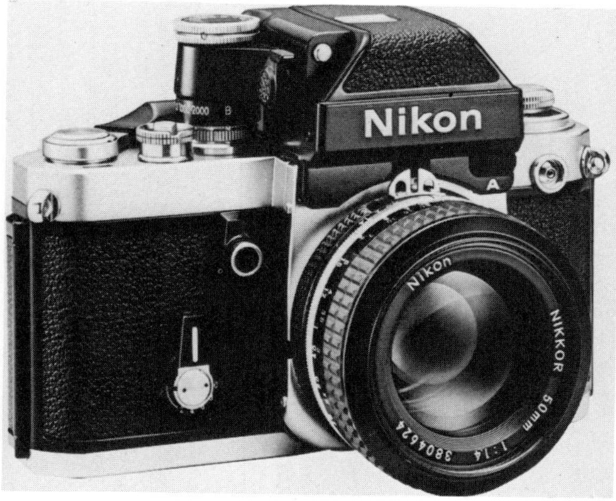

(Left) The Leicaflex SL-2—one of the most expensive of the 35 mm SLRs. Photo courtest E. Leitz. (Right) The Nikon F2AS is the successor to the Nikon F, the camera responsible for the great popularity of the 35 mm SLRs. Photo courtest EPOI, Inc.

5. excellent financial investment (some Leicas will be worth more ten years from now than their original list price).

Disadvantages of the Leica M series are:

1. these models are among the, if not *the,* most expensive rangefinder cameras to purchase
2. weight and size of M4 and M5 approach that of 35 mm SLRs
3. lens choice is limited to Leica-manufactured lenses.

The 35 mm SLR. This camera type began to eclipse other designs about 20 years ago. By virtue of its direct viewing through the lens and its lens interchangeability, it is the most versatile and popular of all currently available quality cameras.

The body of a typical 35 mm SLR is approximately 15 cm (6 in.) long, 9.5 cm (3¾ in.) high, and 10 cm (4 in.) deep and weighs in the neighborhood of 900–1350 g (2–2½ lb.) with the "standard" 50 mm or 55 mm lens mounted in place. Because these cameras are highly acceptable to both amateurs and professionals, manufacturers have gone out of their way to provide every conceivable accessory and gadget for the potential buyer. A representative camera might accept as many as 50 different lenses from the same manufacturer alone. Literally hundreds of additional accessories are also on the market, ranging from $2 rubber eye cups to

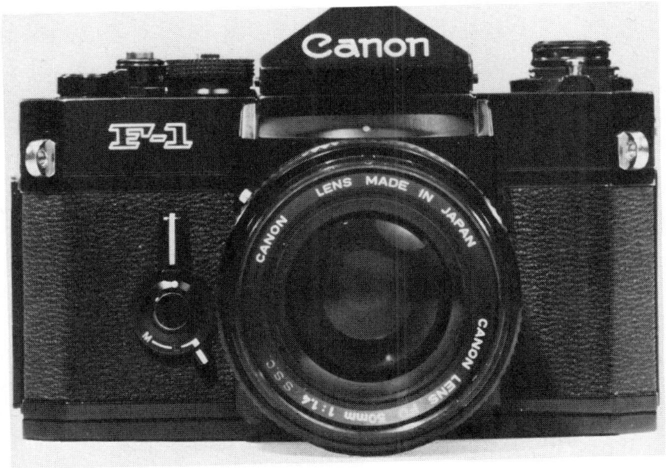

The Canon F-1n is the top line competitor of the Nikon F2AS. Photo courtesy Canon, U.S.A.

$2,000 electronic remote-control units.

This mind-boggling array of lenses and accessories is at best a mixed blessing; at its worst it becomes a gadget-trap for the unwary buyer. In many ways this "burden of riches" defeats the original design purposes of the 35 mm SLR, which were portability, flexibility, and ease of operation. Anyone who has carried an SLR, two or three lenses, and other assorted accessories for several hours will deny the "portability" of his camera. The added weight of a few accessories and lenses may not seem like much; but try hanging that dead weight on your shoulder for a couple of hours and you'll see what we mean.

What seems to have happened is that as designers packed more and more features into the camera, size and weight naturally escalated, too. So did the user's confusion. Consumers seem to succumb to the ad men's visions of all photographers producing pictures of Eugene Smith quality. But it is easy to accumulate two camera bodies, five lenses, one or two flash units, eight or nine filters, alternative viewing screens, cases for everything, a five-pound tripod (marginally portable) and a 20-pound studio tripod (hardly portable)—until we have to consult U-Haul before we can go out in the field. This may sound extreme, but we do want to point out that too much of a good thing can become a genuine encumbrance.

In fact, we're no longer dealing with the question of *portability*. *Flexibility* is what is most hampered, in our view, by the vast array of available what-nots. We end up spending more time changing lenses and accessories than we do shooting. As a consequence, both spontaneity and careful, previsualized picture taking suffer. Many SLR owners will agree that at times we come to depend more on our equipment than on our own senses. Thus, creativity and photography as an art seem

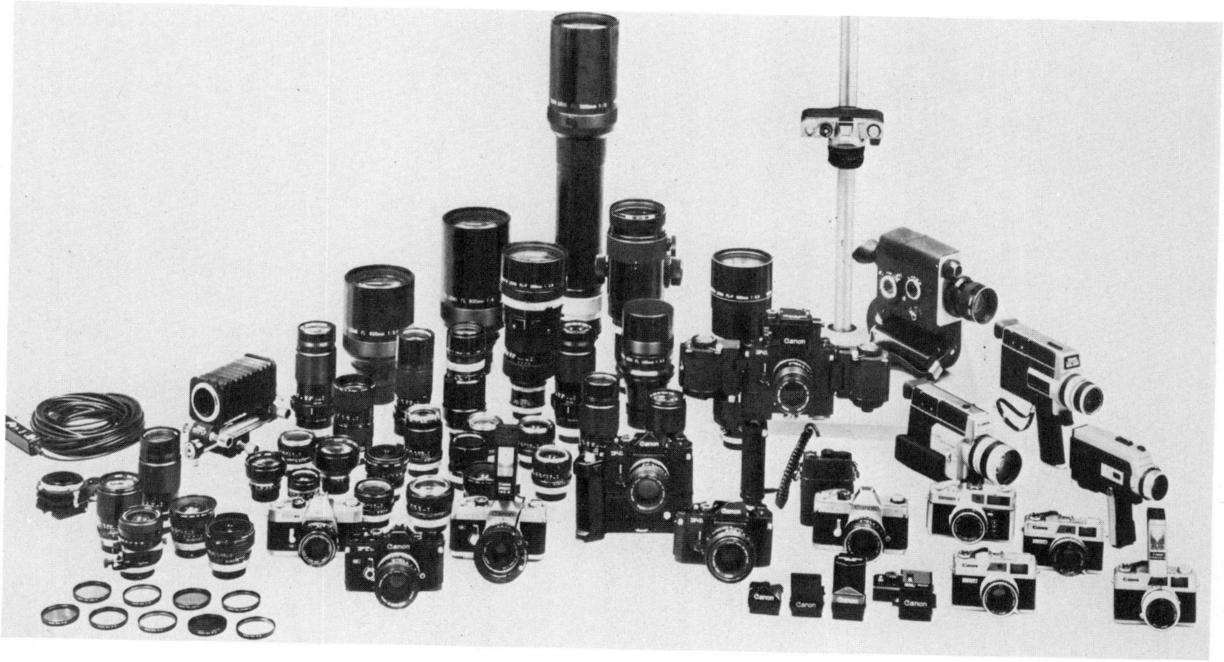

The variety offered by a complete SLR system does not streamline the selection process. Photo courtesy Canon, U.S.A.

bound to flounder a bit.

Enough said about our gadget bias. For more information on buying techniques, read the chapter entitled, "Photoequipment Buying." Let's turn now to a discussion of what the 35 mm SLR is and what it is not.

Historically the SLRs trace back to the turn of the century. In the early 1930's, the then-standard 3¼ × 4¼-inch format of single-lens reflex cameras gave way to smaller types, first the 2¼ × 2¼-inch format and then, in the quest for a camera that retained the advantages inherent in the SLR, the "miniature eye-level reflex." This first miniature was little more than a scaled-down version of the earlier, larger reflexes, with no additions or innovations. From the earliest German-designed Exakta, technology has progressed to a point today where 35 mm SLRs dominate the competitive camera market.

Basically, there are four classes of 35 mm SLRs. Being victims of advertising ourselves, and hopelessly enamored of gadgets, we have as a group used virtually every brand of 35 mm camera on the market. We offer the following analysis and guide to the 35 mm SLR in the hope that you will profit from our purchasing errors and our successes.

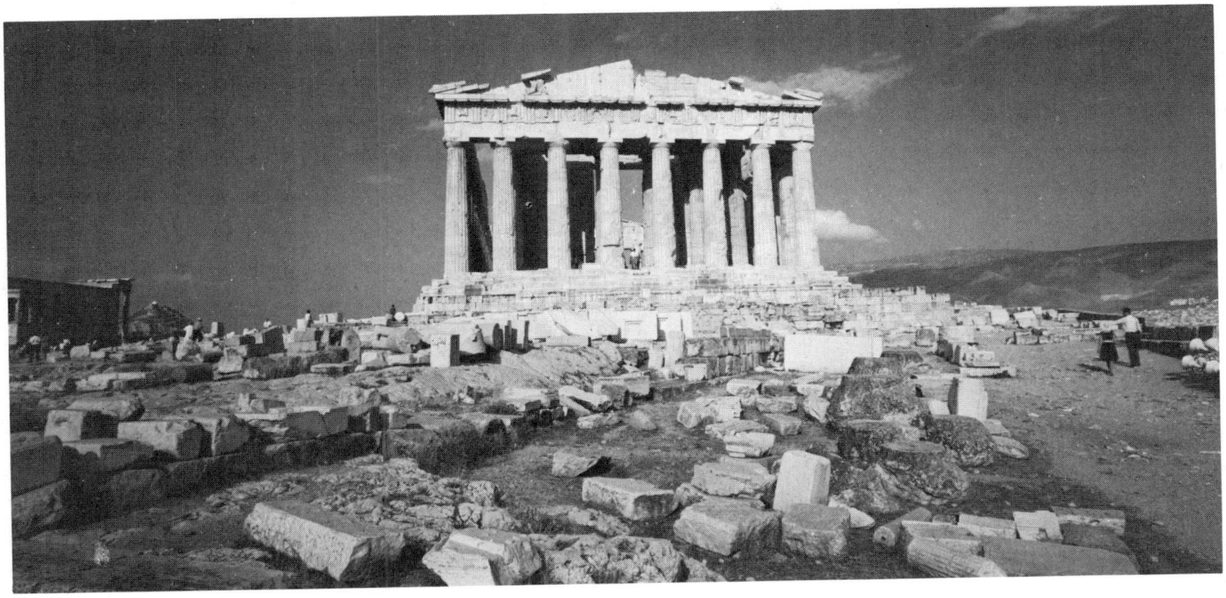

The photograph above, taken with a 35 mm SLR, demonstrates the versatility of a camera system like the Nikon F. Photo by Bill Coleman. The photo below was taken with a Canon Pellix QL with a 200 mm lens. Photo by Bob Baumbach.

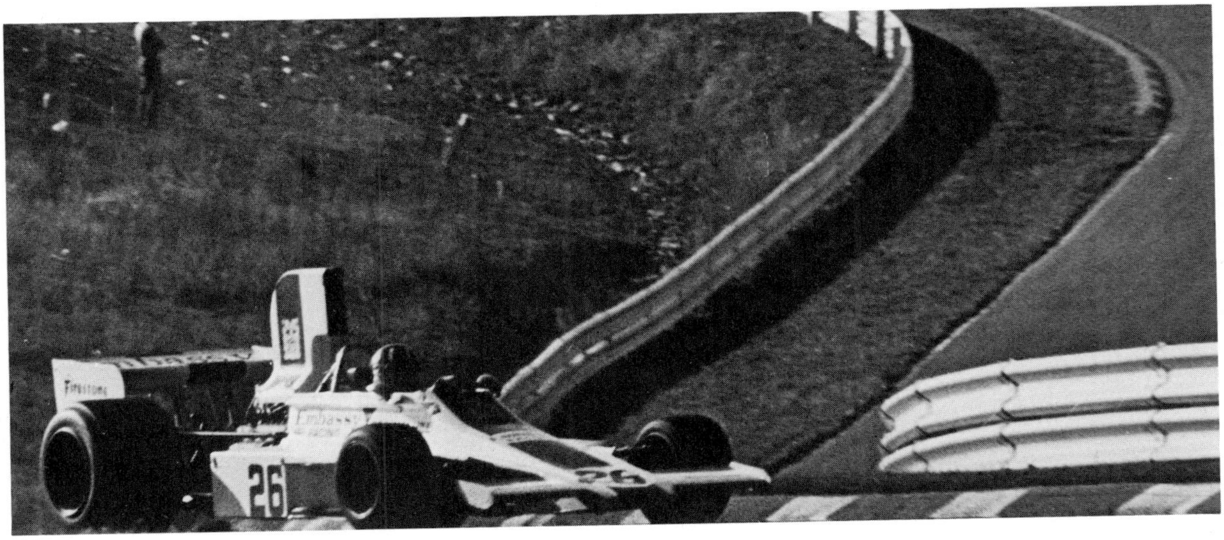

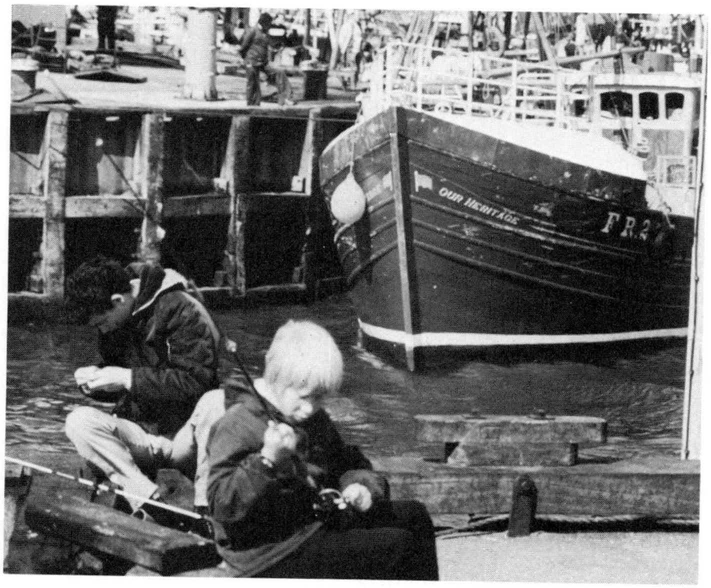

A Canon EF with a 24 mm lens was used to make this photograph. Photo by Marc Levey.

The 35 mm SLR in Detail

Nearly all SLRs share a number of attributes in common.

Behind-the-Lens Exposure Meter. A light-measuring cell inside the camera body measures and indicates to the photographer the proper exposure settings. These metering systems can be further classified as in the following table:

The term *CdS* stands for cadmium disulfide, a material that generates electrical energy in proportion to the amount of light striking it. This chemical has been the standard light-sensitive element used in exposure meters for the last 15 years or so. CdS replaced the selenium cell used in built-in metering systems of the late 1950's and early 1960's.

A more recent development, pioneered by Fuji Photo Film of Japan, is the blue-filtered silicon cell. Silicon overcomes two weaknesses of the CdS meter that have plagued photographers for the last decade. The first is that CdS cells have a "memory": When the CdS cell is exposed to strong light immediately after metering very low light levels, it is technically "blinded" and requires several minutes before it can again give accurate meter readings. The other disadvantage of CdS meters is that their reaction time is not linear; that is, it takes progressively longer for them to meter decreasing amounts of light accurately. Thus, in very dim ambient-light conditions a typical CdS meter is slow to react, and its capability of making a proper reading of the amount of light available is limited.

The latest innovation—first from Pentax and then from Nikon—is galium arsenide (GAP), which has the virtues of the blue-filtered silicon cell but draws less current.

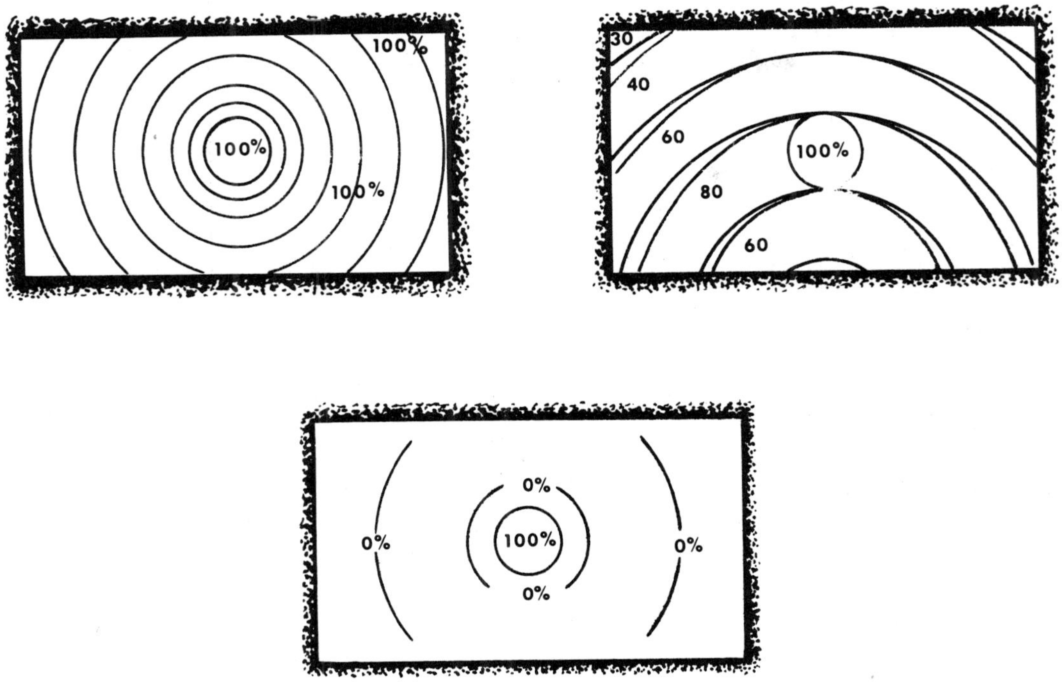

Three basic types of metering patterns found in cameras. (Top left) The *averaging meter* averages the scene, with no emphasis imparted to any one area over another. (Top right) The *center-weighted meter,* which is most commonly in use, emphasizes the center area, decreasing toward the outer edges. (Bottom) The *spot meter* meters only one spot so no gradual reduction in emphasis appears toward the area's periphery.

Both GAP and silicon, unlike CdS, are resistant to "blinding" and exhibit nearly true linear performance because they can "read," or meter, much lower levels of ambient light than the CdS cells can. Another advantage of silicon and GAP is that the manufacturers using them have added a blue filter layer in front of the cells and this, they assert, adjusts the response characteristics of the meter to match more closely the modern color films. Having used both CdS and blue-filtered silicon meters, we can testify that the blue silicon does indeed extend the meter's measuring range and does react much faster in almost all metering situations.

Until very recently meters relied on potentiometers and moving coils to produce the meter indications in the camera's viewfinder. Now miniaturized electronic circuits are replacing mechanical meter components. As we will see in the next section (on shutters), solid-state devices used in place of electromechanical ones provide camera makers with the possibility of designing smaller, lighter, and potentially more accurate and reliable subcomponents.

TYPICAL EXPOSURE-METER ARRANGEMENTS

TYPE	WHAT IS MEASURED	PROS	CONS
CdS: Averaging	All of what you see on viewing screen, equally	Will balance light reading for entire scene	In scenes with great brightness range between light and dark areas, meter tends to indicate an average, possibly rendering some scene elements too dark, others too light
CdS: Center-weighted or Silicon	Same as above, except more meter sensitivity in center of viewing screen, either in upper or lower of center and falling off toward scene's edges	Since most crucial scene elements typically near viewing screen center, more accurate measuring of this element can be made	Fairly nonselective; may lose detail outside area of greatest meter sensitivity
CdS: Semi-spot or Silicon	Large, perhaps 8–10 mm, circle in center of viewing screen is only portion metered	Accurate measurement of area within metering circle	Care must be taken to meter important elements: if more than one, average must be computed
CdS: True-spot or Silicon	Same as semi-spot, but with much smaller area covered by meter	Same as above	Same as above

Focal-Plane Shutters. A focal-plane shutter is a mechanism with either one or two cloth or metal curtains that produce a variable slit through which light passes to expose the film on the rails just behind it (on the focal plane). These shutters travel either vertically or horizontally, depending on their design.

Until rather recently, elaborate systems of gears, pulleys, and levers were needed to time and control the shutter curtains' movements. Many mechanical parts have now been replaced with inherently more accurate solid-state electronic components. Shutters have also been designed to be much smaller and quieter; so smaller overall camera dimensions are now possible.

It should be noted that focal-plane shutters, while convenient in interchangeable-lens cameras, are not used in all cameras. Leaf or iris shutters are used not only in several makes of larger-format cameras but also in less expensive 35 mm rangefinder and viewfinder cameras. When the lens of a particular camera is to be fixed (rather than interchangeable), a leaf shutter is invariably employed as a cheaper, more easily manufactured substitute for the focal-plane shutter.

The real disadvantage of focal-plane shutters is that they can be synchronized with flash units only up to a speed of about 1/125 sec. Leaf shutters, on the other hand, are generally synchronized at any speed throughout their entire operating range. Typical shutters for 35 mm SLRs have a speed range that lies between one second and 1/1000 sec. Several newly developed shutters can extend from 30 seconds to 1/2000 sec. and beyond. Recent electronic shutter designs boast an accuracy through their entire operating range of less than 10 percent deviation from their marked speeds.

From the preceding discussion of meters and shutters it becomes apparent that the quality of future 35 mm SLRs, and for that matter most cameras, will be decided by the advances in the electronics industry. The use of electronic parts makes various subsystems virtually impervious to wear, once they have been properly assembled and sealed.

The disadvantage of these solid-state components, if there is one, is the increasing dependence of cameras on electrical power. There are now several cameras that cannot operate at all without battery power. And, while great strides have been made in the design and production of electronic camera subsystems, the same cannot be said of the batteries needed to power them. The weak point, then, is the power source, because battery technology has not kept pace with camera design: Camera batteries cannot sustain high drain for long periods of time.

Several other innovations have been generated as a result of electronic camera design. First is the electronic information readout in the viewfinder. Some cameras, such as the Nikon FM and the Asahi Pentax ME and MX, present information in the form of light-emitting diodes; others, like the Fuji ST 901 and the new Canon AE-1, by means of calculatorlike digital readouts of shutter speed, *f*-stop, or both. Full digital readouts will probably become standard in the near future. Second, electronic parts are beginning to replace mechanical self-timers and shutter releases.

These and other electronic innovations add up to quieter, lighter, more accurate, and potentially more reliable cameras. In the long run, however, we will pay for these advances in higher repair bills and more reliance than ever on battery power.

Automatic vs. Match-Needle Cameras. The automatic 35 mm SLR is one of the latest adaptations in electronic camera design. While several automatic cameras are fully mechanical, most employ electronics to some degree. The term "automatic camera" is a bit misleading, because the photographer usually must select either the shutter speed or the *f*-stop, even though the camera will adjust the other to allow for proper exposure. There are cameras that are fully automatic, but they are programmed to provide only a set combination of *f*-stop and shutter speed at any given level of light and generally do not offer the user any selective control. (For programed-metering, fully automatic cameras, see the preceding section on 35 mm rangefinders. As of this writing, only one camera—the Canon A1—provides both automatic and programed metering.)

Photographic purists will argue that a hand-held exposure meter is more accurate than the built-in meters, and for truly professional results, some will insist that the photog-

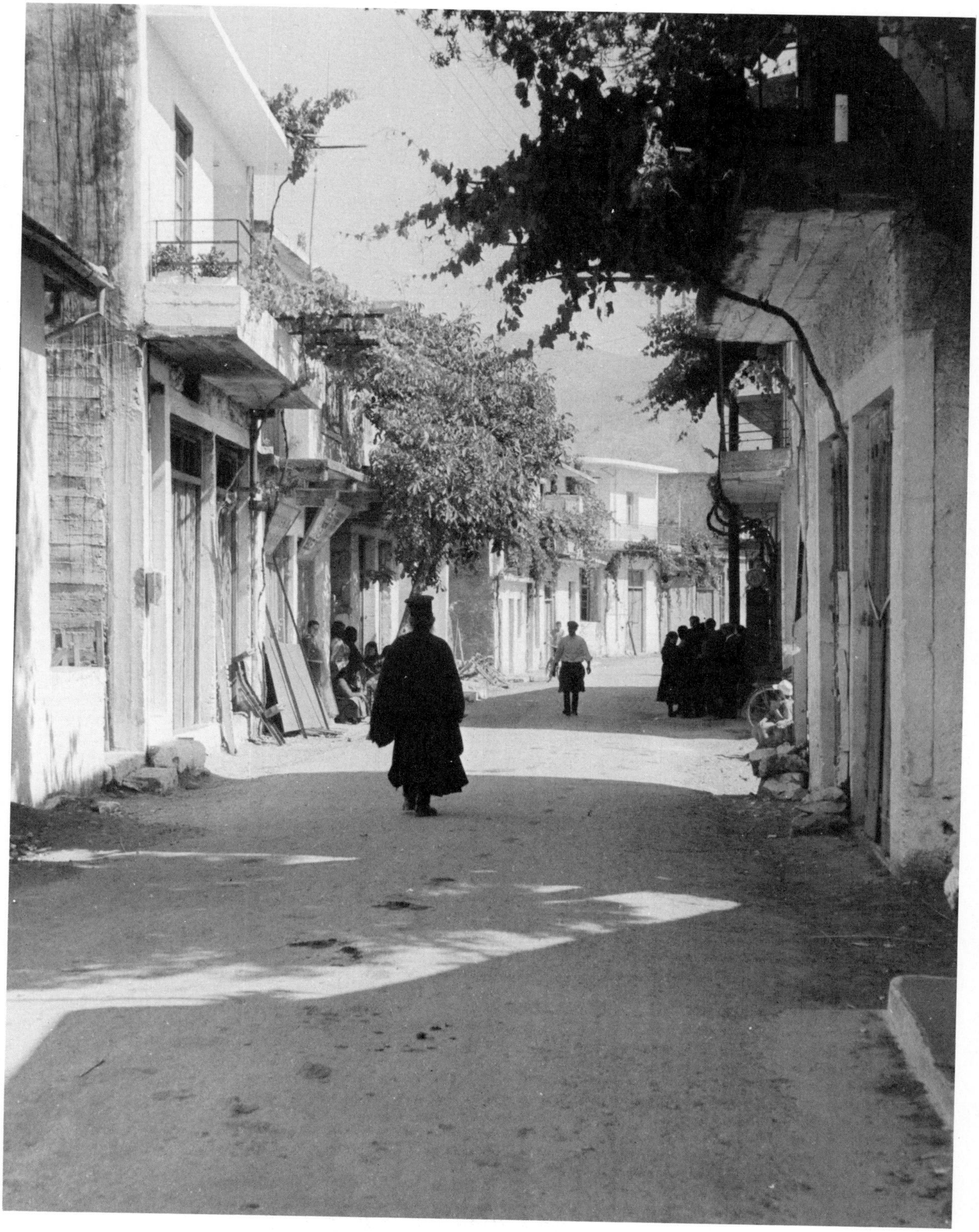

Where the light changes, the automatic feature of shutter-priority cameras is useful. Photo by Bill Coleman.

rapher have full manual control over shutter speed and *f*-stop. Many photographers disagree. We have seen thousands of pictures shot with built-in-exposure-meter cameras and discovered accurate exposure information in 99 percent of the photographic situations represented. The built-in metering system, especially in its automatic form, does seem likely to free the photographer from one more manual task and allow him to concentrate more fully on his subject.

For the last 15 years or so cameras with built-in meters have mostly been of the "match-needle" variety. In these, by turning either the shutter-speed dial or the *f*-stop ring on the lens, the photographer aligns a needle with a reference mark or circle in the viewfinder to set the camera controls for proper exposure. While the system did—and still does—work well, it usually relies on mechanical gears and pulleys, which are necessarily prone to wear and tear. As mentioned earlier, moving coils in exposure meters are subject to the intrusion of dirt, which can damage the fragile needle movement. In addition, bumps and shocks to the camera can knock the meter way off. But perhaps the most significant disadvantage is that the photographer must set shutter speed and *f*-stop manually while trying to concentrate on composition, lighting, and subject at the same time.

Shutter-Priority vs. Aperture-Priority Metering. Automatic metering in modern 35 mm SLRs comes in variations.

1. Shutter priority: The camera mechanism selects the proper *f*-stop after the user has chosen a shutter speed.
2. Aperture priority: The camera mechanism selects the shutter speed after the photographer has picked the *f*-stop.
3. Dual mode, combining 1. and 2.: The camera can select either the proper *f*-stop or the proper shutter speed, or it can select neither and leave all decisions up to the photographer (as in the Minolta XD11 or Canon A-1).

In considering shutter as against aperture priority, the advantages of one are the disadvantages of the other. On the pro side of shutter-priority metering: It does give the user shutter-speed control in case of changing light conditions, and it reduces the chance that camera shake will ruin the photograph. Beginners generally find shutter-priority metering the easier of the two systems. Aperture priority allows you to use manual lenses, bellows, and other accessories on the camera body while retaining its automatic metering function. With aperture priority you needn't purchase specially designed lenses, as you must when the metering gives priority to shutter operation.

Compact 35 mm SLRs. Through time, 35 mm SLRs have grown in size and weight to a point where they are anything but the "miniature reflex cameras" envisioned in the 1930's. But that trend has reversed itself, beginning with the introduction of the Olympus OM-1 a few years ago. The Olympus team, with their many years of expertise in compact camera design, perceived that a quality 35 mm SLR could be made appreciably lighter and smaller than all contemporary models. The resulting OM-1 was about 35 percent smaller and lighter, yet

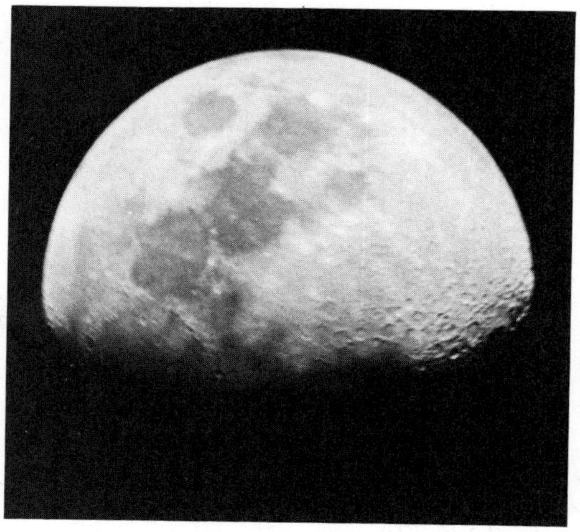

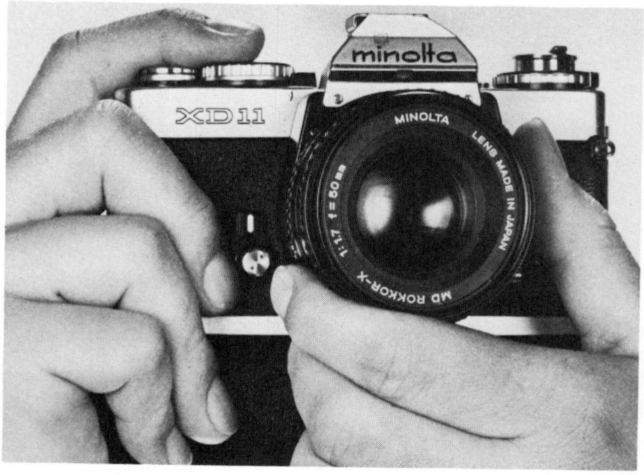

(Left) The aperture-preferred control system allows for constant *f*-stop for maximum depth of field. This can be especially useful when using mirror lenses for a shot. This photo was taken with an Olympus OM-2 Celestron 1250 mm mirror lens, hand-held. Photo by Marc Levey. (Right) The Minolta XD-11 is a compact 35 mm SLR featuring dual metering (either shutter- or aperture-preferred). Motor drive is also available, as shown here. Photo courtesy Minolta, U.S.A.

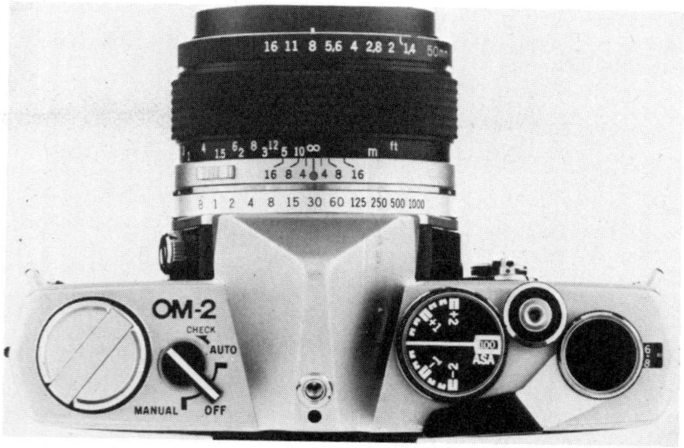

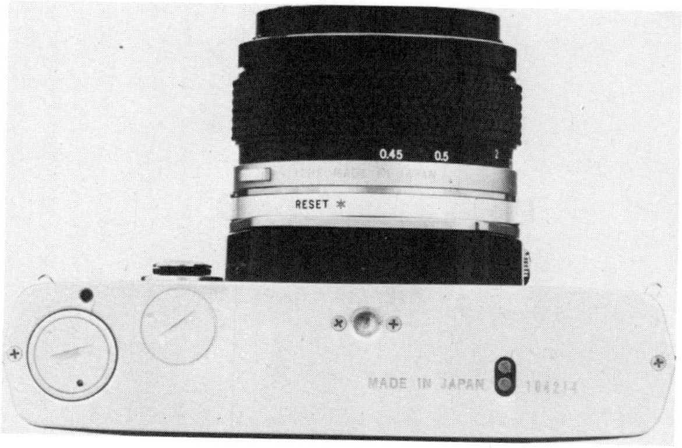

Top and bottom views of the Olympus OM-2 compact 35 mm SLR. At right of the bottom view are shown electrical connections for motor drive. Photo courtesy Vivitar, Inc.

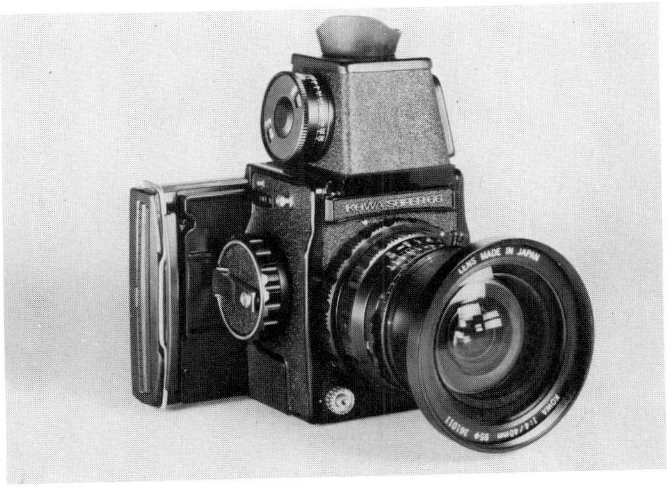

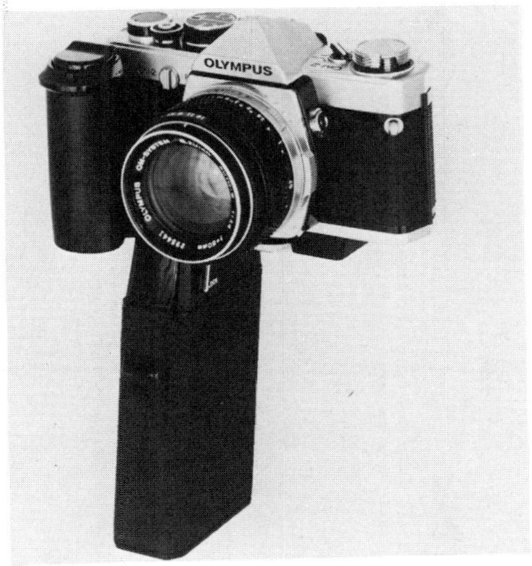

(Left) This Kowa Super 66 2¼"× 2¼"SLR represents a typical medium format camera. Photo courtesy Berkey Marketing Co. (Right) One of the latest in compact 35 mm SLRs is the Olympus OM-2. Photo courtesy Vivitar, Inc.

sacrificed very few features. In the wake of Olympus's enormous success with the OM-1 and OM-2 have come Canon, Pentax, Konica, Minolta, Nikon, and others with their own compact models. No doubt more manufacturers will follow suit. More and more camera designers will turn to computer technology to pack features into shrinking camera bodies, reduce production costs, and improve reliability. As you'll see below, these innovations are much slower in coming to the larger-format cameras.

Medium-Format Cameras

One complaint often heard about 35 mm is that the image produced on the film (24 × 36 mm [1 × 1½ in.]) is too small to manipulate in the darkroom. Posterization and negative retouching are quite difficult with negatives smaller than 6 × 6 cm (2¼ in. square). Small-format films also require a great degree of enlargement when being printed, whether from slides or from negatives. Use of larger-format cameras considerably reduces the degree of enlargement required and makes printing easier. Larger-format cameras do not necessarily result in better-quality prints, but consider that a 35 mm negative requires nearly 10× magnification to produce a 28 × 36 cm (11 × 14 in.) image on an easel. If you work with a 6 × 6 cm (2¼ × 2¼ in.) negative, you only need about 6× magnification to obtain the same 28 × 36 cm (11 × 14 in.) image size. Since enlargement of your negative magnifies not only the image but also the imperfections—such as film grain, dust, and scratches—the less enlargement required, the better.

Another consideration in deciding between camera formats is film, which will be discussed

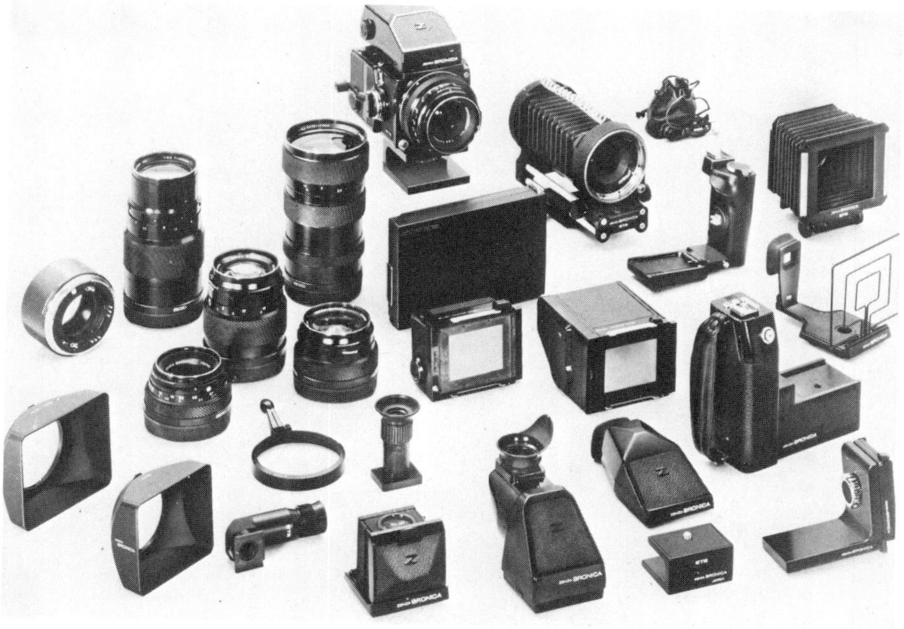

Bronica markets quite a selection of accessories in its medium-format ETR system. Photo courtesy EPOI, Inc.

more particularly later on. For now, think of the active component of film as being made up of silver halide crystals. These crystals have a granular texture, and if sufficiently enlarged this structure will downgrade your image quality and can eventually affect the quality of the finished print. The grain structures of most modern films are such that they can withstand considerable enlargement before the grain becomes obtrusive; nevertheless, if large, smooth, ultrasharp prints are your goal, consider a camera of larger format than the 35 mm.

The 645. This recently introduced "new" series is really the revival of an old film format. It produces an image 6 × 4.5 cm (2¼ × 1¾ in.) on either 120-size or 220-size film, which enlarges comfortably (with little cropping) to 20 × 25 cm (8 × 10 in.), 28 × 36 cm (11 × 14 in.) or 41 × 51 cm (16 × 20 in.).

By designing cameras in this format, manufacturers are saying they can offer you a camera almost as small and light as a 35 mm SLR, yet with an appreciably larger negative. Bronica and Mamiya from Japan are the first to offer the 645's. They claim small size, light weight, easy handling, and a rectangular format like the 35 mm, with virtually three times the negative area of the latter. In fact, they call them "mini-2¼-squares" or "super-35 mm's" and have earmarked considerable capital for extensive accessory development for their basic models. In price, these cameras fall between top-of-the-line 35 mm SLRs and the even-

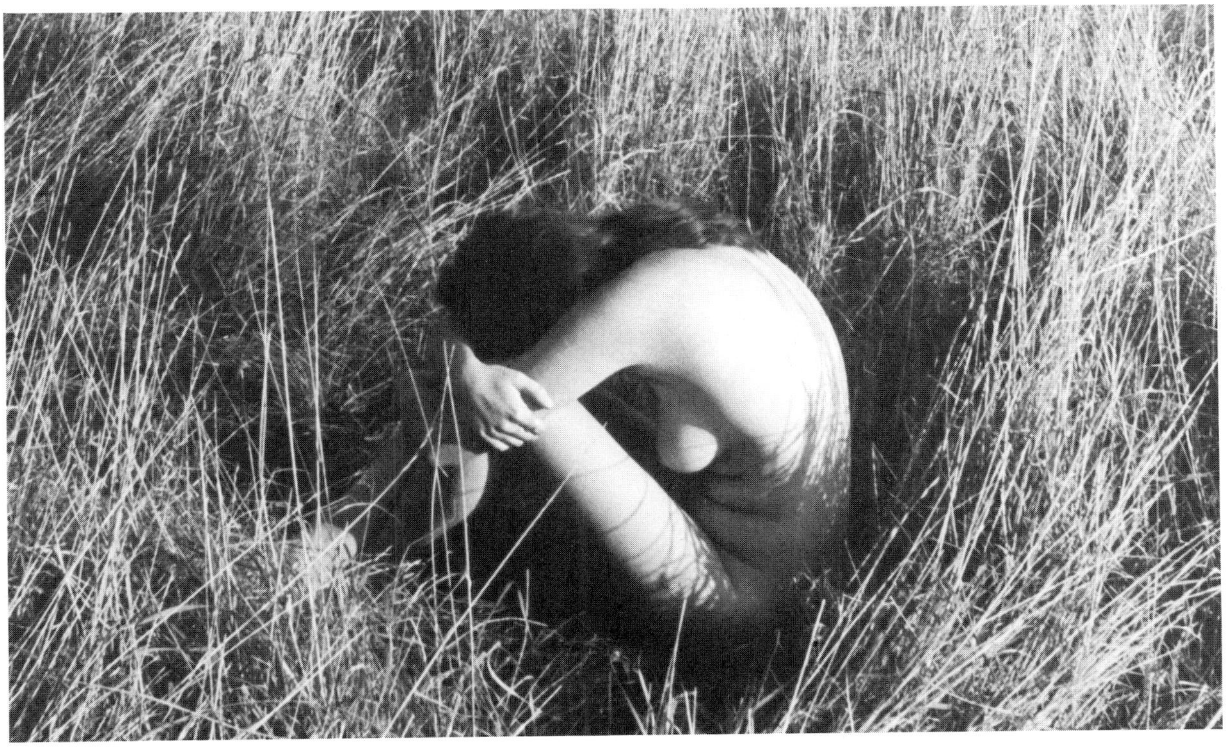

This sensitive figure study photograph was taken with a 2¼" × 2¼" camera. Photo by Jim Lukens.

higher-priced 2¼ × 2¼-inch cameras. Whether we will see a major movement to 645's as alternatives to 35 mm or 2¼ × 2¼-inch cameras is hard to say. They do appear to offer some advantages; so they should not be dismissed without closer examination.

The 2¼ × 2¼-inch-square Camera. This has been the workhorse of professionals for some time. The format produces twelve 6 × 6 cm (2¼ × 2¼ in.) negatives on 120-size film or twenty-four on 220-size film. Unlike 35 mm film, which comes in cassettes and has no backing, 120 and 220 films are backed with a paper strip and come on spools; thus the name "roll films."

There are three variations on this format commonly available: the 2¼-inch twin-lens reflex, the 2¼-inch or 2¾-inch single-lens reflex, and the 2¼ × 2¾-inch single-lens reflex.

Twin-Lens Reflex. The 2¼ TLR (6 × 6 cm [2¼ × 2¼ in.] twin-lens reflex) possesses an optically matched pair of lenses mounted vertically on a rectangular body. The upper lens is used strictly for viewing, composing, and focusing, while the lower one actually makes the photograph. A mirror fixed at 45 degrees behind the upper lens reflects incoming light onto a ground-glass viewing screen for composition and focusing. Since the mirror is fixed in place, the scene being photographed is always in view, even during the instant of exposure. Due to its basically simple design with few moving parts, a TLR operates quietly. TLR cameras are generally sturdy, the best seeming to be virtually indestructible.

Sounds terrific, you say? There are, however, a few photographic flies in the ointment. Lenses for TLRs—and very, very few of the cameras take interchangeable lenses—tend to be large (therefore heavy) and slow (virtually no TLR lenses are faster than *f*/2.8). *Parallax error,* caused by using separate lenses for viewing and picture taking, cannot be fully compensated for. Still, the cameras *are* robust and simple. For decades they've served as standard cameras for pros working at weddings and news events. But with the introduction of new and different 2¼-inch designs, most TLRs have slowly gone the way of the horse and buggy.

A few camera makers continue to market TLRs. Rollei in Germany produces a series of quality cameras that take advantage of this design. Two varieties come from Japan: Yashica offers a moderately priced TLR with coupled CdS metering and fixed lenses. Mamiya is unique in that it offers the only interchangeable-lens 2¼-inch TLR on the market. In addition, Mamiya offers an extensive accessory line, along with a rather complete lens line. The Mamiya C220/C330F series probably comes closest to a photographic "system" in the TLR field.

Twin-lens reflexes may have diminished in importance in the marketplace, but the faithful swear by them. Just ask an owner.

The Mid-Size SLRs. Arriving on the scene some 20 years ago, the *2¼ × 2¼-inch SLR* and the *2¼ × 2¾-inch* ("ideal" format) *SLR* contributed to the TLR's demise. Using size 120 or 220 roll film, these cameras possessed both the advantages of larger film size and through-the-lens viewing, which eliminated the parallax difficulty. Originally they were introduced to overcome a major TLR drawback: the lack of lens interchangeability. Users soon found several more advantages, and for the last 15 years or so medium-format SLRs have appeared on the market, coming from several camera manufacturers.

In talking about these designs, the Swedish Hasselblad must be discussed first. The Hasselblad 1000F's introduction made a big splash in 1949. Superbly crafted and impeccably finished, this camera quickly became the staff of life for working professionals. Then complaints of shutter problems began cropping up. Hasselblad redesigned the shutter and lens system, replacing the original focal-plane shutter with leaf shutters built into each individual lens. The new shutter design offered the additional advantage of fully synchronized flash at all shutter speeds, in place of the limited range available with the focal-plane-shutter-equipped 1000F. This second Hasselblad design (the 500) and subsequent relatives have become legendary in the history of photography. The answer to whether Hasselblads deserve their unique status as *the* superlative

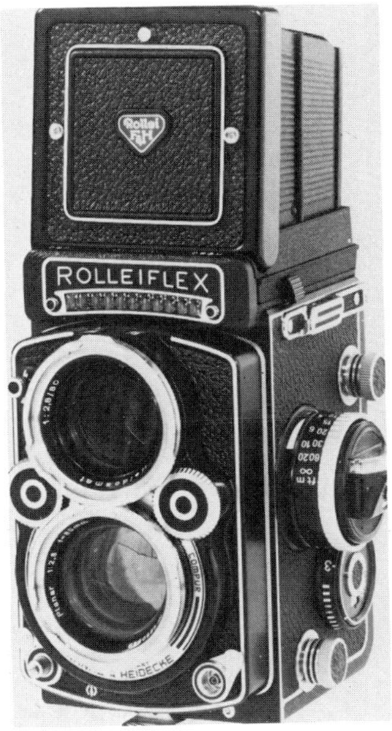

(Left) The Rolleiflex 2.8F is the latest in a long line of distinguished cameras. Photo courtesy EPOI, Inc. (Below) This fine study was taken with an old Minolta Autocord. Photo by James Forkner.

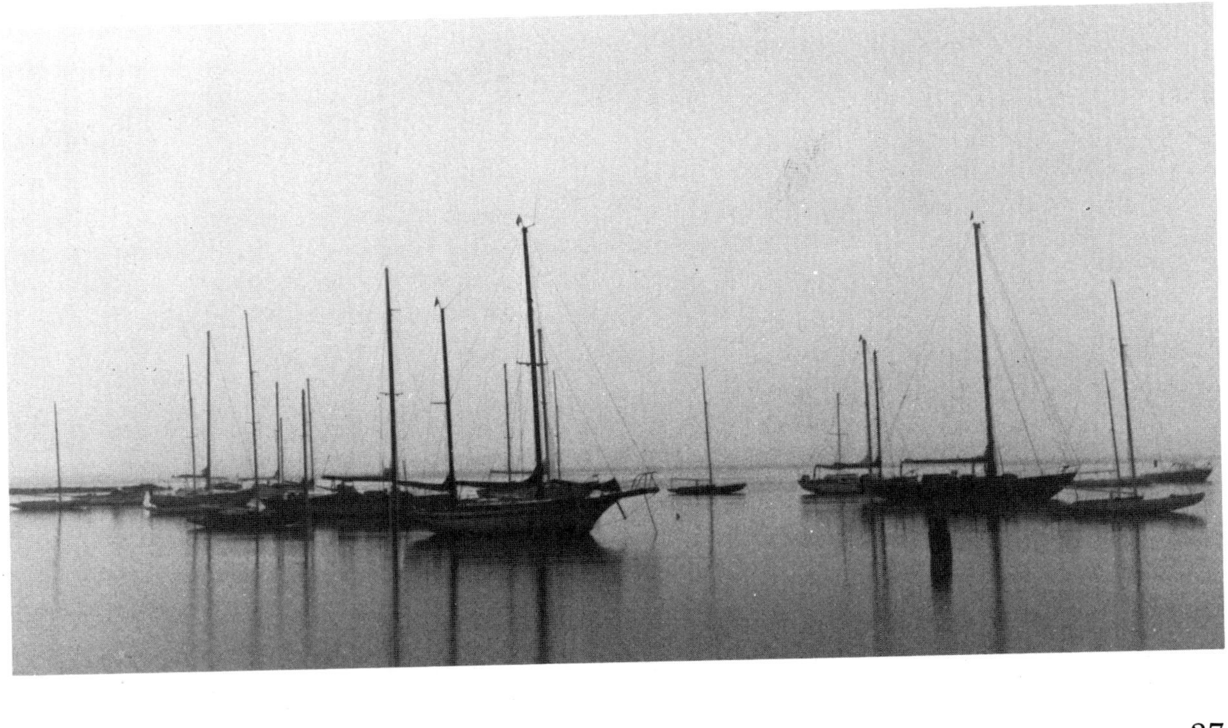

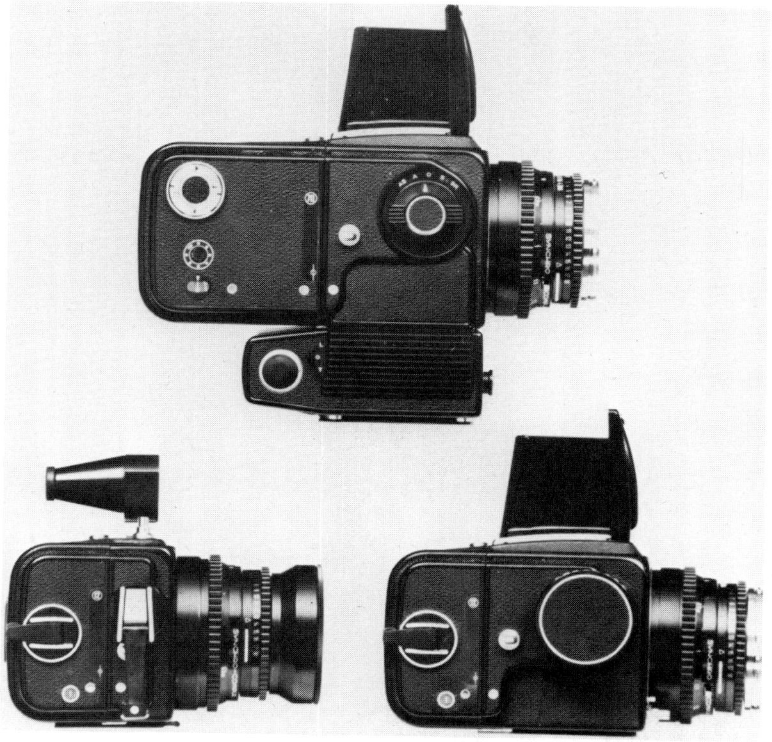

Hasselblad's dependability and performance have made it the professionals' choice for years. Shown from top to bottom: Hasselblad ELM, Hasselblad Super Wide, and Hasselblad 500 CM. Photo courtesy Braun, North America.

medium-format camera is hardly a simple yes or no. The same question can be raised in the 35 mm field with regard to the Leica. Leica has continued to update its models, incorporating behind-the-lens metering systems; but the Hasselblad 500C is essentially the same camera as it was ten years ago.

While the 500CM (the latest model) is a jewel of craftsmanship, with its lenses among the best-performing available, the Hasselblad is without an instant-return mirror or a fully coupled exposure meter. Perhaps another drawback is that, in spite of numerous accessories and gadgets to facilitate eye-level viewing, the Hasselblad 500CM still feels and performs best at waist level.

A pertinent question is whether a Hasselblad is worth its premium price. Consider that the 500CM body, with one back for 120 film and a standard 80 mm Zeiss Planar lens, will list for more than $1400, and additional lenses cost at least $600 each. While you needn't be a Rockefeller, it would help if you're planning to buy into the Hasselblad family. Some photographers say the quality built into a Hasselblad will more than compensate for the initial investment in years of dependable performance. Yet the design is something of an anachronism, in that Hasselblad has refused to update it by incorporating an instant-return mirror. SLRs have moving mirrors that flip out of the way at the instant of exposure; most re-

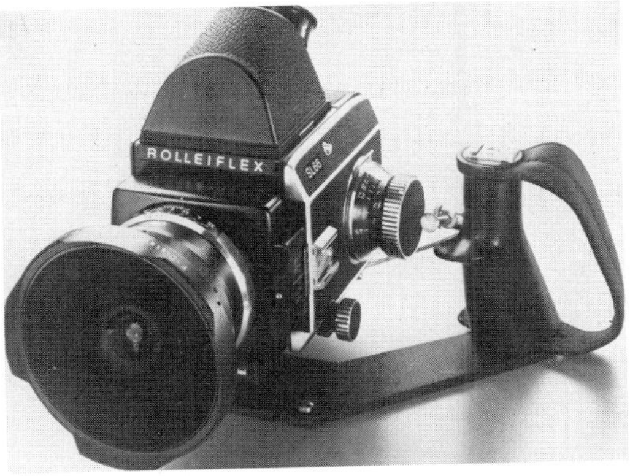

(Left) The Rollei SL-66 has a list price of approximately $1800. It is shown here with a 30 mm fisheye lens and handgrip. Photo courtesy Rollei/EPOI, Inc. (Below) Like many professional-grade medium-format cameras, the Rolleiflex SL-66 comes with a variety of viewfinders and lens. Photo courtesy EPOI, Inc.

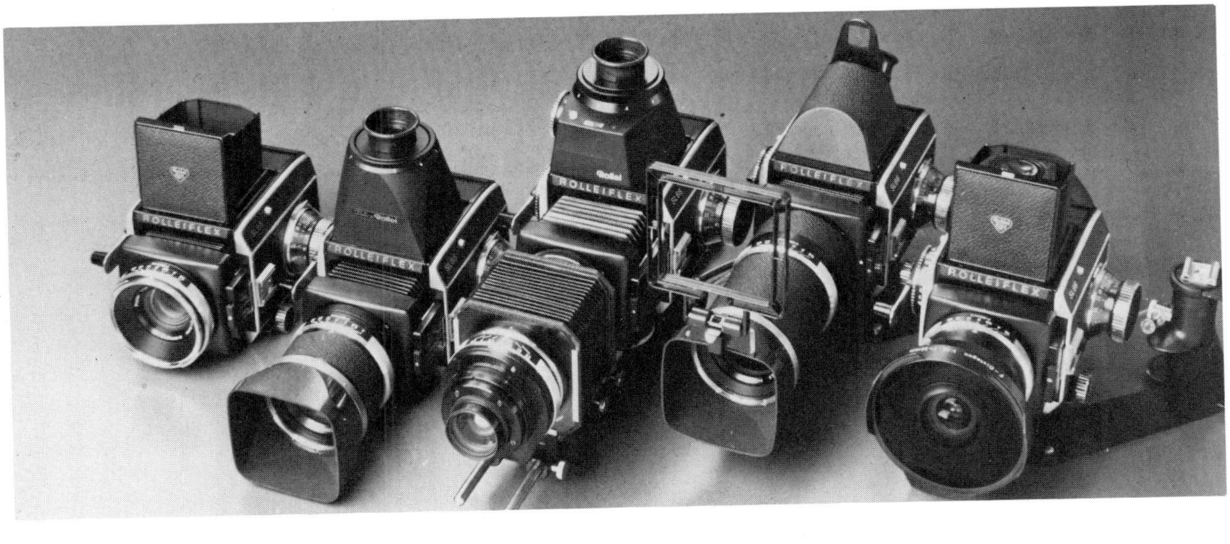

turn instantly after the exposure is completed. The Hasselblad photographer has to crank the shutter-winding–film-advance mechanism before he can view the scene again. Naturally this operation can slow down action photography. Other problems with Hasselblads are their weight—especially with long lenses mounted—and the difficulty of operating the narrow focusing rings on many of the lenses.

These criticisms aside, the Hasselblad does represent an exceptionally well-built camera, with hundreds of accessories available for nearly every conceivable application. You will have to decide whether the not-impossible investment is justified in terms of your own needs and desires.

This year Hasselblad's first new camera since the 500 series was being shipped to dis-

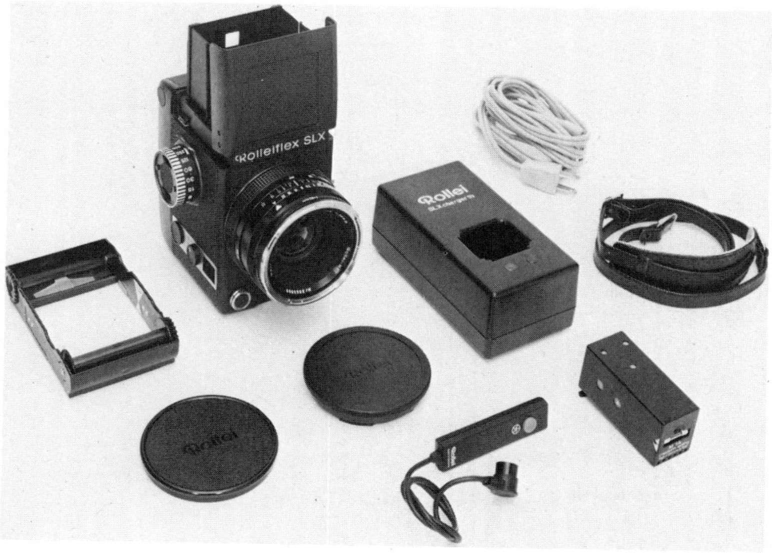

The SLX model marketed by Rollei features linear motors, automatic through-the-lens metering, and integral motor drive. This is probably a good reflection of the state of the technology in the mid to late 1970s. Photo courtesy EPOI, Inc.

tributors. Among its features are an electronically governed focal-plane shutter, provision for double exposures, and a new fast-*f*-stop lens series that focuses appreciably closer than its predecessors. Initial price estimates hit $2000-plus just for the camera body with standard lens and camera back.

If we've led you to believe Hasselblad is all there is in quality medium-format cameras, it isn't really so. The medium-format cameras may not be as numerous as the smaller 35 mm SLRs, but there *are* several choices. They fall into two categories: 6 × 6 cm (2¼ × 2¼ in.) SLR (Hasselblad, Bronica, Norita, and Rollei) and 6 × 7 cm (2¼ × 2¾ in.)—the so-called "ideal" format—SLR (Pentax and Mamiya).

Rollei's SL66, newer in design than the Hasselblad, offers decent competition to it. Priced even higher than the Hasselblad, the Rollei SL66 has several unusual features above and beyond the standard virtues of the single-lens reflex camera. It incorporates a long bellows, which allows it to be used in near-macro (close-focusing) range with its standard 80 mm lens. The user also can tilt the lens on its vertical axis, which allows the photographer considerable gains in depth of field without changing the lens's *f*-stop. The workmanship is excellent throughout; in fact, Rollei's lenses are manufactured by the same people who make Hasselblad's.

Rollei does market numerous accessories, more than enough for all but the most specialized uses.

Third in the 6 × 6 cm field come three Bronica cameras. Similar in shape to the Hasselblad and Rollei, the Bronicas are horizontal rectangles about 10 cm (4 in.) high, 13 cm (5 in.) wide, and 18 cm (7 in.) deep, ranging in weight from 1.9 kg (4 lb 3 oz) to 2 kg (4 lb 5 oz).

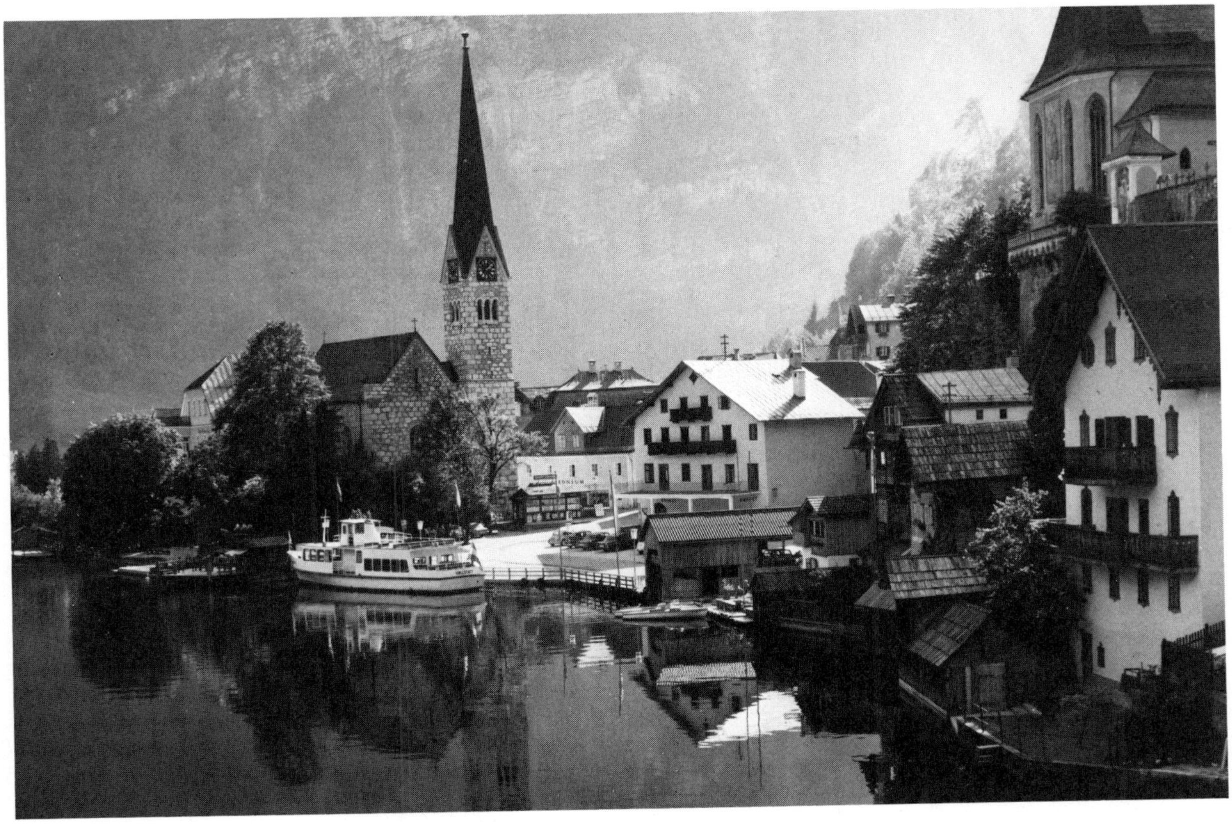

This photo demonstrates the great depth of field and fine detail possible from a 2¼"× 2¼"negative. Photo by L. P. Greenhill, F.R.P.S.

Several of Bronica's recent camera designs incorporate electronic rather than mechanical shutter operation as well as coupled and built-in meters. In general, as mechanical and electronic sophistication increases so does price. Bronica's top cameras now approach the cost of Hasselblads ($900) and Rolleis ($1000-plus), although their standard S2A camera body and accessories are considerably less expensive ($700 at the maximum) than those of competitors.

All three lines of cameras possess advantages and disadvantages. If money is the key to your selection and you are set on a medium-format camera, you might look at the Bronica S2A. This camera owes much of its design to the original Hasselblad. Equipped with a standard 75 mm Nikkor lens, it should prove a fine picture taker. "Bugs" in the shutter's gear train have been eliminated, to a point where most recent tests indicate the camera should stand up reliably to prolonged professional use.

Sharing the virtues of 2¼ × 2¼-inch square SLRs, but having particular pluses and minuses of their own, is the second group mentioned above, the 6 × 7 cm (2¼ × 2¾ in.) "ideal" format SLRs of Pentax and Mamiya. Design philosophy differs radically in these two cameras. While the Mamiya RB67 is essentially a larger-appearing 2¼ × 2¼-inch, the Honeywell Pentax 6 × 7 looks like a 35 mm SLR with a thyroid condition. The Pentax looks and feels like a 35 mm, but on the grandest scale; it is the only medium-format camera designed at the start to be used at eye level. It has impressive dimensions, weighing about 2.5 kg (5½ lb) and measuring 19 cm (7½ in.) wide, 14 cm (5¾ in.) high, and 15 cm (6 in.) deep.

By way of contrast, the Mamiya RB67 is a waist-level reflex that has earned wide accep-

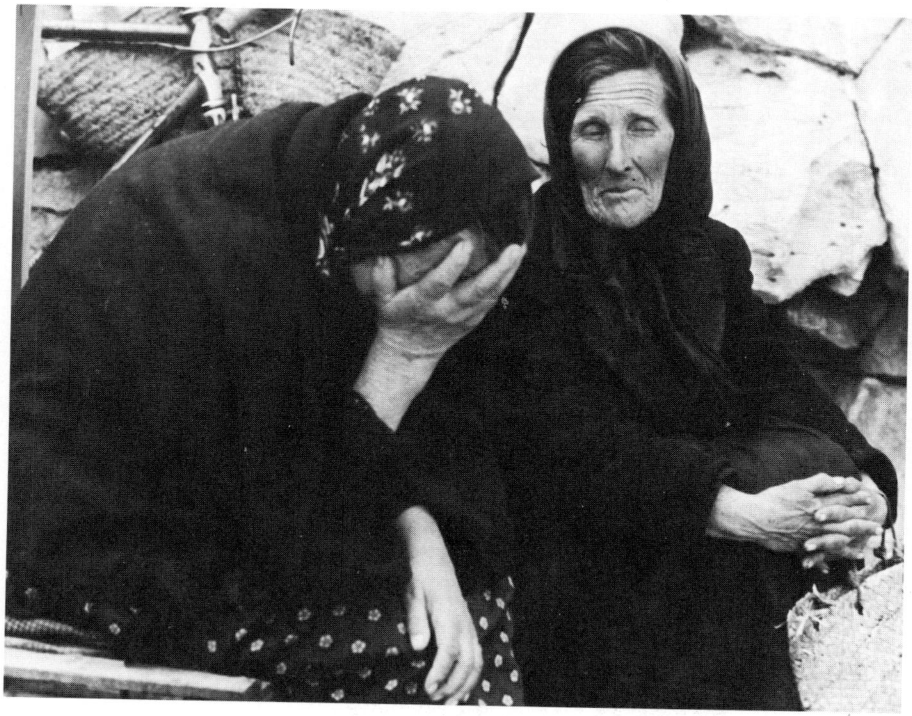

This scene of great emotional impact was photographed with a Hasselblad 500C with an 80 mm lens. Photo by Bill Coleman

tance among professionals. It has a rectangular body, a rotating film magazine, and long bellows for close-up work.

The makers of 6 × 7 cm cameras say their format provides a more usable-sized negative when enlarging to standard sizes, such as 20 × 25 cm (8 × 10 in.), 28 × 36 cm (11 × 14 in.), and 41 × 51 cm (16 × 20 in.). It's much the same argument as that presented for the 645 format. You will notice that in order to get this larger size there have been considerable increases, both in physical dimension and in weight, of the 6 × 7 cm cameras when compared with the 6 × 6 cm format (2¼ × 2¼ in.). We feel that the former cannot really be hand-held with long lenses: We're talking about a combined weight of 3.6–4.5 kg (8–10 lb) for camera and lens. Other problems might arise from the fact that most of the lenses are slow, typically *f*/4.5. But for studio, wedding, or other commercial uses, the "ideals" are good choices.

As with the 35 mm SLRs, several medium-format cameras are currently in the works. Rollei has already shown a preproduction version of a highly advanced 2¼ × 2¼-inch cameras incorporating behind-the-lens silicon metering, built-in motor drive, and several other exotic features.

Larger Formats

There are several cameras in the 4 × 5 in. through 8 × 10 in. range; some are even larger.

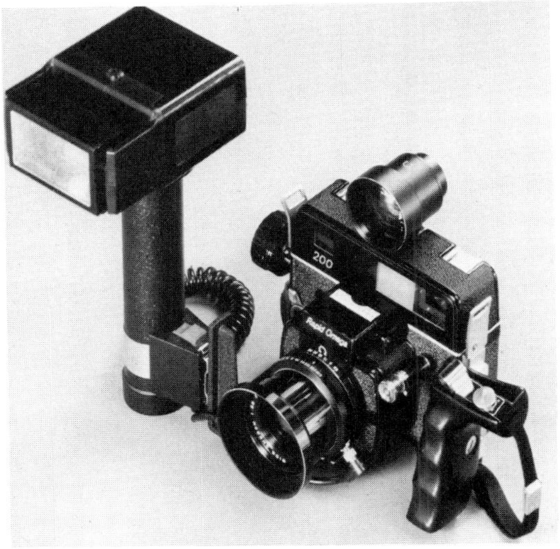

The Rapid Omega 200 is the only medium-format 2¼" × 2¼" rangefinder available. Photo courtesy Berkey Marketing Company.

The larger-format cameras generally use cut sheet film and require manual operation. They consist of a lens-and-shutter combination mounted on a square front standard, a bellows or similar focusing device, and a film holder attached to a swinging rear standard. Many offer complete control over perspective because of their movable lens boards and swinging back standards. To those dedicated enough to work slowly and produce large negatives under controlled conditions, "view cameras" are definitely the thing.

For all their unique advantages, though, view cameras are relatively unportable and so may not suit many photographers. The lenses are slow, although the best can produce great results in the hands of an earnest photographer. If murals are your specialty these cameras are essential, as they allow you to produce negatives that have enormous enlargement potential. There are no built-in meters, automatic diaphragms, or auto-anything-else; so there's very little to break down.

Medium-Format Rangefinder Cameras

In the 1930's, 1940's, and even into the 1950's the working pro's camera was the press camera—the good old folding Speed Graphic. Even though the 35 mm and 2¼ × 2¼-inch-square format single-lens reflexes have largely won the day, a few cameras still carry on the tradition of the press camera. Mamiya and Omega market medium-format cameras, using size 120 or 220 roll film, that provide rangefinder focusing, interchangeable lenses, and reasonable portability.

"Instant Picture" Cameras

Instant-picture photography has its adherents, mostly in the quick-snapshot-photographer group. Since control is virtually

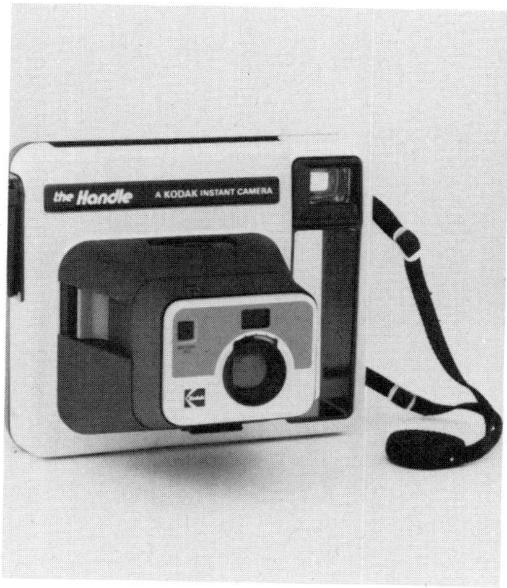

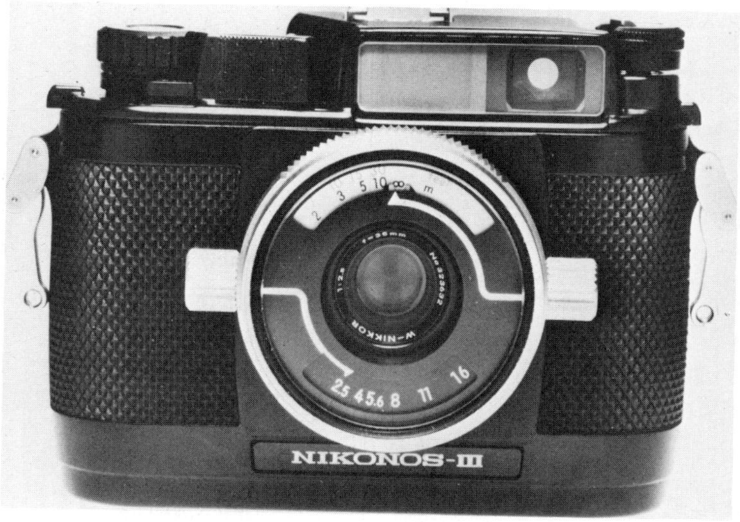

(Left) The Handle by Kodak is one of the less expensive instant cameras available today. Photo courtesy Eastman Kodak Co. (Right) The Nikonos is the only underwater camera available. The most recent model, the Nikonos III, is self-contained, good to a depth of 150 feet, and features interchangeable lenses. Photo courtesy EPOI.

automatic in all but one of the available Polaroid still cameras and there is only one film that produces negatives in addition to prints, these cameras have limited appeal to or use for the serious photographer. That is not to imply they are useless—many professionals use them to preview lighting, for instance.

Since photographic companies other than Polaroid have now introduced "instant picture" cameras—and rumors have it that still others are being designed—the field seems to have great potential. Imagine a professional type of camera offering instant black-and-white or color negatives, prints, or transparencies. We'll probably see that, and more, in the not-too-distant future. Watch the developments in the next five years or so.

Underwater Cameras

The Nikonos III is the only such camera available at this time, but underwater housings are made for many sorts of cameras.

While we have tried to cover all currently available types of cameras, we probably have missed a few Suffice it to say we discussed all types currently in production and on the market. Below you'll find a comparison chart that we hope will be helpful to you.

CAMERA COMPARISON CHART

CAMERA TYPE	FILM FORMAT	DIMENSIONS (LENGTH × WIDTH × DEPTH)	WEIGHT W/ STANDARD LENS	METER TYPE (BUILT-IN)	MAXIMUM SHUTTER SPEED (SEC.)	COMMENTS
Pocket Drop-in Cartridge	110	13 × 2.5 × 3.2 cm 5″ × 2″ × 1¼″	198–340 g 7–12 oz	Programed CdS or silicon	Most 1/250 Some 1/500	Increasing sophistication, zoom lenses, SLRs, *f*/2 lenses
Compact 35 mm Rangefinder	35 mm	13 × 7.6 × 8 cm 5″ × 3″ × 3¼″	454–907 g 16–24 oz	Automatic CdS	1/500	Many automatic and available below $100
High-priced 35 mm Rangefinder	35 mm	15.9 × 8.9 × 7.6 cm 6¼″ × 3½″ ×3″	992 g 2 lb 3 oz	Match-needle CdS	1/1000	Limited production; $600, $1000, and up
Compact SLR	35 mm	13.3 × 7.6 × 8.2 cm 5¼″ × 3″ × 3¼	737 g 1 lb 10 oz	Match-needle CdS	1/1000	Electronics permit size reduction without loss of features
Compact Auto SLR	35 mm	13 × 8.9 × 8.3 cm 5″ × 3½″ × 3⁵⁄₁₆″	907 g 2 lb	Auto silicon	1/1000	Small lenses and electronic shutters
Standard SLR	35 mm	15 × 9.5 × 10 cm 5¾″ × 3¾″ × 4″	1.1 kg 2 lb 8 oz	Match-needle or auto CdS/silicon	1/1000–1/2000	Refined over years, feature-laden, over two dozen types available
Medium-format Standard (SLR)	6 × 6 cm 2¼″ × 2¼″	14 × 11 × 16 cm 5½″ × 4½″ × 6¼″	1.4–2.3 kg 3–5 lb	Usually no meter	1/500–1/1000	Optional meter prisms; full system of accessories
645	6 × 6 cm 2¼″ × 2¼″	13 × 15 × 16 cm 5″ × 5¾″ × 6¼″	1.4 kg 3 lb		1/500	
Ideal Format 6 × 7	6 × 7 cm 2¼″ × 2¾″	13.3 × 14 × 22 cm 5¼″ × 5½″ × 8⅝″	2.3 kg 5 lb		1/500	
TLR	6 × 6 cm 2¼″ × 2¼″	10 × 15 × 10 cm 4″ × 5¾″ × 4″	1.4 kg 3 lb	Usually no meter	1/500	Swinging back; system of accessories
Polaroid SX 70	8.9 × 8.9 cm 3½″ × 3½″	18 × 10 × 15 cm 7″ × 4″ × 6″	624 g 1½ lb	Auto programed	1/180	
2¼″ × 2¼″ Rangefinder	6 × 6 cm 2¼″ × 2¼″	20 × 13.3 × 15 cm 8″ × 5¼″ × 5¾″	2.3 kg 5 lb	No meter	1/500	Interchangeable lens, bright focusing
4″ × 5″ View Cameras (or larger)	10 × 13 cm, 4″ × 5″	18 × 20 × 7.6 cm 7″ × 8″ × 3″	3.6–4.5 kg 8–10 lb	No meter	Depends on shutter in lens	Separate shutters, lenses, swings, tilts, etc.

LENSES

With all the different types of lenses on today's photographic market, it can be an excruciating experience to decide which lens is best for you. To help you choose, we have established six functional categories for our discussion of lenses for both 35 mm interchangeable systems and the larger film formats. These categories are *wide angle, normal, telephoto, mirror, macro,* and *zoom.*

Before we jump into this material we need to consider what a photographic lens is. Lenses are combinations of spherical or aspherical elements, usually of glass, designed to focus incoming light sharply on a single plane (in this case, the film) with little change in color rendition. Further, each lens is designed to reproduce the subject in focus in a specific manner. For instance, a wide-angle lens takes in wide angles of coverage, but with decreased subject magnification. A telephoto lens, on the other hand, covers narrow angles but gives increased subject magnification. (See the accompanying line drawing.)

You should realize that all lenses have aberrations, or defects. However, having multiple elements of specific shapes and materials tends to reduce and, in some cases, even eliminate these flaws. Moreover, modern lenses are coated with a variety of materials to increase transmission of light through the lens to the film, thus compensating for aberrations in certain portions of the color spectrum.

Multicoatings. Modern lenses are coated with such materials as magnesium fluoride to improve effective transmission of light. New technological processes now make possible ultrathin precision multiple coatings of various materials on lens surfaces. Contrary to manufacturers' advertisements, so-called *multicoating* reduces lens flare very little. What multicoating does do is allow a higher percentage of the light entering the lens to pass through to the film. In a complex zoom lens, with as many as 20 individual glass lens elements, multicoating is particularly useful. In independent tests a 15-element zoom lens with a standard single coating on the lens elements transmitted only 67 percent of the light entering the lens, as opposed to 83 percent for the same lens after multicoating.

The practical importance of increased light transmission becomes evident in comparing the maximum marked *f-stop* against the *T-stop* of a particular lens. In the example above the regular coated lens was marked for a maximum *f*-stop of *f*/3.5, when in reality the maximum T-stop (essentially the true *f*-stop measured at the film plane) was approximately *f*/4.5, or about ⅓ *f*-stop less. Multicoating decreased the lens's transmission loss to about ¼ *f*-stop; so, practically speaking, the loss could be forgotten in all but the most critical metering situations.

A final word about multicoating. Many manufacturers claim it improves performance dramatically. Actually, the opposite may be true unless multicoating is computed as part of the lens's optical design. To keep up with the times, some lens manufacturers have multicoated older optics just so they can say the lenses are multicoated. Other lens makers, notably Canon, frankly admit that multicoating does not improve the performance of all their lenses and restrict its use to those for which the process is most useful. Canon lenses

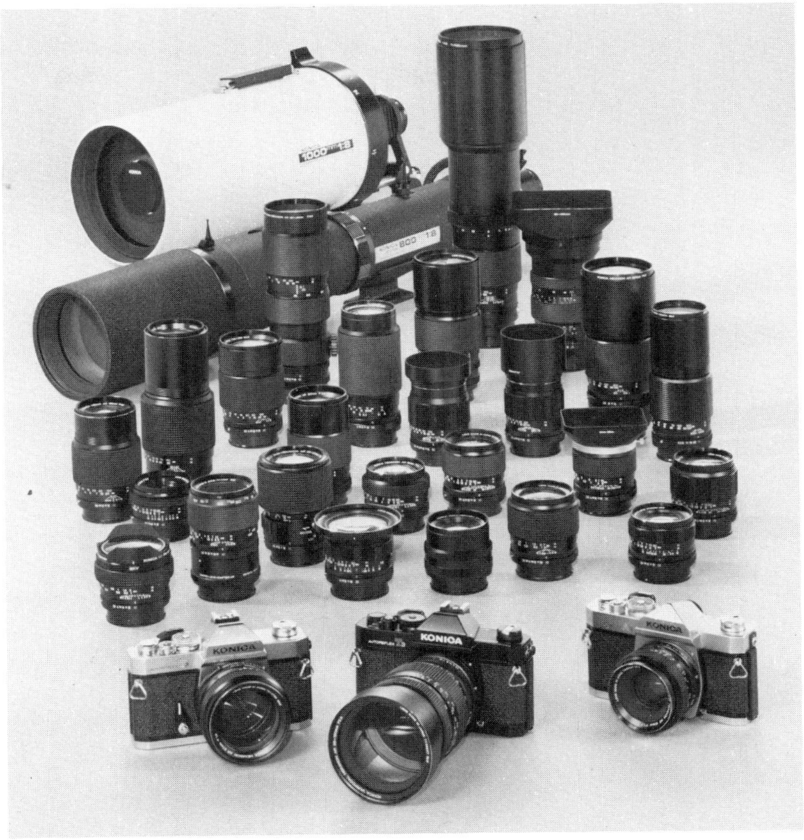

A quality 35 mm SLR camera possesses quite a lens system from which to choose. Photo courtesy Konica Camera Co.

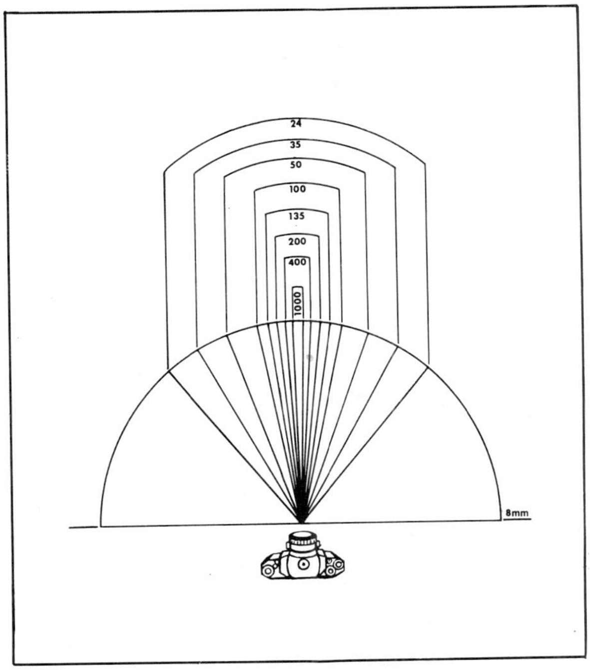

Different focal lengths provide varying angles of coverage.

1000mm: 2.5°
400mm: 6°
200mm: 12°
135mm: 18°
100mm: 24°
50mm: 46°
35mm: 63°
24mm: 82°
8mm: 180°

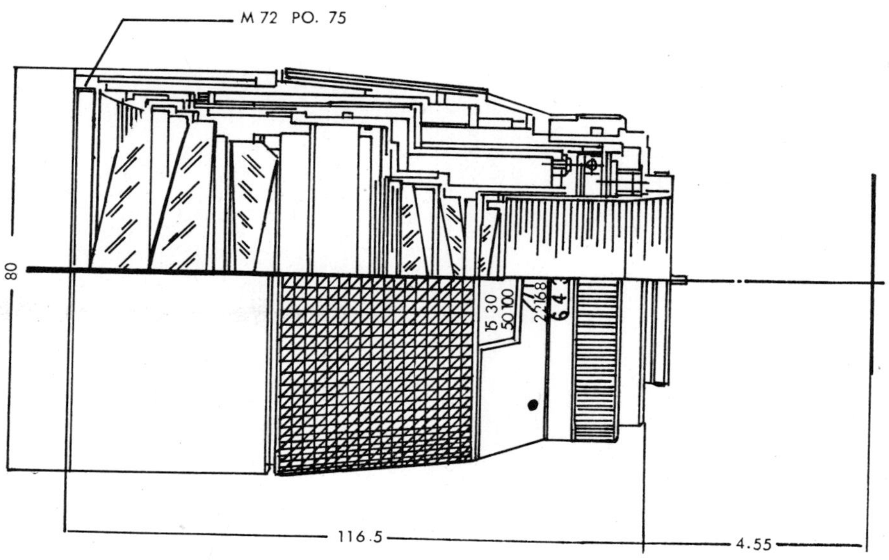

Modern telephoto lenses are generally constructed as shown. Higher performance demands more complexity. Drawing by Joan Jablonski.

are clearly marked to indicate which are multicoated and which are not—a frankness uncommon in the photoequipment market.

So beware. Multicoating is no panacea. A bad job can cause wild color shifts as well as reduced sharpness. A good non-multicoated optic remains preferable to a badly made multicoated lens.

Lens Construction (Reliability vs. Appearance)

Modern lenses are complex interactions of cams, key ways, glass, aluminum or steel, and various retaining devices. A single lens might contain hundreds of separate parts, the failure of any one of which could render the lens inoperable. Lens manufacturers (most of them Japanese) select the material and design for a particular lens to sell in a specific price range. As a potential buyer you should be aware that the price you pay in large part determines not only what materials will be used but also how they will be constructed.

It has been estimated that at least 75 percent of photographic equipment's cost goes for labor. Thus, a lens producer can cut his production costs by reducing manufacturing tolerances and the number of precision processes required. So while the lens may be attractive cosmetically, it can be poorly constructed. Unfortunately, this might not be evident in the first few months of use; it could prove disastrous later on. Cheap construction typically employs heavy grease in place of fine-machined focusing threads. The greased-up lens will focus very smoothly in the store; but eventually the grease dries out, and the lens is then virtually useless. Another common difficulty with sloppily assembled lenses is lens-element decentering. To achieve top performance, *all* lens elements require precise alignment. Poor assembly often results in decentering of one or more elements and thus in downgraded optical performance.

In most respects, you get what you pay for. Most camera makers market an accessory line bearing their names. To uphold their business reputation, it behooves them to see to it that their lenses are well made and finished—which is usually the case. Naturally, the lenses are also quite expensive. If quality is uppermost in your mind and price is secondary, you might do well to stick with your camera manufacturer's lenses.

Of course that general rule has its exceptions. There are several independent lens producers who market quality lenses at considerably lower prices than those of the camera manufacturers. Among these are Vivitar, Tamron, Soligor, and Sigma. They offer several lens lines in different price ranges; but their premium lenses are made and finished—and perform—as well as, or in some cases perhaps better than, many of the camera manufacturers' original-equipment lenses. And at no little saving to the consumer.

These independent lens producers frequently offer innovative options before the generally more conservative camera manufacturers do. For example, independents led the way in developing close-focusing zoom lenses with first-class optical performance. Vivitar's 70–210 mm Series I zoom pioneered a whole new lens-design series now being explored by the camera manufacturers.

Another thing to consider in regard to independent lens makers is that they often are prepared to offer more liberal warranties than their camera-producing competition. Original-equipment lenses are typically guaranteed for one year, sometimes two. On the other hand, Soligor offers a three-year warranty and Vivitar a five-year warranty period.

Figuring Your Costs

Finally you, the purchaser, must do a cost/benefit analysis. If you intend to use a wide-angle lens just three or four times a year, you might consider one of the cheaper versions. But if you intend to use it often and your investment is a one-time affair, it might be wise to spend the money for a top-quality optic.

There is considerably less difference optically than there is mechanically between lenses of different prices. So before you buy, do these three things:

1. talk to friends who own different brands of lenses;
2. read the test reports in the photographic magazines;
3. personally handle the lens or lenses you are considering, and also shoot a test roll if at all possible.

Lens selection is highly personal and subjective; so feel and ease-of-handling strike each of us differently. But be advised that even the most prestigious lens manufacturer occasionally lets a "dud" slip through. Simply because your lens costs $300 to $500, don't assume it will be a super performer. Check it out both in the store and at home.

Looking at Lenses

Now for a discussion of specific lens types, their uses, and the advantages and disadvantages of each.

The Wide Angles. By definition, a *wide-angle* lens is one whose coverage across the

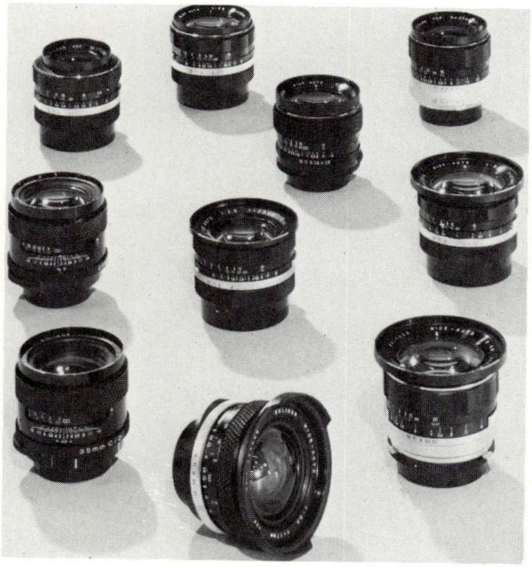

There are numerous wide-angle lenses from any one of a dozen manufacturers to choose from. Photo courtesy A.I.C.

film's diagonal measures at least a 60-degree angle. The subcategories of this lens type are: (1) the fisheye, 6.5–16 mm, with an angular coverage to 220 degrees; (2) the extreme wide angle, 17–24 mm, with angular coverage of 110–84 degrees; and (3) the wide angle, 28–35 mm, with 75–63 degree coverage. The categories are somewhat arbitrary but still represent useful descriptive distinctions between lenses.

(1) *Fisheye Optics.* We have all seen (especially in ads) the circular photographs that take in enormous amounts of space. This fisheye effect provides a view of the subject in a perspective that is extremely distorted toward the picture's edges as well as highly distorting to the objects nearest the lens. Such photographs have become commonplace, and we feel this particular lens has limited usefulness for most photographers, especially when you consider the price you must pay for a good one ($150 to $500) and the relative scarcity of scenes suggesting its use. If you feel you must have this one, we can suggest an alternative lens that you can make at home for less than $10 (see Book 2, Chapter III, on creative applications).

Because of their extremely short focal length, fisheye lenses possess tremendous depth of field. At *f*/8, a typical fisheye might have a sharp-focus field ranging in depth from 30 cm (less than a foot) to infinity. Most such lenses are relatively slow, with a maximum *f*-stop of *f*/4 or *f*/5.6. The first fisheye was the Hill Cloud Lens, developed in 1924 and used to observe sky phenomenon, which of course demanded a very broad angle of view.

(2) *Extreme Wide Angles.* These lenses have intermediate angular coverage (110–84 degrees) between the fisheye and the wide angle. Because these lenses can take in very large angles of coverage, they are useful for panoramic outdoor shots. They also come in handy for indoor photographs where you can-

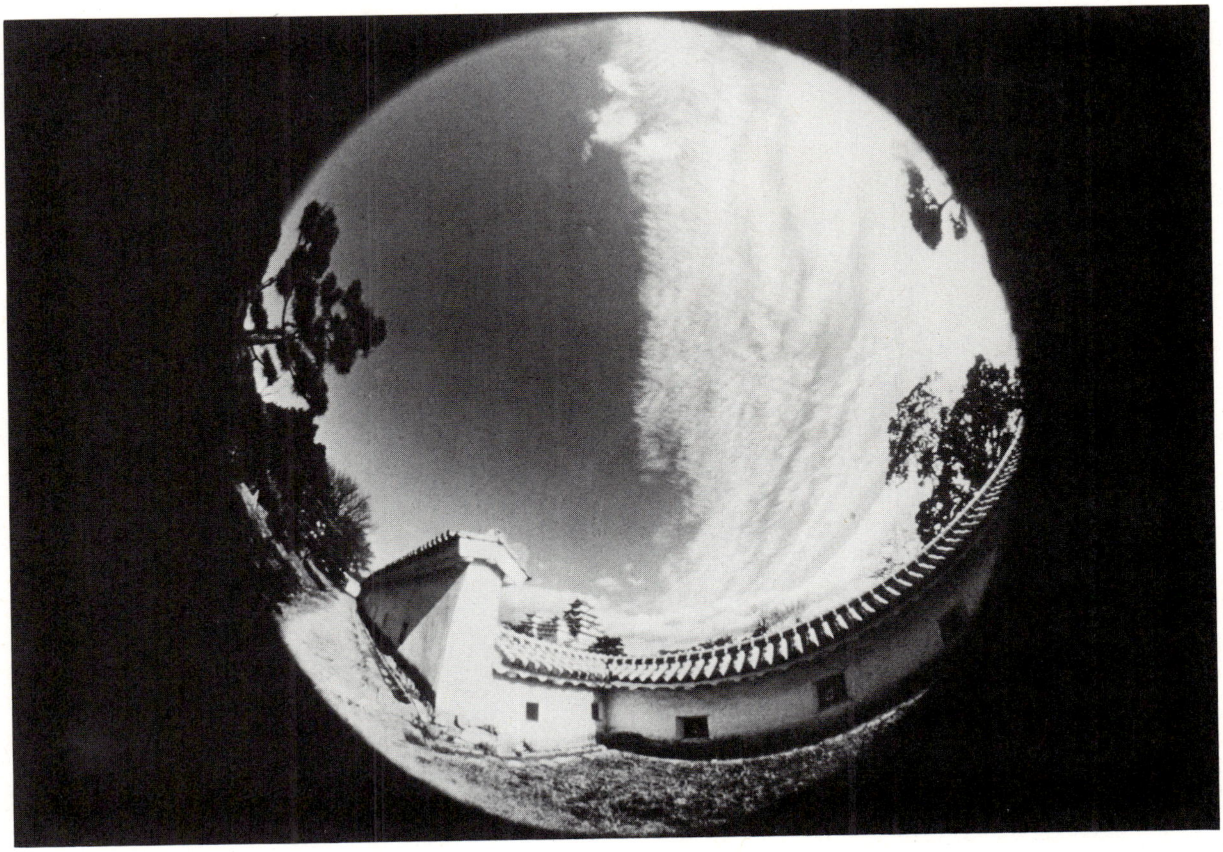

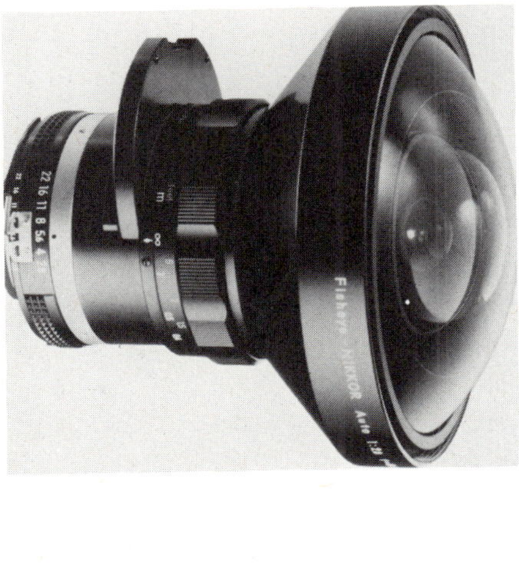

This photo was taken with a Rokkor-X 7.5 mm fisheye lens. Photo courtesy Minolta, U.S.A. (Left) Nikon's 8 mm *f*/2.8 fisheye lens produces a 180° circular image. Photo courtesy EPOI.

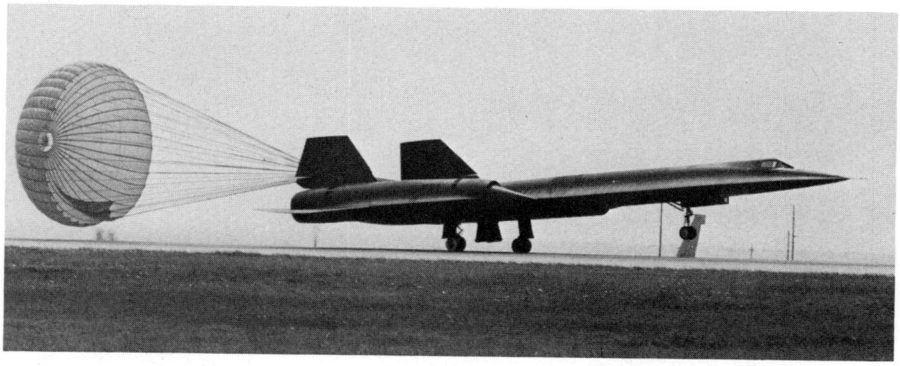

This photograph was taken with a 20 mm extreme-wide-angle lens. Photo by Marc Levey.

not back far enough away from your intended subject to take it all in—say, in a museum setting or a narrow street.

The inherent design of these lenses produces apparent distortion of the subject matter. A general guideline to be aware of is: *The wider the angular coverage of the lens, the shorter the focal length, and the harder the lens is to control* in regard to distortion. For example, an extreme-wide-angle lens used up close distorts the image to such an extent that wild, impressionistic (possibly even grotesque) photographs result. Still, these lenses can be used as creative tools and some noted photographers have produced interesting portraits with them. For the average photographer, though, they are probably best suited to scenic photography.

The one characteristic of ultrawide angles, and to a lesser extent wide angles, is the extent of their depth of field, which is great at any given aperture in comparison with that of normal or long lenses. Another useful rule of thumb is: *When focused at the same distance, short-focal-length lenses will deliver greater depth of field at comparable* f-*stops than longer-focal-length lenses.* So if you have two 35 mm SLRs—one with a 50 mm lens mounted on it and the other with a 24 mm—and, using an opening of *f*/8, you focus both cameras on an object ten feet away, you will be able to see that everything from 1.4 m (4½ ft) to infinity will be in focus in the photo from the 24 mm lens, while with the 50 mm only objects from 2.6 m to 4.6 m (8½–15 ft) will appear in focus. That's quite a difference. It is therefore an advantage for the photographer wishing to keep widely separated things in focus to use the 24 mm lens.

The price you will pay for this advantage, aside from the cost, is difficulty in *precise* focusing. There can be so much depth of field that it is very tricky to find the exact plane of focus. Further, extreme-wide-angle lenses rarely are faster than *f*/2.8. Viewing and focusing with extreme-wide-angle lenses with less than *f*/2.8 can be quite a chore under all but high light levels. Then, too, ultrawide-angle optics have a tendency to add fullness or roundness to the subject matter. To photograph overweight people with this lens would be to accentuate their bulk unkindly.

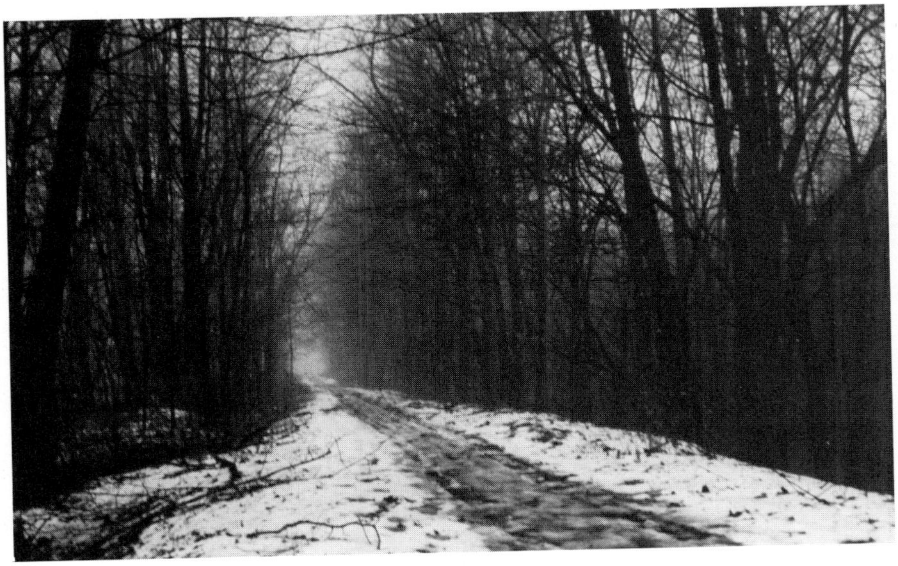

A 28 mm wide-angle lens was used to make this photograph. Photo by Samuel Kazdan.

Unless you have a special reason for wanting one or have had experience with extreme-wide-angle lenses, 24 mm is about as far down the focal-length scale as you probably want to venture. The 24 mm can be controlled, and still it gives impressive coverage. Beyond that focal length, problems such as the ones described above can develop. The present trend is to go in for exotic lenses and expensively achieved effects, but our experience has proved the middle ground is preferable in terms of practicality and usefulness.

(3) *Wide Angles.* These 28–35 mm lenses have a 75–63 degree angle of coverage, which has become the standard in wide angles. They possess more inherent depth of field and cover more picture area than normal lenses, but they are more tolerant of focusing errors than normals or telephotos. Several newer wide-angle designs boast maximum *f*-stops of 2 or faster. Canon and Nikon recently introduced a 24 mm *f*/1.4 lens. The typical 35 mm or 28 mm sports a maximum *f*-stop around *f*/2.8, which is sufficiently bright for focusing and composing in most picture-taking situations.

When choosing between the 28 mm and the 35 mm lenses, we lean toward a 28 mm for the following reason: A 35 mm lens covers 63 degrees, while the standard 50 mm lens covers about 46 degrees. In practical picture-taking terms, that's not too much of a difference. There's not much of an advantage, then, in buying a 35 mm if you already own a 50 mm. In addition, the introduction of fast 35 mm and 28 mm lenses has led numerous photographers to select wide angles as their standard lenses in place of 50 mm optics. For indoor and action shots you don't need a fast 50 mm now, since the advent of 28 mm *f*/2 or *f*/1.8 lenses allows for added depth of field.

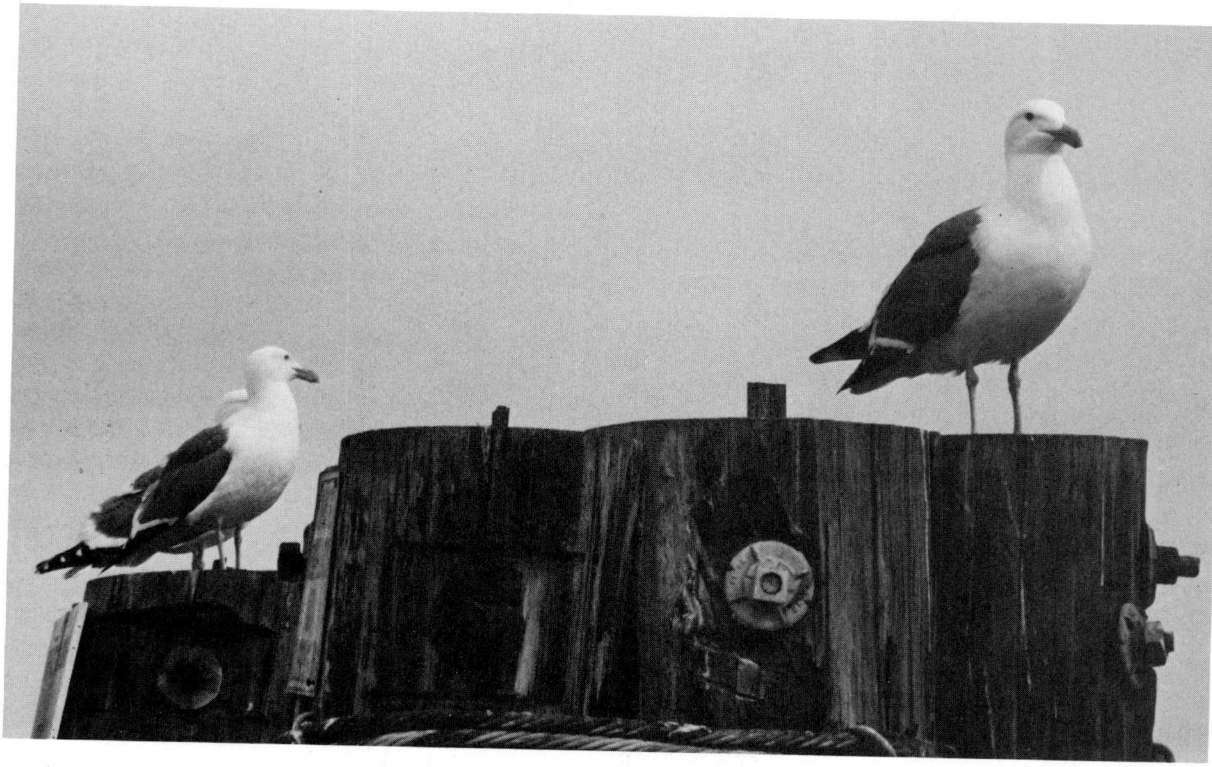

Normals. The 50 mm lens produces an image in which the subject appears in about the same size as our eyes see it. Lenses in the 45–58 mm range are called "normal" somewhat arbitrarily by camera manufacturers who want to merchandise camera bodies and lenses as packages. The truth is that bodies and lenses for virtually every good 35 mm SLR come separately and can be bought singly.

The most significant advantage of normal lenses is that their optical design produces the highest image quality, in terms of resolution and contrast, of any lens type. They generally also have the largest maximum *f*-stop of any kind of lens, with common *f*-stops of *f*/1.8, *f*/1.4, and even *f*/1.2. Resolution in the best of normals, in terms of lines per millimetre, approaches modern color-film limits. In some cases the lens can actually resolve (that is, sharply define) even more lines per millimetre than the film can.

If your forte is low-ambient-light photography, a high-speed normal is an excellent investment. Keep in mind, however, that shooting most of your photos at *f*/4 or *f*/5.6 with a lens sporting an impressive glass expanse out front is somewhat a waste. Remember, 80–90 percent of all photographs are taken between *f*/4 and *f*/11 and at shutter speeds between 1/30 sec. and 1/500 sec. That isn't a pattern you are tied to, but it's definitely something to consider before investing money in what might prove to be extraneous equipment.

Telephotos. Any lens with a greater-than-60 mm focal length falls into this category, including the "portrait" and "short tele" lenses (up to 105 mm or so). Telephotos aim to provide an image on film that is larger than that produced by a normal lens and therefore larger than that seen by the naked eye. The degree of magnification as compared to normal lenses is called the *lens magnification factor.* In general, telephotos are longer and heavier than normal lenses and most wide-angles. The telephotos' physical characteristics and ability

(Facing page) This photograph was taken with a 50 mm normal lens focused at a distance of seven feet. Photo by James Forkner.

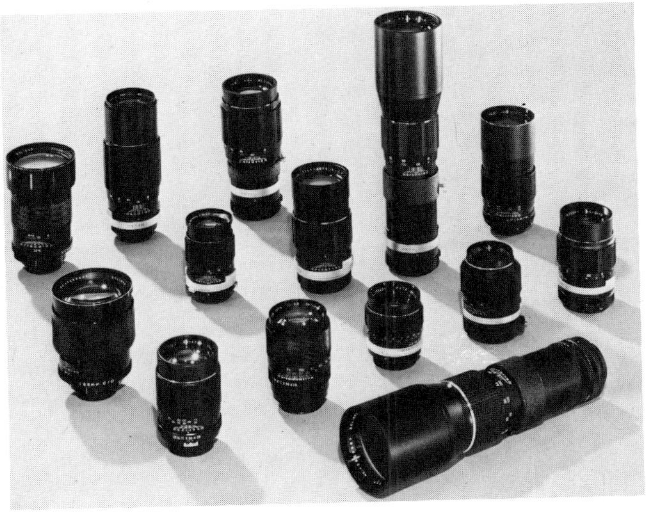

This photo represents a typical manufacturer's lineup of telephoto lenses. Photo courtesy A.I.C.

to magnify compound the usually controllable effects of camera shake. Acting much like the arm of a fulcrum, a hand-held telephoto can really frustrate the user because of the sheer weight and length of the lens housing. The unsteadiness associated with its use often results in unsharp pictures. Camera shake is probably more responsible than anything else for bad pictures.

Up to a focal length of about 135 mm, telephotos are fairly compact and their weight is manageable. With shutter speeds of 1/125 sec. or faster, most photographers should be able to produce acceptably sharp photos with 135 mm lenses. If you have never tried a telephoto before, don't expect instant success. Some practice will probably be necessary. Any support you use will help: A tree, a fence, the windowsill—even better a tripod—will reduce camera shake.

Bear in mind that camera shake is magnified by the lens's magnification factor. A 200 mm lens fitted to a 35 mm SLR gives you a magnification of 4X when compared with normal lenses, and all camera movement will consequently be four times as severe. The farther you move up the focal-length scale, the more acute the problem becomes. A 400 mm telephoto magnifies, not just the image but also the internal and external camera shake, eight times. You can see here both the practical limits of hand-holding long lenses and the outright necessity for a sturdy tripod.

To minimize the image-degradation effects of camera movement, it helps to select the highest practical shutter speed. Supporting your camera-and-lens combination with a good tripod will also reduce the shakes. In our experience, pictures taken with a tripod-mounted camera always appear sharper than hand-held shots. Others seem to agree with us: In tests conducted by a number of photography magazines under controlled conditions, virtually all the photos taken with cameras mounted on a tripod were sharper than the same pictures taken in a hand-held mode. In

LENSES IN DIFFERENT CAMERA FORMATS

CAMERA FORMAT	FOCAL LENGTH	MAX. *f*-STOP	ANGLE of VIEW	WEIGHT	TYPICAL LENGTH	BARREL DIA.	MIN. FOCUS DISTANCE	COMMENTS
Pocket Drop-in Cartridge	23–26 mm	*f*/4–5.6	43°–50°	7–12 oz	6″	Integral	3′–5′ ft	
35 mm	W/A 8–15 mm Fisheye	*f*/4	180°	16–24 oz	2″–8″	2½″–3″	8″–1′	Built-in filters
	18 mm	*f*/3.5–4	100°	24 oz	2¼″–2¾″	2¾″	8″–1′	
	20 mm	*f*/4	94°	24 oz	2½″	2½″	1′	
	24 mm	*f*/2.8	84°	20 oz	2½″	2½″	1′	
	28 mm	*f*/2.8	75°	18 oz	2½″	2″	1′	Becoming standard WA
	35 mm	*f*/2.8	63°	12 oz	2″	2″	1′	
	Standard 50 mm	*f*/1.2–2	46°	12 oz	2″	2″	18″–2′	Except for macros, sharpest of all lenses
	Short Telephoto 85 mm	*f*/1.8	28°30′	12–18 oz	2¾″	2¼″	3′	Many use so-called "portrait lenses" as standard
	100 mm	*f*/2.8	24°	16 oz	2½″	3″	3½′–4′	
	Telephoto 135 mm	*f*/2.8	18°	1½ lb	3½″–4″	3″	5′	Standard telephoto
	200 mm	*f*/3.5	12°	1½–2 lb	5½″	3″	6′–10′	
	300 mm	*f*/4.5	8°15′	2½ lb	7″	3″	12′–15′	
	400 mm	*f*/5.5–6.3	6°10′	8 lb	10″	3½″	15′	Equipped with rotating tripod socket
	600 mm	*f*/5.6	4°10′	10 lb	10″	3½″	30′	
	800 mm	*f*/8.0	3°06′	12 lb	18″	3½″	60′	
	1200 mm	*f*/11	2°05′	15 lb	32″	3½″	100′	
	Mirror Lenses 500 mm	*f*/8	5°	4½ lb	8″	5½″	12′	
	1000 mm	*f*/11	2°30′	6–7 lb	8″–10″	6″	20′	Fixed aperture, rotating focusing wheel built in
	Macro Lenses 50 mm	*f*/2.8–3.5	46°	18 oz	3½″	2¼″	6″	Focuses to 1:1 magnification ratio
	100 mm	*f*/2.8	24°	20 oz	4½″	2½″	14″	Recessed front lens element
	Zoom Lenses 24–40 mm	*f*/3.5	84–55°	31 oz	4″	3″	3′	Close-focusing capability
	35–100 mm	*f*/3.5	63–24°	24 oz	4½″	3″	3½′	"
	100–200 mm	*f*/5.6	24–12°	18 oz	5″–6″	2½″	5′	Lightweight zoom
	70–210 mm	*f*/3.5	34–11°40′	32 oz	6½″	2¾″	6′	Half-lifesize capability in some "macro zooms"
	85–300 mm	*f*/4.5	28°30′–8°15′	3 lb	9½″	3″	8′	

LENSES IN DIFFERENT CAMERA FORMATS (continued)

CAMERA FORMAT	FOCAL LENGTH	MAX. *f*-STOP	ANGLE of VIEW	WEIGHT	TYPICAL LENGTH	BARREL DIA.	MIN. FOCUS DISTANCE	COMMENTS
6 × 6 cm (2¼″ × 2¼″)	W/A 30 mm Fisheye	f/3.5	180°	36 oz	4″	3½″		Built-in lens shade
	40 mm	f/4.0	88°	28 oz	3¾″	3″		
	50 mm	f/3.5	75°	32 oz	4″	3″		
	Standard 80 mm	f/2.8	52°	24 oz	2¾″	2¾″	3′	
	Telephoto 100 mm	f/3.5	43°	24 oz	3″	2¾″	3½′	
	120 mm	f/4.5	36°	30 oz	4″	″	3½′	
	150 mm	f/4.0	30°	40 oz	5″	″	5′	
	250 mm	f/5.6	18°	3 lb	6½″	3″	8′	
	350 mm	f/5.6	13°	4½ lb	11″	3½″	15′	
	500 mm	f/8.0	9°	6 lb	16″	4″	30′	
6 × 7 cm 2¼″ × 2¾″	W/A 35 mm Fisheye	f/4.5	180°	2½ lb	4″	3″	1½′	
	55 mm	f/3.5	78°	2 lb	3½″	″	1½′	
	75 mm	f/4.5	61°	1½ lb	3″	″	2′	
	Standard 90 mm	f/2.8	52½°	1½ lb	3½″	3″	2½′	
	105 mm	f/2.8	45°	20 oz	4½″	3¼″	3½′	
	Telephoto 135 mm	f/4.0	36°	28 oz	5″	3″	3′	
	200 mm	″	26°	32 oz	4½″	″	8′	
	300 mm	″	17°	3 lb	7½″	3½″	16′	
	400 mm	″	12°	5 lb	8″	″	26′	
	600 mm	f/8.0	8°	11 lb	15″	4″	40′	
	800 mm	f/8.0	6°	30 lb	24″	″	70′	
	1000 mm Mirror	f/8.0	5°	13 lb	14″	8″	60′	Built-in filler wheel

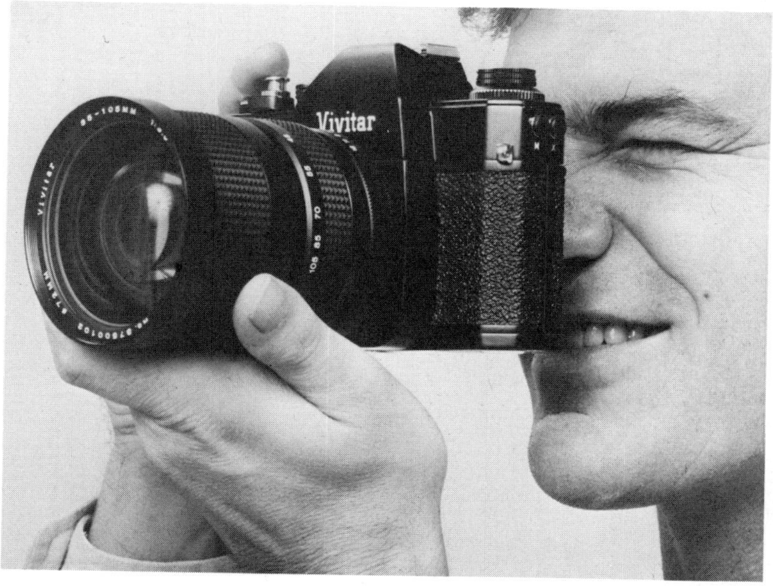

For better balance and stability, use the palm of your hand to cradle the lens. Photo courtesy Vivitar, Inc.

fact, pictures of distant scenes (lens focused at infinity) confirmed that tripod-mounted cameras produce sharper images not only at the same shutter speed but also at two or three speeds slower than were possible with the hand-held cameras. (All tests were conducted with the same camera-and-lens combination and the same subject.)

What do you do in situations where tripods are either impractical or prohibited, as in some museums? If you want to get a closeup of an art object you cannot physically move in on, you have to use a telephoto lens; but there are alternatives to tripods. Various designers offer chest pods, gunstocks, and harnesses as steadying devices for this sort of situation. We have found most work fairly well. But camera unsteadiness, especially with long lenses, is produced as much by improper body positioning as by the weight of your camera and lens.

Try using your own body as a vertical support. Have you noticed photographers all scrunched up, their cameras seemingly growing out of their foreheads? That's a technique you can practice to improve steadiness. First, press the camera body firmly against your face. Then tuck your elbows into your sides and take a wide, comfortable stance and a deep breath. Just as you begin exhaling, steadily squeeze the shutter release. Do not punch, poke, or jab it, but *squeeze* it. If you've ever fired a rifle you'll see it's the same smooth motion you would use to squeeze a trigger. You can steady the camera further by holding the camera body in one hand and *cradling,* rather than gripping, the lens barrel about halfway down its length with the other hand.

Because of their design, telephotos give you a much shallower depth of field than normal or wide-angle lenses at the same focused

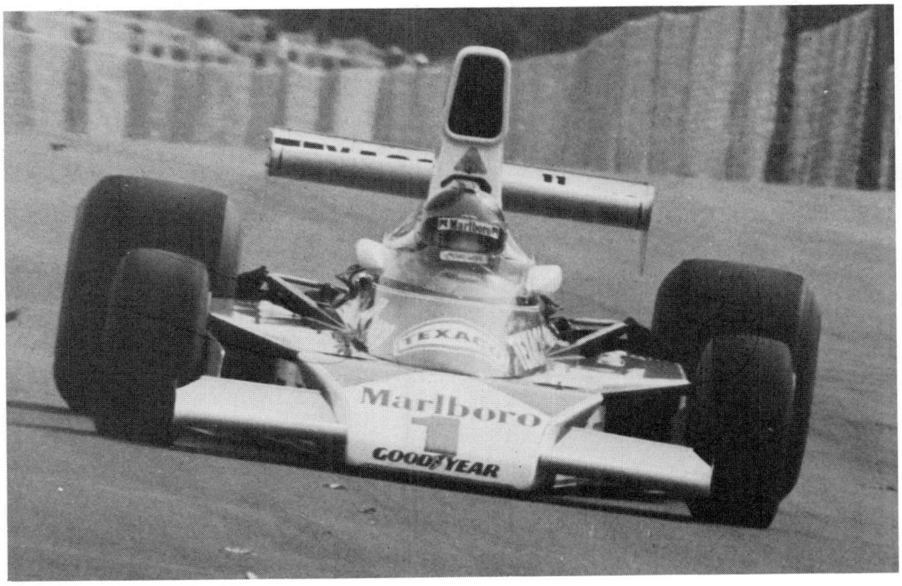

A 500 mm lens used on a bright, sunny day produced this compressed image with some noticeably hazy effects. Photo by Dave Reasinger.

distance and *f*-stops: As focal length increases, depth of field decreases. Thus the problem of focusing accuracy that was mentioned in the discussion of wide-angle lenses is not present in telephoto-lens use. You will probably find that images leap in and out of focus with astonishing ease. The limited depth of field presents a different caution: Closeups with a telephoto must be focused with extreme care and, since most telephoto lenses have small maximum *f*-stops, slow shutter speeds are usually necessary. All the more reason for using a tripod.

One more problem you're likely to encounter, especially with lenses longer than 300 mm, is atmospheric haze. Airborne dust particles tend to obscure a scene and diminish the quality of telephoto picture taking. Manmade air pollution obviously compounds the problem. Ultraviolet or haze filters help, as do polarizers, but no filter can altogether eliminate the particles' effect. Also, hot summer days literally produce waves of heated air that rise from the earth and disturb the air between camera and subject, if the two are far apart. The only way to combat this atmospheric disturbance is to shoot early in the day.

Telephoto pictures characteristically compress and flatten the objects appearing in them. The "telephoto effect" tends to reduce the apparent separation in distance between objects, as well as to present them as more linear than they seem to the eye. As you will see, these effects become more pronounced as focal length increases.

Telephoto Focal Lengths

85–105 mm. These lenses are often referred to as "short" or "portrait" telephotos and

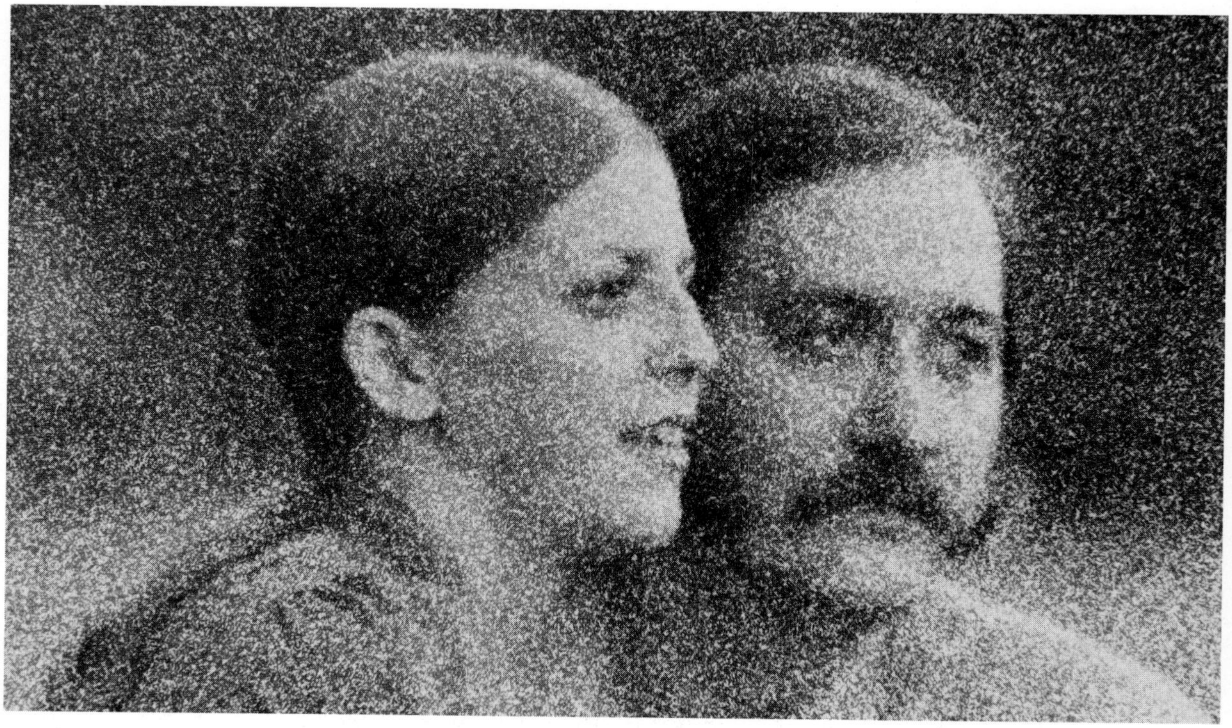

are favored by many professional photographers. Their merits are several, the most important perhaps being that short telephotos are usually very fast, with maximum *f*-stops of *f*/2, *f*/1.8, or even *f*/1.7. They are short in length, relatively lightweight, and often physically indistinguishable from 50 mm lenses. Actually, many people use 85 mm as their "normal" lens. While having roughly the same speed as the 50 mm's, the 85 mm's have more magnification; so they allow the photographer greater distance from his subject and some freedom of movement. Even close up these lenses do not unduly exaggerate apparent proportion.

These optics are easily hand-held because of the large *f*-stops available, which permit high shutter speeds, and because of their short length and light weight, which reduce the danger of camera shake. High speed, small size and weight, and increased image magnification make the short telephotos ideal general-purpose lenses. You might consider shopping for an 85 mm lens–35 mm SLR combination, rather than a 50 mm lens—we don't think you would be at all disappointed.

A rung up the focal-length ladder are the 100–105 mm lenses, which can be used the same way as the 85 mm's but which are a little slower. They tend to render the different objects in a scene in the same proportions as the human eye does, and so are well suited to portrait shooting. The 100–105 mm lenses flatten subjects just enough to produce pleasing results, especially when shooting head-and-shoulder portraits. Lens producers have come up with exceptionally sharp 100–105 mm lenses with high contrast, and if maximum *f*-stops of *f*/2.5–2.8 aren't too slow for you, they make really outstanding all-purpose lenses.

135–200 mm. Many of the attributes of the 100–105 mm lenses are applicable to these next lenses, at least to some extent. In general, 135–200 mm lenses produce too flattened a perspective to be ideal for portraiture. Some photographers do use the 135 mm's for portrait

(Facing page) This self-portrait of the photographer and his wife was taken with a short telephoto. Note the darkroom addition of a texture screen to enhance the serenity of the scene. Photo by Dave Reasinger. (Right) A short telephoto can make a very good all-purpose lens for some photographers. This photo was made with a 105 mm Nikkor lens mounted on a Nikon F body. Photo by Bill Coleman.

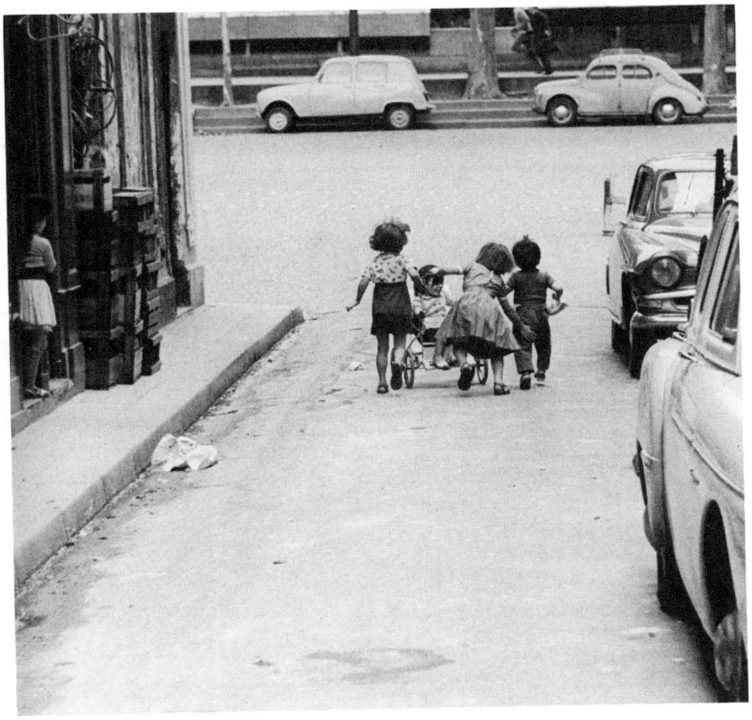

work; but the 200 mm sees far more use for moderate-distance action or nature than for formal portraiture. You may not be aware that 135 mm lenses have been sold as standard telephotos for years, basically for the same reasons that 50 mm lenses are now sold as standard "normals": They are both good compromises. These particular telephotos are neither too heavy nor too long, and their magnification is moderate and so more easily contained. Above all, good-quality 135 mm's with maximum *f*-stops of *f*/2.8 or so are for the most part easily manufactured, and so are often priced very reasonably and found in abundance.

If it's a lens for action photography you want, however, 135 mm's fall a little short of ideal. In many situations they simply do not offer enough magnification. It is our firm belief that a 200 mm lens of *f*/3.5 or faster is pretty much the lower limit for action shots. To bring you into the thick of a football game from the sidelines, for example, 4× magnification puts you no more than 20 yards away from your farthest subject if you are at the 50-yard line. Using high-speed film, a hand-held 200 mm makes basketball shots practical. Rather dramatic effects can often be achieved with a 200 mm, because at large *f*-stops this lens allows you to separate the main subject visually from its background and thus emphasize it. In other words, you can blur the background, allowing only the main subject to remain in sharp focus.

300–400 mm. At a focal length of about 300 mm, subject-compression and isolation effects typical of telephoto lenses become very pronounced. There are several lenses in this focal length that permit the photographer to focus as close as 3–4.6 m (10–15 ft). But most 300–400 mm lenses are heavy (1.4 kg [3 lb] or more) and tend to be from 20 to 30 cm (8–12 in.) long, which increases the likelihood of camera shake.

While there are a few 300 mm's with maximum *f*-stops of *f*/4, *f*/5.6 is the norm. The

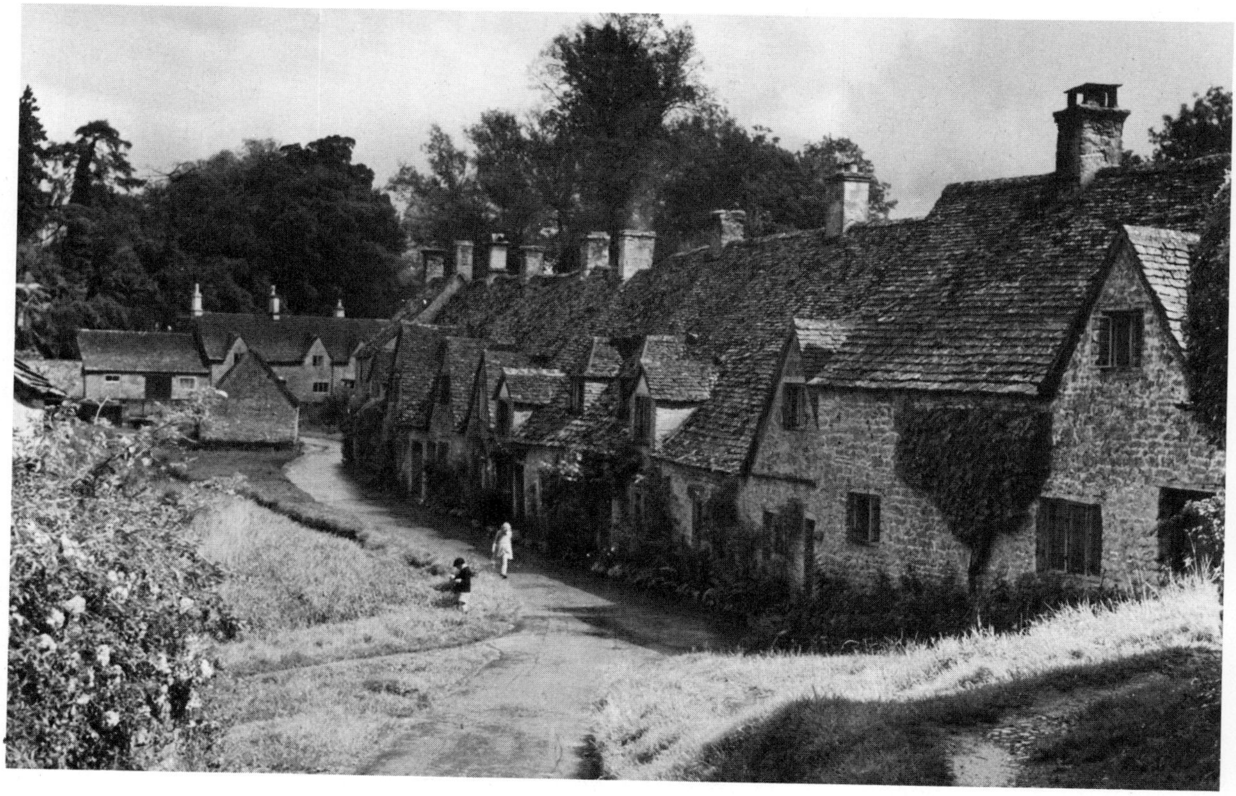

(Above) Arlington Row, Bibury, England, as seen through a medium (135 mm) telephoto lens mounted on a Minolta SRT 101. Photo by L.P. Greenhill, F.R.P.S. (Below) This long telephoto shot was taken with a 400 mm lens. Photo by James Forkner.

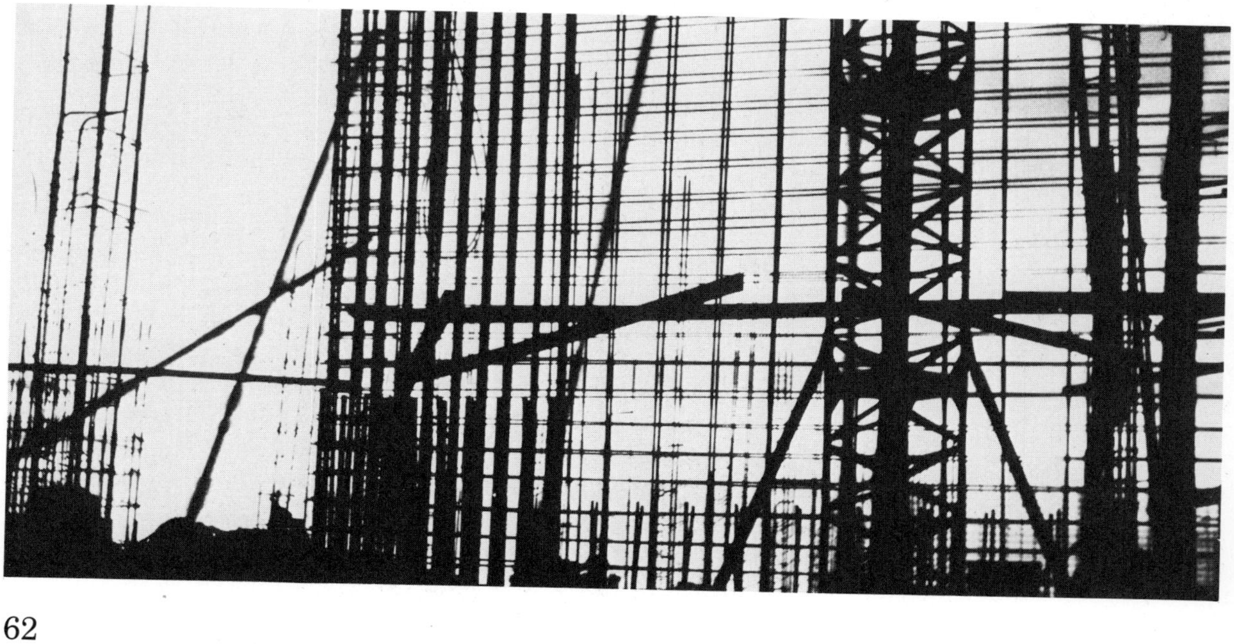

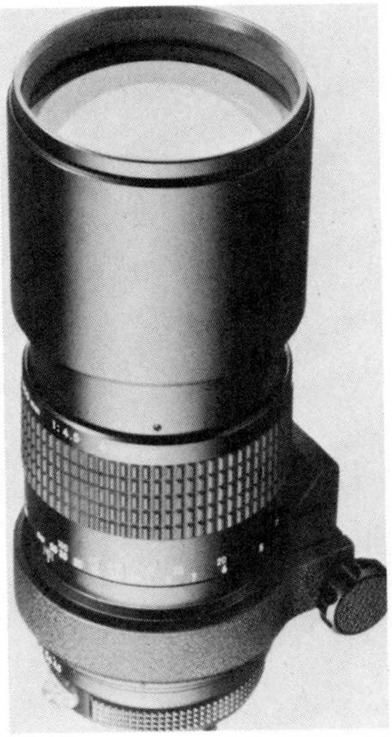

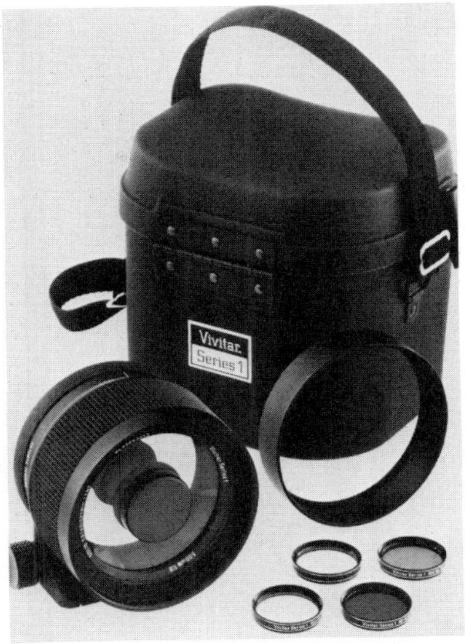

(Far left) This 300 mm *f*/4.5 Nikkor telephoto lens has a sturdy tripod-mounting collar which is an absolute must with longer lenses. Photo courtesy EPOI. (Left) Shown here is the Vivitar 600 mm *f*/8 "Solid Cat" catadioptric lens with case and accessories. Photo courtesy Vivitar, Inc.

400 mm's generally have a maximum of no more than *f*/6.3. In low light they are hard to focus. Focusing is especially tricky with the general-purpose split-image viewing screens found in many 35 mm SLRs because half of the split-image viewing screen circle has a nasty habit of going black on you. While viewing screens especially designed for these lenses are available, the expense probably outweighs their usefulness: They do not work well with lenses of shorter focal lengths.

So there are problems associated with using long-focal-length lenses, although we feel these can be managed. In good light, with high-speed film, careful focusing, and some support other than your own body, you can produce fine, sharp pictures with the unique look only long lenses can provide.

500 mm and Up. These highly specialized lenses possess all the problems of the 300–400 mm's and more. We have discovered that, with the exception of the 500 mm mirror optics (more about them in a bit), no ultralong telephotos made of glass can be hand-held and still produce consistently sharp photographs. We wouldn't advise your counting on finding an exception to this rule, although you may have more luck than we have had.

For sports, though, or other action photography the 500–600 mm (or even longer) lenses are really in their element. Once mounted on a sturdy tripod, they draw you right into the middle of the action. Obviously, high-speed film will be essential with these optics. Nevertheless, we feel that 500 mm or longer lenses are not practical investments for most people. No matter how well-suited they seem, not many of us are likely to spend hours lugging a 2.3-kilo, 38-centimetre lens (5 pounds in weight, 15 inches in length) around the woods in search of interesting scenes or wildlife.

If you are determined to take the ultralong-lens plunge anyway, why not investigate the mirror optics, more technically called *catadioptric,* or "cat," lenses? They duplicate telescope design but with drastically reduced physical length, owing to a system of optical "folding" with mirrors and glass elements. They provide the same long focal length at generally less than half the length of their all-glass counterparts. Unfortunately, mirror lenses do not permit incorporation of a diaphragm; so the amount of light reaching the film (i.e., the exposure) must generally be controlled by shutter speed alone. Some mirror lenses do incorporate neutral density filters. These are mounted on a rotating ring in the lens's light path in such a way that the filters can be used to vary the lens aperture.

Vivitar recently introduced a new mirror lens that reduces the required physical length even more. Their 600 mm Series I mirror lens is a little over 7.6 cm (3 in.) long and weighs about 1.6 kg (3½ lb). According to the manufacturer, this lens (hand-held, yet) makes ultralong telephotography practical at shutter speeds considerably slower than those of normal mirror or all-glass ultralong lenses. These claims seem reasonable, but it's a case of not believing until you have seen. A 1.6 kg (3½ lb) lens on an SLR is still quite a handful, and remember that any camera motion or subject motion would be magnified 12 times over the camera shake you might expect from a 50 mm optic. We have used Celestron's mirror lenses extensively and have found them to be excellent performers. It is unfortunate that the nature of mirror-optic design really limits these lenses' usefulness.

New technology and exotic glass or even plastics may dramatically reduce lens weight and size in the near future. Both Minolta and Spiratone have already introduced very compact 500 mm mirror optics of excellent quality. The Spiratone lens can be adapted to any SLR.

Macro Lenses. True macros have lens designs specifically formulated to produce best results at half- to full-life-size magnification ratios. They can be focused very close to the subject (13–25 cm [5–10 in.] subject-to-film-plane distance) and produce negatives or slides that lose very little in sharpness or contrast from center to edge. Since normal and telephoto lenses function best when focused at infinity, they aren't as well suited to macro work as lenses specifically designed for close work.

The most common macro lenses for 35 mm cameras fall in the range of 50–60 mm focal length. Several manufacturers now offer 90–100 mm macros, which have some definite and obvious advantages over the 50–60 mm's. A 100 mm provides double the subject-to-film-plane distance at any given magnification ratio, compared with its 50 mm macro cousins.

Quality macros usually cannot be found outside the camera manufacturer's lens lineups, but at least three independent lens makers (Vivitar, Sigma, and Soligor) have introduced macros for most 35 mm SLRs.

If you can accept relatively slow maximum *f*-stops (*f*/2.8 to *f*/4), you might consider a macro as a highly versatile standard lens. While macros have been designed for close-up work, they usually perform well at longer focusing distances, too.

The real advantage of good macros lies in their ability to reproduce fine detail and line-copy. They resolve as many lines per millimetre, if not more, than virtually any other lenses, and they do so over their entire field. Quality macros are designed to make any unwanted curve caused by the optics less noticeable, and thus are able to control the tendency of a picture taken at very close distances to show either pincushion or barrel distortion at the edges. Macros are also quite compact and lightweight, but those benefits might be overshadowed by their rather steep price. If you're planning to shoot a lot of closeups, especially of stamps, coins, documents, or flowers, macro would be a wise, probably a necessary, investment.

Zoom Lenses. If it's versatility you want, the zoom cannot be beaten. Finally, after a lot of bad press, zooms that rival fixed-focal-length

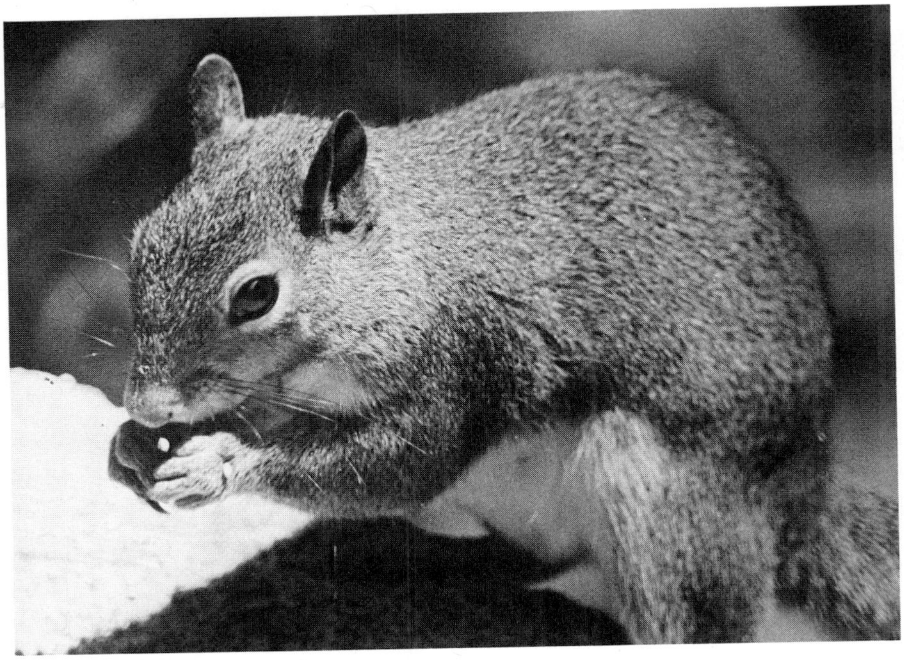

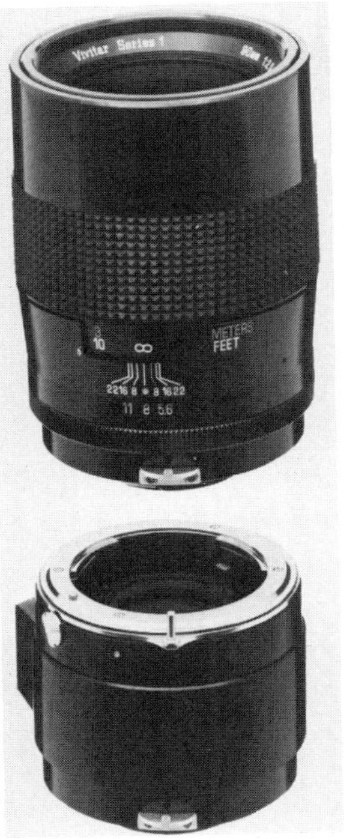

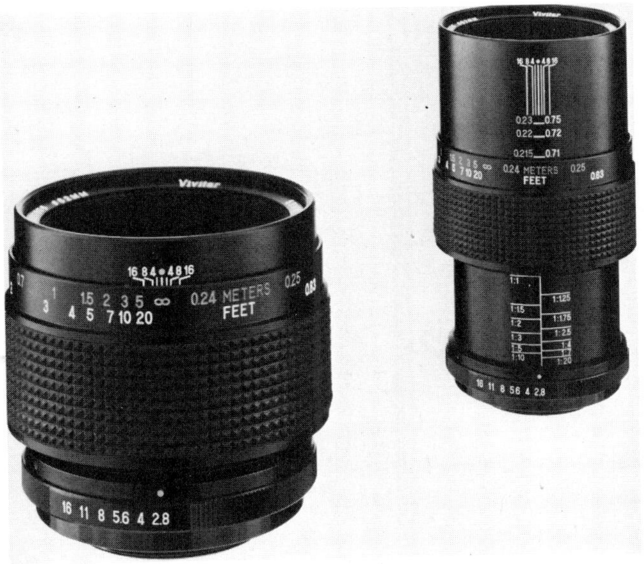

(Above left) This photograph was taken with a tripod-mounted Celestron 1250 mm *f*/10 lens at 1/250 sec. Photo courtesy Celestron, Int. (Above right) A 90 mm focal-length puts some space between the lens and the subject. This is a Vivitar Series 1 90 mm *f*/2.5 lens. (Left) This 55 mm macro lens has a 1:1 focal length ratio without the addition of tubes. Photo courtesy Vivitar, Inc.

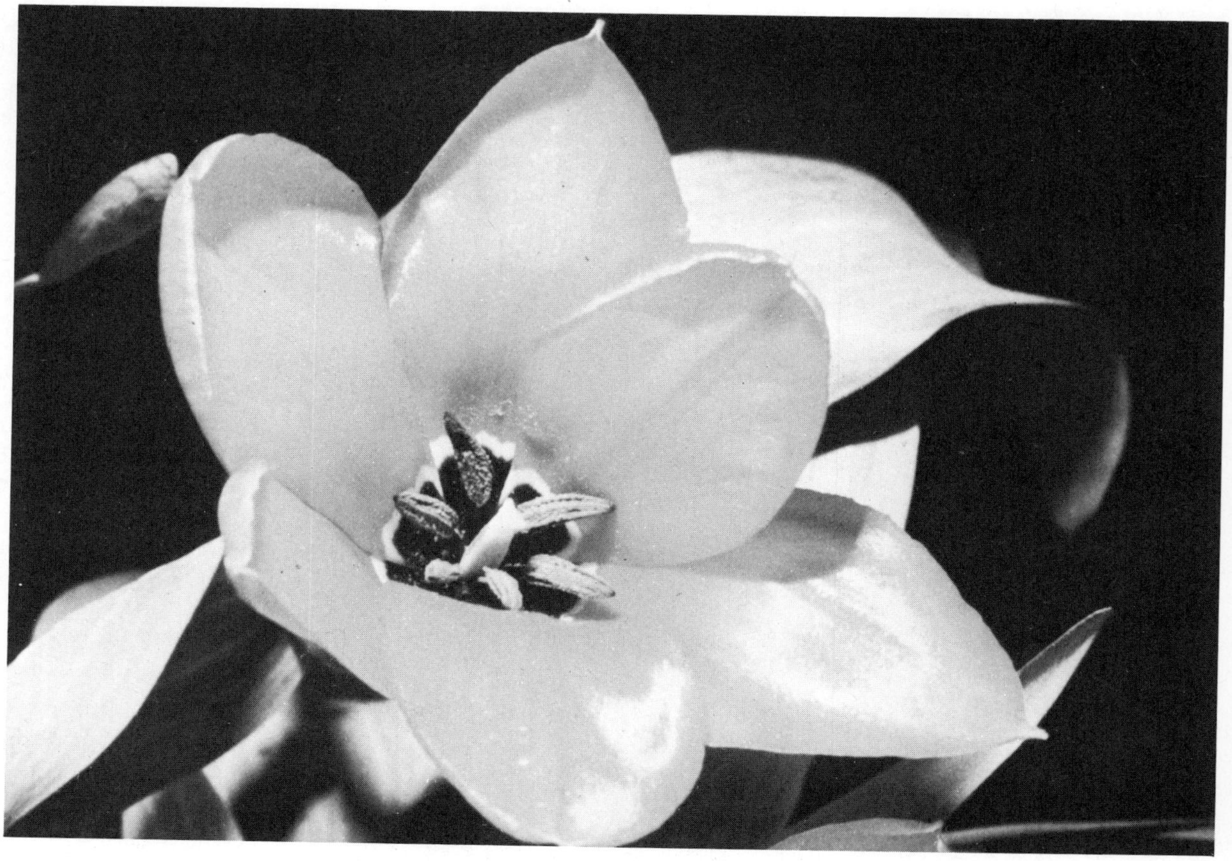

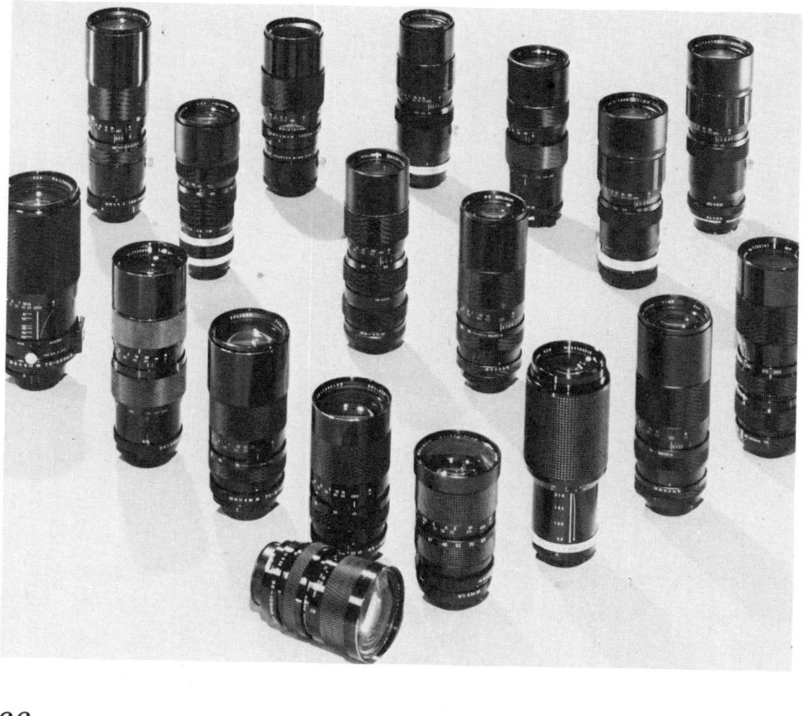

(Above) This macro shot is one-half life size. Photo by Marc Levey. (Left) There are zooms for everybody on todays market, varying widely in speed, focal length, and price. Photo courtesy A.I.C.

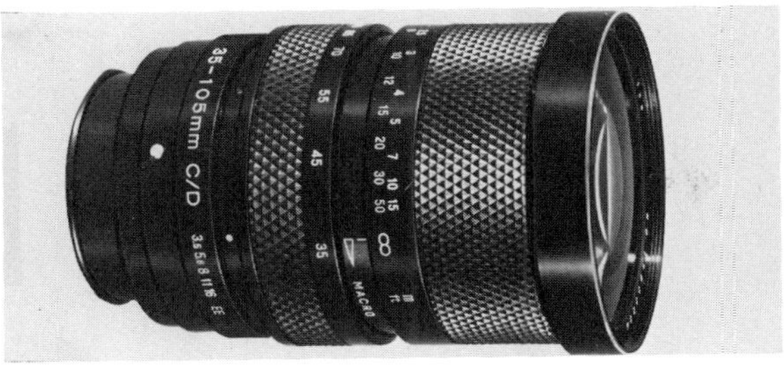

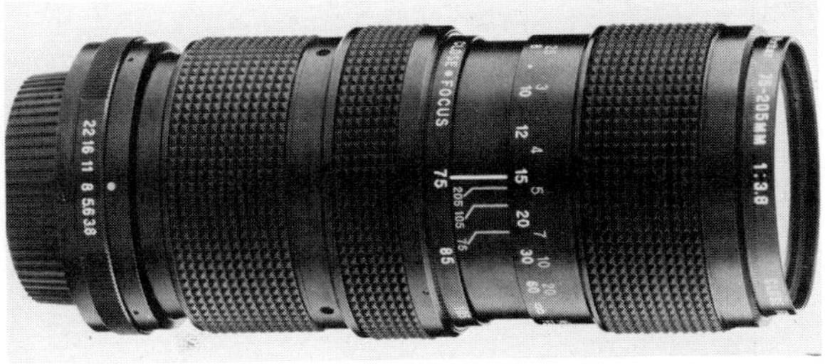

(Left) A popular moderate-wide-angle to short-telephoto zoom lens is the Soligor 35-105 mm *f*/3.5 C/D lens. Photo courtesy A.I.C. (Right) This is the Vivitar 75-205 mm *f*/3.8 C/F zoom lens. Photo courtesy Vivitar, Inc.

lenses in sharpness are now being offered to the photographic public. For years zooms were considered gimmick lenses no self-respecting photographer would admit to owning; but recent advances in computer technology and new kinds of glass and coatings have improved zoom-lens performance to a point worthy of serious consideration. As an alternative to fixed-focal-length lenses, zooms provide a tremendous choice in focal lengths within their designed ranges. Zoom ratios of 3:1 (ratio of shortest to longest focal length) are common, and a number of more exotic lenses, with 6:1 zoom ratios, are also available.

To many people a zoom lens seems ideal for 35 mm photography. In our opinion, it is—but with some qualifications. While it is a versatile and creative optic, a zoom is also heavy, highly complex, and expensive. Also consider that often a low-cost fixed-focal-length lens can yield surprisingly good results where a low-cost zoom will generally produce barely acceptable or even downright awful results. Zooms always demand much more precision in their manufacture than their fixed-focal-length relatives do, and so cost-cutting has a more drastic effect on zoom quality.

Yet it seems that a month doesn't go by without the advent of yet another zoom lens. The first zooms for the still-photography popular market appeared a good decade or more ago; they covered the 80–200 mm range and offered maximum *f*-stops in the area of *f*/4. Then about three years ago Vivitar introduced its 70–210 mm Series I macro zoom. This close-focusing long lens really shook up the market, both because its makers proclaimed it to be as good as fine fixed-focal-length lenses in terms of resolution and contrast and especially because it possessed near-macro capability all the way down to half life size. Thus began the race, and every lens manufacturer went to the designing board and the computer to engineer its own "dream" lens. Lenses in the 75–260 mm, 200–600 mm, and 50–300 mm ranges resulted. Most incorporated close-focusing, or macro, capability; some lenses added the macro ability as an afterthought, with no redesign of the optics.

Undoubtedly, a well-made 70–210 mm zoom lens capable of rendering 1:2 image magnification is a truly versatile lens. But even the best of the type are in some ways compromises. Lens technology has not yet been able to provide a relatively wide zoom range, good performance at all focal lengths, and true macro lens performance at close focusing distances. Some zooms do well at normally focused distances but fall short on close-up work. To produce any lens that does both equally well appears to require monumental technological achievement. Many photographers find macro zooms satisfactory in all but the most critical applications, where flatness of field and critically sharp resolution from center to edge are required.

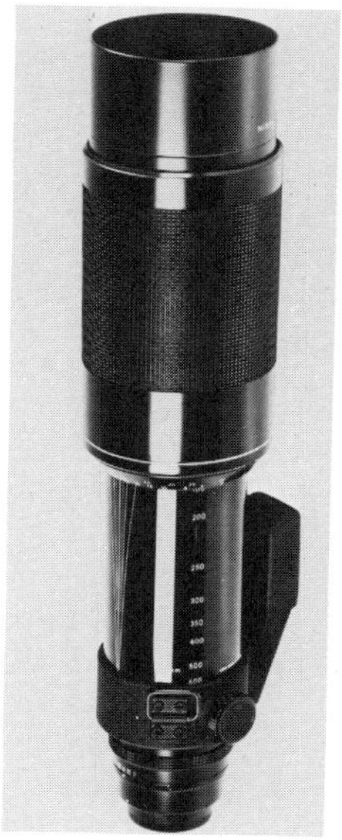

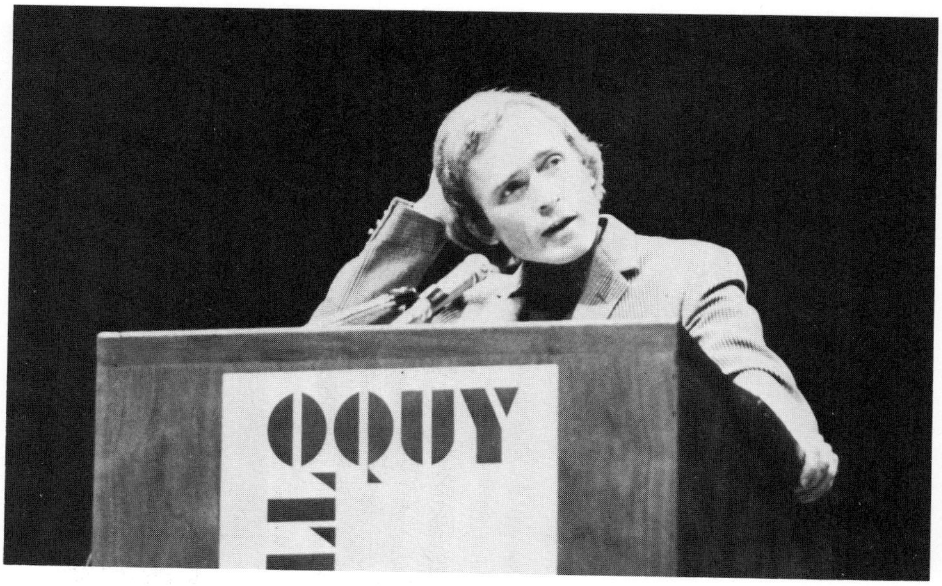

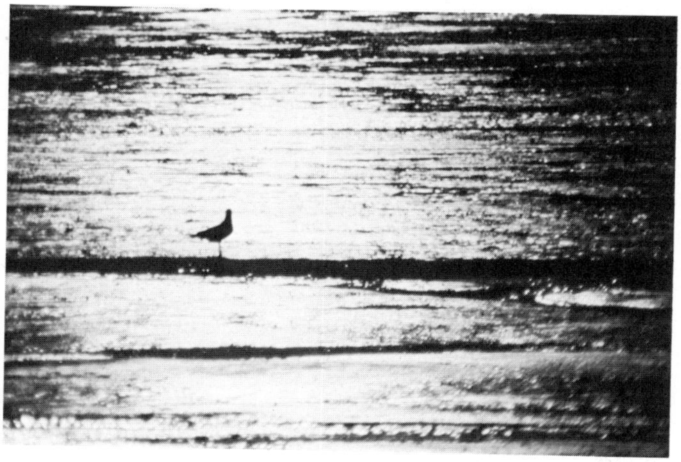

(Above left) The longest available zoom lens is the Nikkor 180-600 mm *f*/8. Photo courtesy EPOI, Inc. (Above) This hand-held photograph was taken with a zoom lens at 200 mm. Photo by Marc Levey. (Left) This zoom-lens photo was taken at 100 mm. Photo by Samuel Kazdan.

For dramatic nature shots, super-close-up portraiture, and similar uses, the best of the macro zooms perform admirably. Vivitar Series I 70–210 mm, Soligor 70–210 mm, and Sun/Spiratone 80–240 mm are among the top macro zooms available. In the non-macro category of zoom lenses, Nikon's 80–200 mm is said to be a superior optic. At the present rate of introduction, many more zooms are likely to show by the time this book is in print; so before rushing out to snatch up the latest marvel in optic design, read Chapter IV on the not-so-gentle art of photoequipment buying. It might save you a lot of grief.

Second to the telephoto-macro zoom comes a more recent development in zoom-lens technology, the zoom wide-angle lenses. Usually in the 35–50 mm, 35–105 mm, and most recently the 28–50 mm range, this kind of lens poses more design and construction obstacles than even the zoom telephotos. Consequently, these lenses possess modest maximum *f*-stops of *f*/3.5 or so and are appreciably more expensive than their tele counterparts.

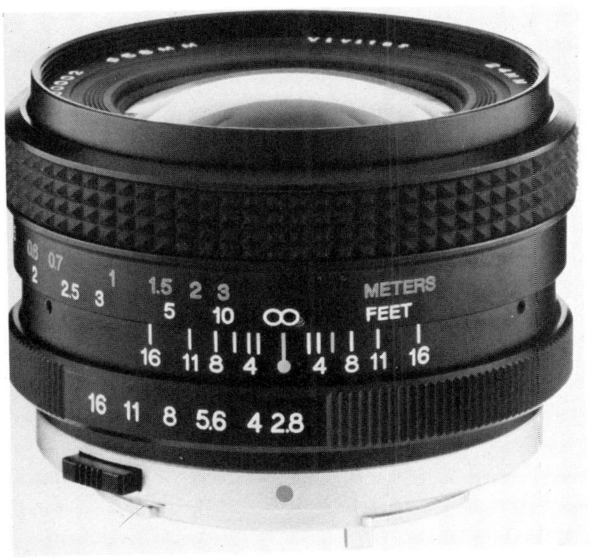

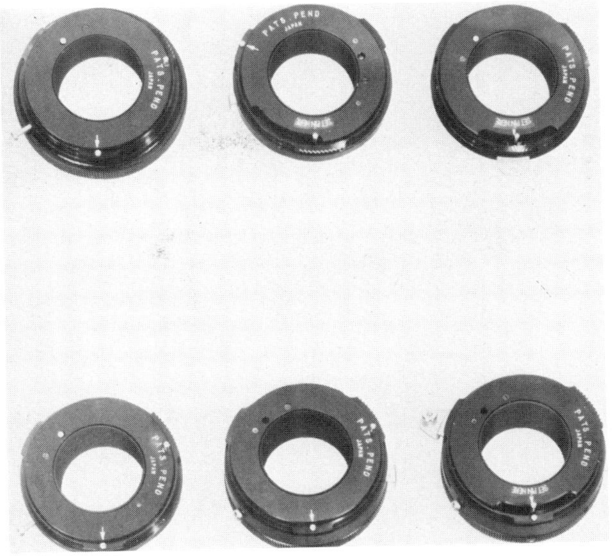

(Left) This lens is fitted with a fixed bayonet mount. Photo courtesy Vivitar, Inc. (Right) A variety of T-4 mounts for interchangeable-mount lenses are available. If you own different camera bodies, one lens with several mounts will suffice for all. Photo courtesy A.I.C.

Several manufacturers have gone the varifocal lens route in recent years. Unlike the true zoom, which maintains its focus while zooming from one focal length to another, the varifocal lens requires refocusing at each focal length. This simplifies the optical and mechanical construction and moves towards offsetting problems inherent in zoom-wide-angle design.

We expect to see in the near future quality zooms covering the 70–250 mm range and having 1:1 magnification capability, as well as 24–50 mm zoom wide-angles that focus to near-macro range. These two lenses would replace, if they performed at all well, an entire bag of fixed-focal-length lenses. In combination, they could increase the speed, versatility, and handling ease of camera systems.

For now, we willingly accept the limitations of existing macro zooms in return for their infinitely greater flexibility over fixed-focal-length lenses. In all but great enlargements (larger than 28 × 36 cm [11 × 14 in.]), the difference isn't detectable, especially when medium *f*-stops of *f*/5.6–11 are used. We feel it wise to consider one good zoom as an alternative to a series of fixed-focal-length lenses, for it would offer you greater opportunities to create unique images unobtainable with conventional lenses.

Lens-Mounting Systems

The debate over fixed mounts vs. interchangeable mounts still rages. Lenses, particularly the 35 mm variety, come with permanently fixed mounts or in interchangeable mounts that are not an integral part of the lens. The advantage of interchangeable systems (known by such baffling codes as YS, TX, Adaptall, T-4, etc.) is that if you decide to change camera makes, you only need to buy one additional mount, at a cost of $7 to $20. At one time these mounts weren't sufficiently rigid, nor were the alignment of lens and body or the meter coupling precise enough to deliver consistently sharp pictures. In the newest mounts, especially Vivitar's TX and Tamron's Adaptall series, many of these deficiencies have been minimized or totally eliminated.

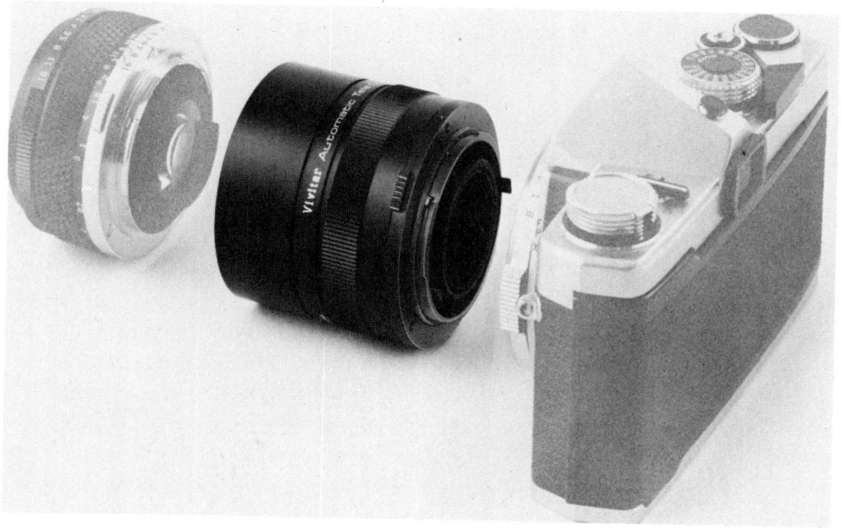

Teleconverters fit between the lens and the body to increase the effective focal length of the prime lens. Photo courtesy Vivitar, Inc.

We feel, however, that in most cases a fixed lens-mount system is still preferable because it can be constructed more precisely and has fewer chances of malfunction. The interchangeable mount cannot ensure such accurate lens alignment and focusing.

There are at present three commonly available mounts for interchangeable lenses: the screw, the bayonet, and the breech-bayonet. A word of caution here: Just because two camera makers advertise bayonet mounts for their lenses, don't assume the bayonets are interchangeable with one another; in fact, quite the opposite is true. It seems as if camera makers deliberately design lens mounts to be incompatible with camera bodies other than their own. Numerous attempts have been made to adapt one manufacturer's lenses to another's cameras, but with little or no success to date.

Screw Mount. Also called a "universal mount," this is simply a threaded "male" lens mounted to a threaded "female" camera body. The advantage this type offers is tremendous lens selection and interchangeability by brand. Its disadvantage is the possibility that the thread could strip and the lens could back out from the mount. In addition, screw mounts take longer to attach than other types do. Pentax and Praktica offer mounts of this kind.

Bayonet Mount. This mount is currently the most popular in quality cameras. It consists of three or more "male" protrusions that lock into "female" slots on the camera body. A simple twist locks the lens into the mount.

Breech-Bayonet Mount. This one combines the virtues of the bayonet type—notably, rapid mounting and dismounting—with a locking collar that applies constant and ever-greater pressure to the mounting surface as the mount wears, over time.

Teleconverters. For years photography writers have argued the merits and liabilities of optical gadgets, variously called teleconverters, doublers, tele-extenders and so on. And although no clear consensus has been achieved, one thing is certain: A lot of teleconverters are used daily throughout the world.

Simply put, a teleconverter consists of a tube containing from four to seven optical elements. The tube is mounted between camera body and lens, usually with some provision made to connect the converter and lens to the camera's metering system.

Basically, these extenders increase the effective focal length of attached lenses while adding a mere couple of centimetres to the total length and only a few grams to the weight of

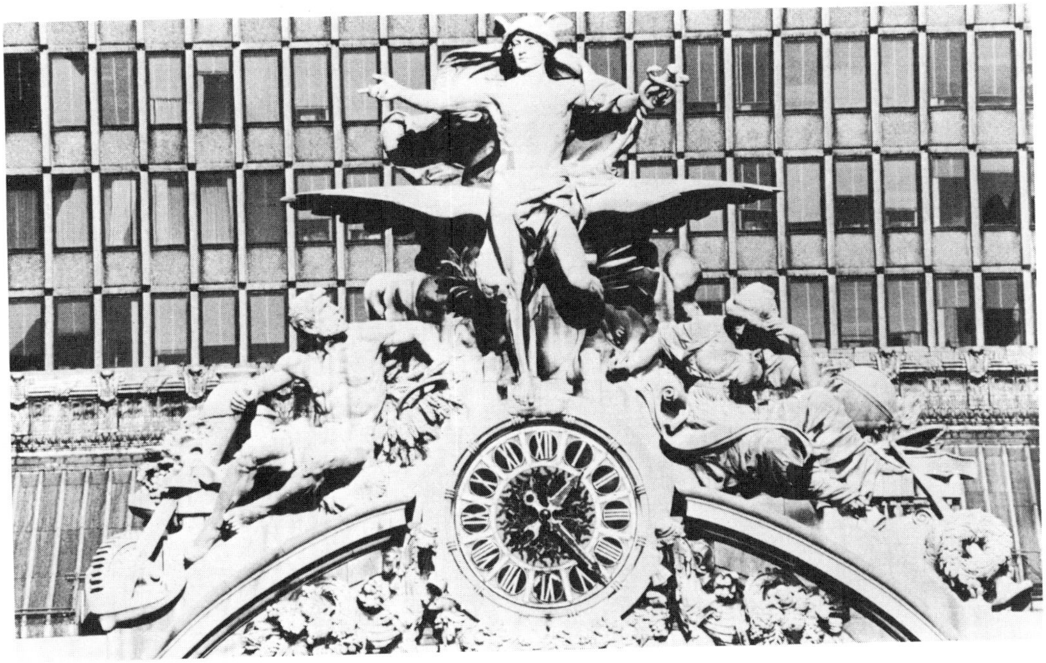

The scene above was photographed with a Rokkor X 400 mm *f*/5.6 APO lens. (Below) The same scene was photographed with the same lens, but a 2× converter was added. Photos courtesy Minolta, U.S.A.

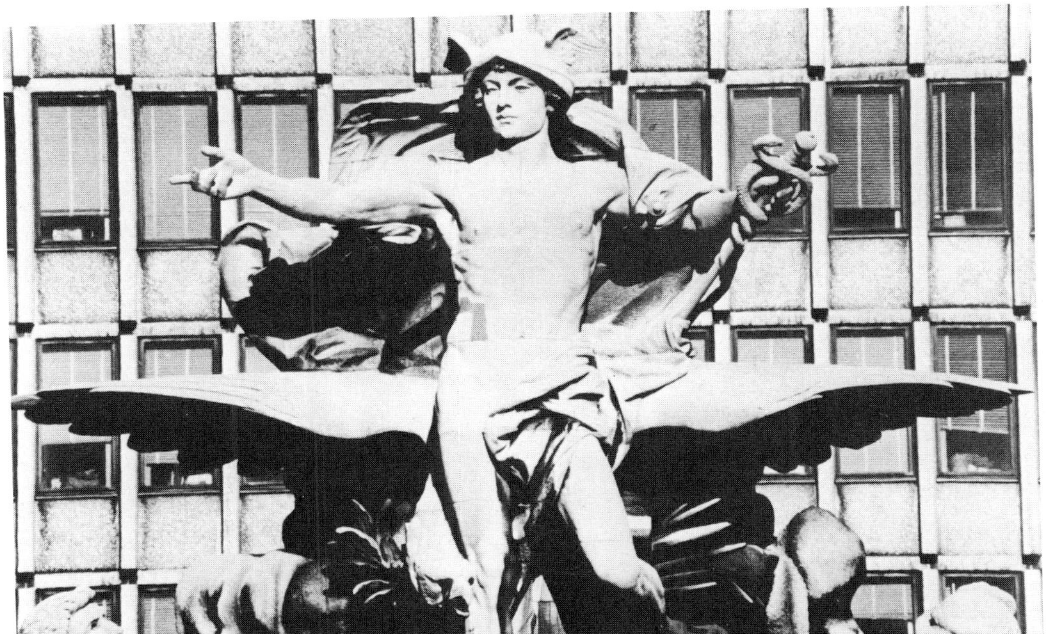

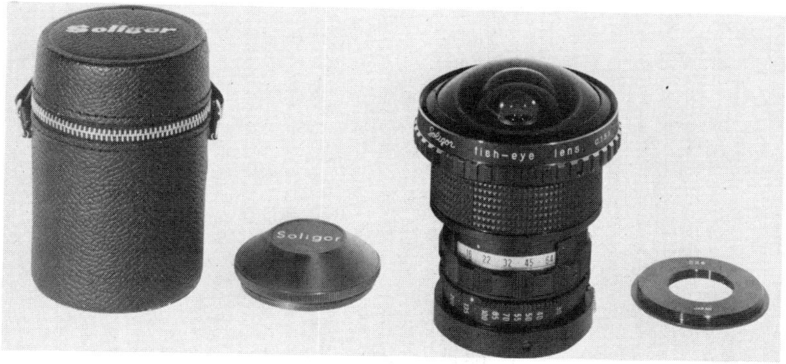

The fisheye converter screws in front of a normal lens and converts it to a 160° fisheye. Photo courtesy A.I.C.

the combination. They come in 1.5×, 2×, and 3× versions. When a 2× converter is mounted with a 135 mm lens, the lens-and-teleconverter combo produces an effective focal length of 270 mm. If the 35 mm alone focuses to 152 cm (5 ft), so does the converter-lens combination. A 3× teleconverter with 135 mm lens results in a 405 mm that focuses as close as 152 cm (5 ft). Sounds too simple and good to be true, doesn't it? Well, in a few ways it is.

First of all, converters do absorb light. In the case of a 2× converter used with a 135 mm *f*/2.8 lens, the effective maximum *f*-stop is reduced to *f*/5.6—two full *f*-stops; with a 3× converter, even more light is lost. Most of us can live with small *f*-stops in long-focal-length lenses; but what about loss of quality?

Several independent tests we've seen indicate a reduction in sharpness, induced flare, and reduced contrast inherent in teleconverter use. How much quality loss is acceptable remains a matter of opinion. Our own in-use tests have shown that a well-made converter mounted on a *sharp* tele lens of at least 100 mm stopped down to about *f*/8 or smaller can produce good results. You should be aware, however, that such a combination will not perform as well as a good 200 mm lens used by itself.

If weight and size are important to you and you don't plan to use long-focal-length lenses often, though, a teleconverter merits some consideration.

On a final note, Nikon has introduced a series of converters specifically formulated for their own telephoto lenses. Initial reports indicate they are of very high optical quality and promise results thus far unobtainable with converters. The single fly in the ointment is that the price of these Nikon converters is likely to approach the cost of their telephoto lenses themselves. Canon and Minolta have produced 2× converters for specific long lenses of their own, but these are available only by special order and useful only in conjunction with the lens for which they're designed.

Will other manufacturers investigate top-quality converter production? Time will tell. Until then, only well-heeled Canon, Minolta, or Nikon owners can take advantage of the "superconverter." For the rest of us, \$20–\$40 converters are available—and in an emergency they certainly are handy.

III

Accessories

"One Man's Junk Is Another Man's Prize"

Besides cameras and lenses, many of us buy accessories. For the amateur as well as the professional, buying photoequipment quickly becomes an affliction. We concluded a long time ago that for us it is congenital and terminal, and have accepted it as a condition of our photographic existences. We have tried virtually every camera attachment ever produced and have discovered to our surprise that many work as advertised. Suffice it to say that most add-on accessories won't make you any better a photographer than you are without them, with perhaps one major exception: a *tripod.*

TRIPODS

As mentioned earlier, camera shake—induced by the photographer or by the camera itself—comes at the top of the list of image destroyers. Again we suggest that with a tripod—used correctly—you will produce far more acceptable pictures than if you hand-hold the camera. We don't mean that just any spindly old three-legged contraption will do. We've learned through bitter experience how to distinguish a useful tripod from one that will hurt more than it will help.

(1) If you plan to use your tripod in the field, you'll need one that *weighs at least two kilograms* (*five pounds*). It makes no sense to mount your $700 camera and tele lens on a one- or two-kilo (two-to-four pound) tripod that could be blown over by a mild breeze.

(2) Typical tripods extend to about 1.5 m (5 ft) and fold to 61–76 cm (1–1½ ft). This is just what you need.

(3) Check the controls while you're in the store. Can you pan smoothly? Do the controls lock easily? When locked, do they slip at all?

(4) How much flexibility does this particular tripod give? Can you shoot verticals easily?

(5) Do the legs extend smoothly and lock with ease?

(6) Extend the legs from the center to their maximum extension and lock the controls securely. Then, with the palm of your hand, put as much weight as you can on the camera platform. If the legs begin to spread, or if you land on your back, try another model.

(7) When you've found the model to meet your needs, mount your camera and largest lens on it. Make sure you can operate the focusing and aperture rings because, while many tripods meet all other criteria, their camera platforms often are poorly designed and can interfere with proper manipulation of the lens.

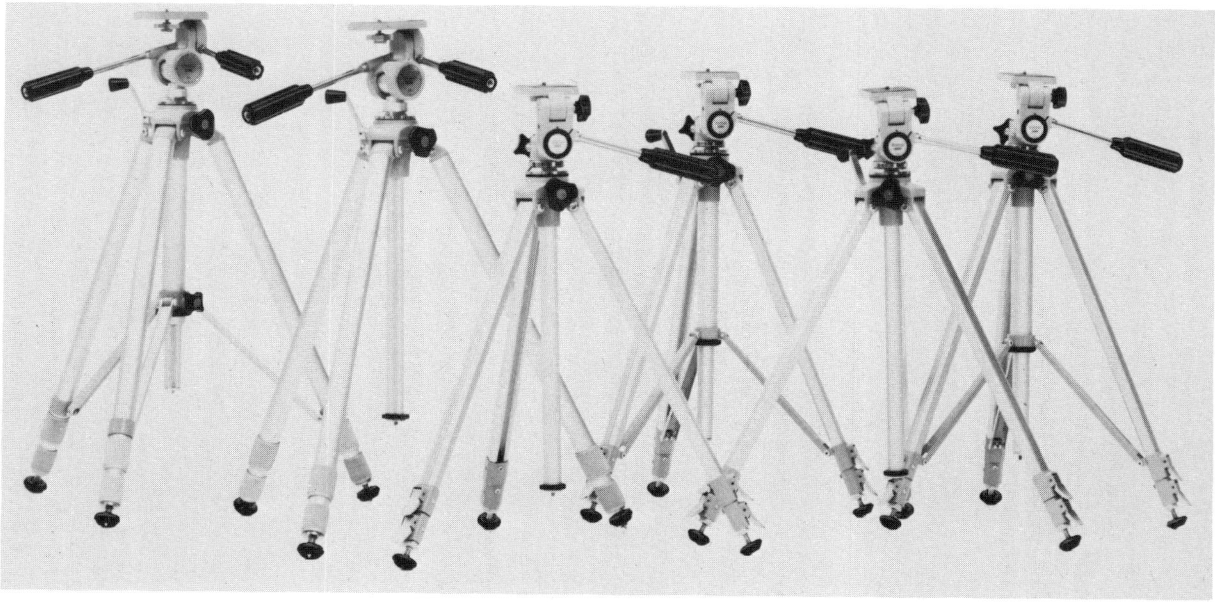

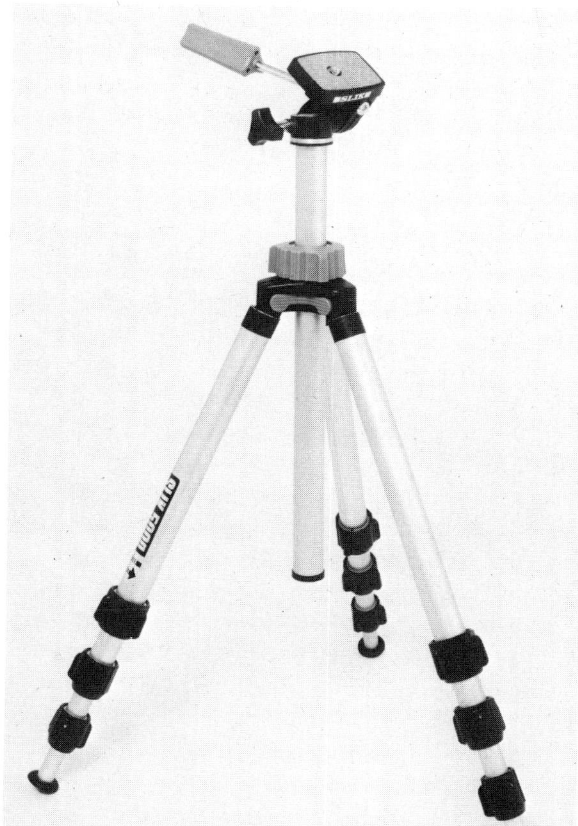

(Above) Complete tripod line from (l–r) studio to lightweight. Photo courtesy Vivitar, Inc. (Left) The small, lightweight but efficient SLIK 500G is one of only a few lightweight tripods worth their price.

For a tripod meeting all the above criteria, you can expect to shell out a minimum of $40 to $80. You can pay several times as much, if you choose; but if you plan to use a camera no bigger than 6.4 × 6.9 cm (2¼ × 2¾ in.), you shouldn't have to pay more.

Several manufacturers offer good-quality tripods. Among them you'll find Vivitar, Quick-Set, Gitzo, Slik, Linhof, Star-D, and Leitz. The last two offer tripods deserving of special mention. Both are essentially the same basic tripod (the D26) and differ only in the finish and the shape of some controls. While the D26 design distributed by Leitz (the Leica people) is finished in a stunning anodized black and operates a hair more smoothly, it is more expensive than the Star-D's by about $35. In our view it is probably no more serviceable or dependable in nonprofessional use than the Star-D, which we feel is the best buy at about $55. Slik tripods, though relatively new in the United States, seem very well made and many have unique features.

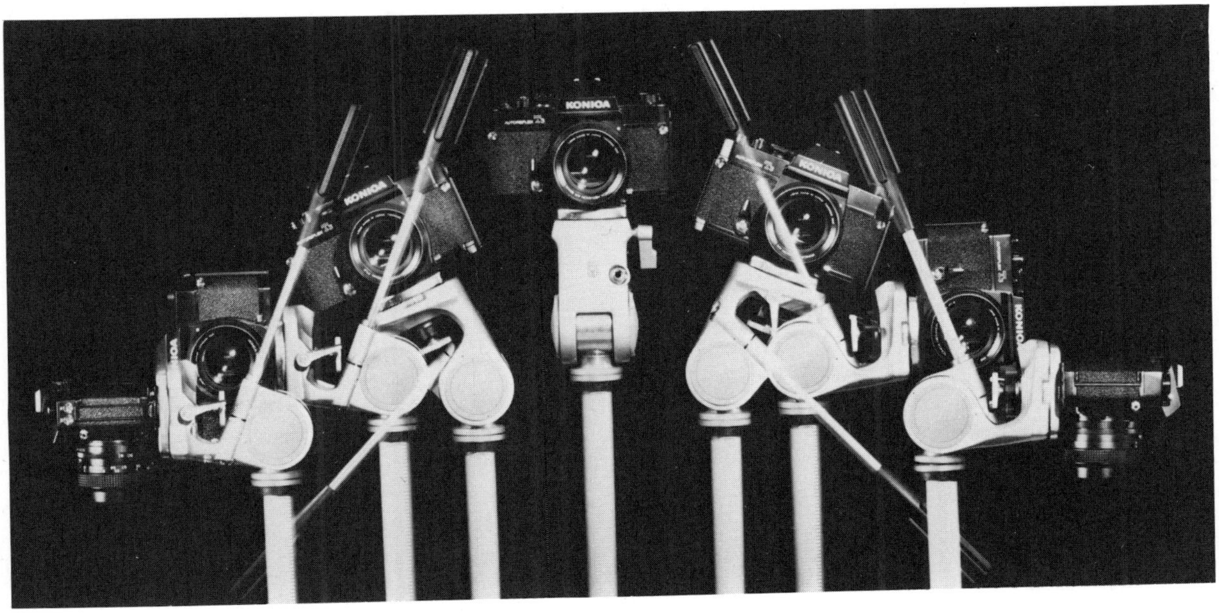

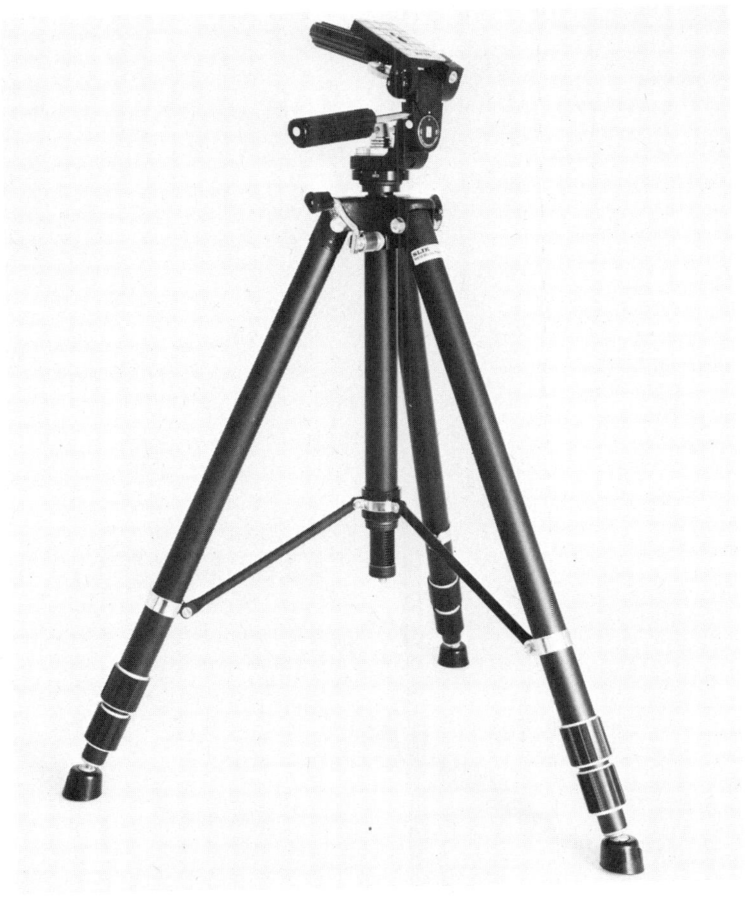

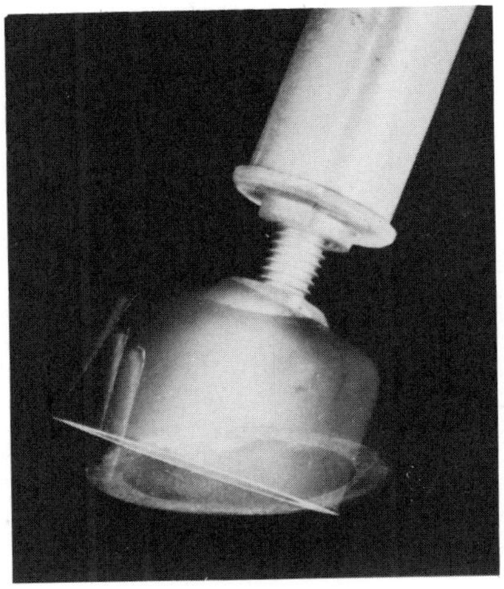

(Above) This is the sort of head movement to check for, as shown in this photo of a medium-priced tripod. Photo courtesy Vivitar, Inc. (Left) SLIK 410M is an excellent medium-weight tripod. Note the oversized panhead controls and the added leg bracing. Photo courtesy Berkey Marketing Co.

FILTERS

Polarizers

The other accessory most likely to improve your photographs dramatically is a polarizer. This filter usually attaches to the front of a lens and alters the character of the light before it reaches the film. There's no real mystery to it. In effect, a polarizing filter organizes light rays (which oscillate in all directions) so that they move in only one direction as they pass through the filter. Think of the way venetian blinds control the passage of light through a window and you'll have a better grasp of the theory involved here. Actually, the theory isn't all that important. What matters is what a polarizer can and cannot do.

First, polarizers are the only filters that can darken and intensify a blue sky without (in color photography) substantially altering the colors of the other objects in the scene. An additional beneficial characteristic of polarizers is that as you intensify the sky's blue (cyan, actually), white clouds literally leap out as if they were suddenly dropped there by an unseen hand.

Second, polarizers can and do reduce the glare from nonmetallic surfaces—water, glass, foliage, and so on. (A polarizer will have little effect on glare from shiny metallic surfaces because most metal does not reflect polarized light anyway.) Depending on the angle of the light source to the object, and thus the resulting angle of reflection, a polarizer will reduce either all or virtually none of the reflection. The polarizer's construction lets you previsualize its effects, as you can rotate the polarizing material. For those of us with SLRs, the polarizer's effect will be apparent immediately in the viewfinder. Various means have been tried to help rangefinder owners with previsualization. The most successful attachment, pioneered by Leica for their 35 mm rangefinders, has an accessory arm linked on one end to the polarizer's rotating ring. On the other end is a smaller ring with an auxiliary polarizer, which can be positioned over the rangefinder/viewfinder window to approximate the effect the main polarizer is having on the lens. A bit cumbersome, perhaps, but this arrangement does work, after a fashion.

Third, the polarizer functions as a rather strong ultraviolet/haze filter. Since many airborne particles produce reflections, desaturate color, and generally reduce contrast, the haze-minimizing qualities of a polarizer can supersaturate your colors. The first time photographers see the results of scenics shot with polarizers they are usually astounded. Flowers and foliage seem to benefit particularly from the "polarizer effect," since the reduction of reflection allows for the more accurate recording of delicate veining and plant texture. One home for polarizer use is the museum, although other places where you'll find it handy are practically unlimited. Some photographers choose to place large sheets of polarizing material over their studio floodlights rather than mount a polarizer in front of their lenses. This provides perfectly glare-free lighting and is a good technique to remember for studio work.

As with all other areas of photography, you must pay for what you get. In the case of polarizers, you'll suffer light loss. Their filter factor is generally quoted at 2.5, roughly a 1⅓ *f*-stop loss. If your camera has a through-the-lens meter, however, the light loss will automatically be accounted for. Be advised that

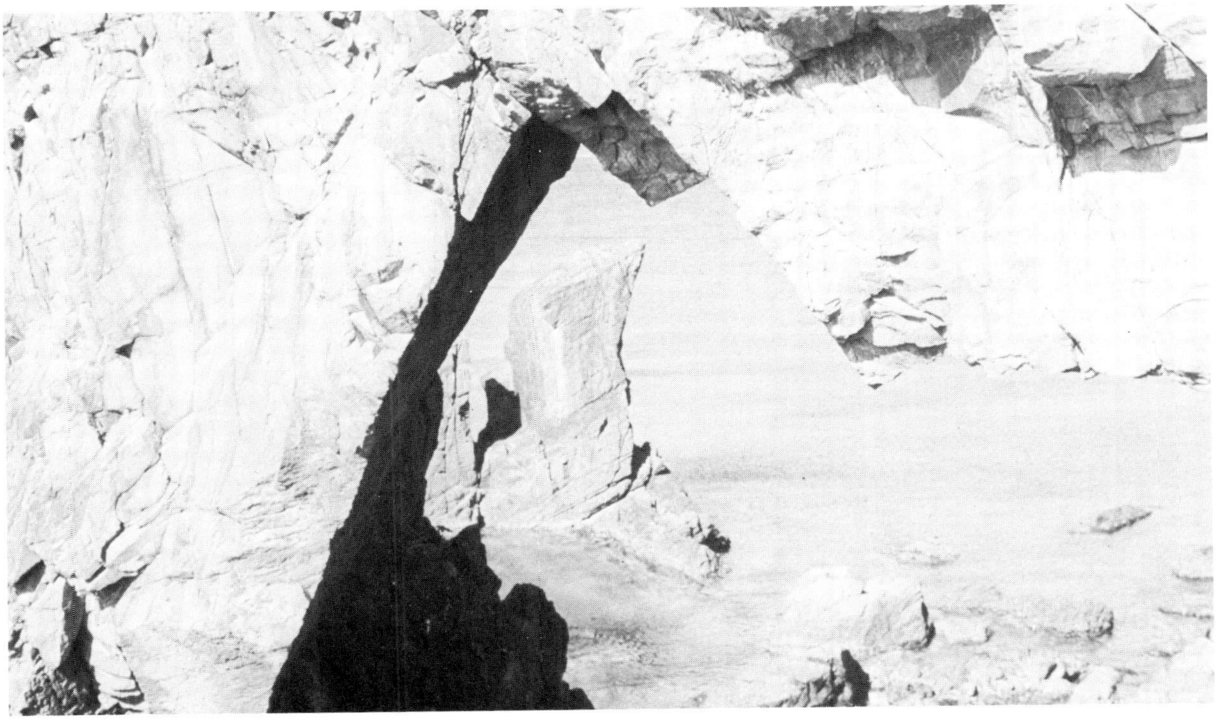

(Above) An unpolarized scenic can appear washed out. (Below) Use of a polarizer can really improve a scenic's rendering. Photos by Marc Levey.

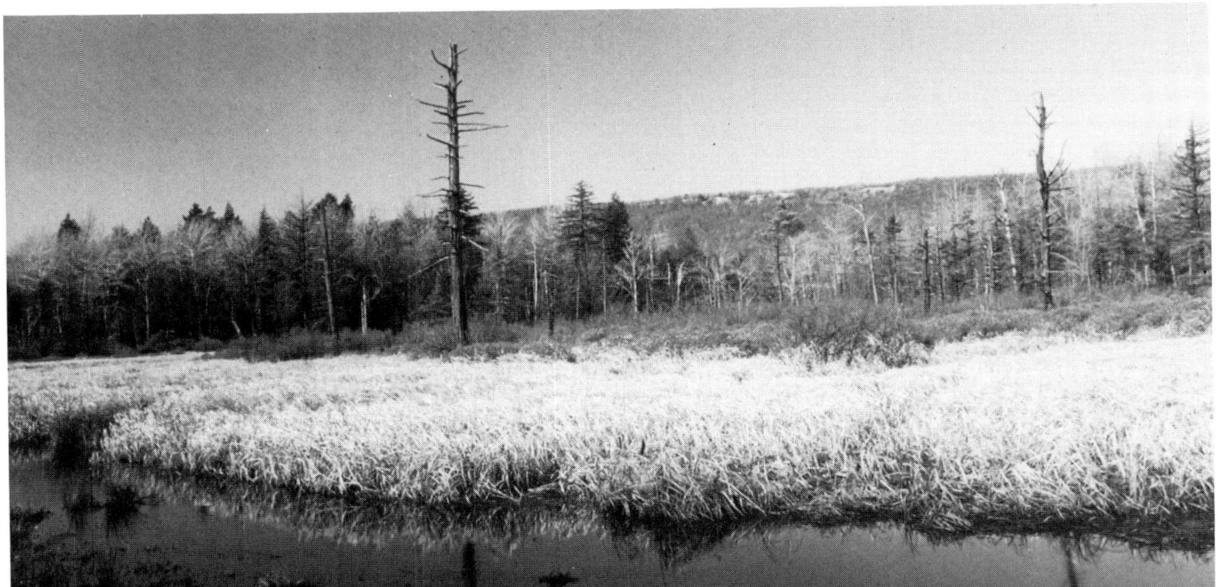

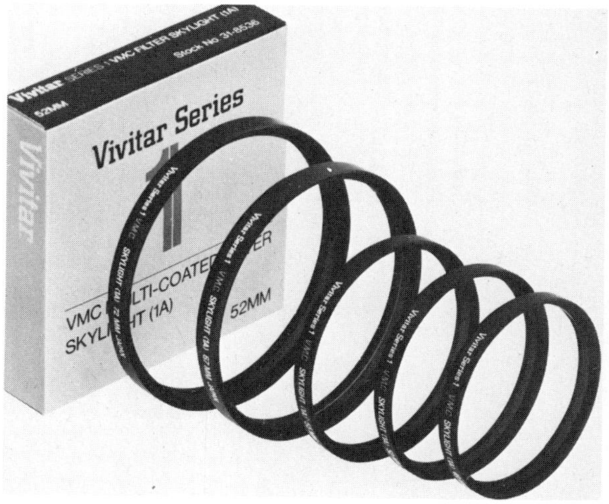

Filters are available in a wide variety of sizes to fit virtually every lens made. Photo courtesy Vivitar, Inc.

some through-the-lens metering systems—those referred to as *beam splitters* and found in some Canon, Mamiya, and Leicaflex models—will not compensate accurately for the loss. Most other metering systems will compute an accurate exposure even with a polarizer in place. While 1⅓ *f*-stop loss is a good guideline, the direction of the light source can alter that factor by as much as one full *f*-stop.

In the main, we have found polarizers very useful tools. Yet pictures without glare can be flat and dull, without apparent depth or emphasis. And some folks just don't like supersaturated colors. In fact, many subjects lend themselves to more subtle renderings in pastels and would look artificial and perhaps gaudy if polarized. We recommend trying a polarizer. Find out for yourself what applications are best for you—there are certain to be a few.

Other Filters

These filters are not exactly what we'd call necessities, but they should be of interest to you. For black-and-white photography, a variety of color filters can accentuate or increase a scene's contrast. For color there are filters referred to as color compensating and color correcting series. Rather than go into an elaborate and necessarily technical discussion of each, we'll refer you to the charts here.

Now, a few observations about filters in general.

Cheap filters are to be avoided. Your lens probably is a fine balance of special glasses and coatings; so throwing a cheap filter in front of it will definitely degrade the image produced. If you can't afford good ones, it's better not to use filters at all, particularly in conjunction with complex multicoated lenses. In some cases non-multicoated filters pull more flare than you get shooting directly into the sun with no filter at all.

Another caution: Never fail to refocus once you have added a filter to your lens. The thickness of a filter can alter precise focus, especially in close-up work.

It has been our experience that cheap filters can shift color balance dramatically. Take care when purchasing filters, especially polarizers. Cheap polarizers tend to have "light leaks" of nonpolarized light around their edges.

You ought to take the time to learn the basics of filter cleaning. Like lens elements, filters require some special care. They are delicate. Their coatings are relatively soft, and so they can be scratched easily. If fingerprints get on, as they're bound to, remove them promptly but gently. Use lens-cleaning solutions only (such as Kodak Lens Cleaning Fluid) in small amounts applied with photographic lens-cleaning tissue. Tear the tissue and gently

FILTERS FOR BLACK-AND-WHITE AND COLOR FILMS *

FILTER TYPE	COLOR OR DESCRIPTION	*f*-STOP INCREASE DAYLIGHT	TUNGSTEN LIGHT	USES
1A	Clear or salmon color	0	0	To protect lens's front element. Reduces ultraviolet, removes excessive blue in hazy outdoor scenes. Restores natural balance to scenes in open shade.
UV/Haze	Clear	0	0	Same as above, only more so.
Polarizing	Photoneutral (light gray)	1⅓ to 2½	1⅓ to 2½	Reduces reflections from nonmetallic surfaces, darkens blue sky without affecting other colors, increases color saturation in many situations, penetrates haze.
ND	Neutral density	Varies with filter strength—2 ×, 4 ×, 8 × most common	Same as daylight	Uniformly reduces amount of light without altering color rendition. Use with high-speed film in strong light (beach, snow scenes, high altitude). Allows use of slow shutter speeds for creative zooming, etc.

* There are literally hundreds of filters, but these are most common.

FILTERS MOST OFTEN USED FOR BLACK-AND-WHITE PHOTOGRAPHY*

FILTER TYPE	COLOR OR DESCRIPTION	*f*-STOP INCREASE DAYLIGHT	TUNGSTEN LIGHT	USES
K2 or #8	Yellow	1	⅔	Renders daylight scene accurately as eye sees it.
(6) or #15	Deep yellow	1⅔	1	Emphasizes contrast, increases sunset's brilliance.
(XI) or #11	Light green	2	2	Renders accurate skin tones in the way eye sees. Increases contrast in scene.
02	Orange	2⅓	2	Dramatizes contrast between blue sky and clouds, increases overall contrast.
#25(A)	Red	3	2⅓	Creates night-light effects in daylight. Simulates moonlight, if underexposed. Increases contrast greatly. Used with infrared color and with black-and-white film.

* Also can be used for creative color work.

FILTERS MOST OFTEN USED FOR COLOR FILM

FILTER TYPE	RECOMMENDED FILM TYPE	LIGHTING	f-STOP INCREASE	USES
80A	Daylight	3200 K lamps	2	A cooling filter. Converts daylight to 3200 K (approx. 3200–5500 K) when used with normal incandescent lights.
80B	Daylight	3400 K lamps	$1\frac{2}{3}$	Same as above, except converts daylight to 3400 K (3400–5500 K).
81A	Daylight and Type B	Daylight, strobe, and 3400 K lamps	$\frac{1}{3}$	A warming filter that prevents excessive blue in open shade or with Ektachrome, warms up cloudy scenes, corrects 3200 K to 3400 K.
82A	Daylight and Type A	Daylight and 3200 K lamps	$\frac{1}{3}$	A cooling filter. Reduces excessive warmth of light in early morning and before twilight. Also balances 3400 K for use with 3200 K lighting.
85	Type A	Daylight	$\frac{2}{3}$	Converts Type A film for use in daylight.
85B	Type B	Daylight	$\frac{2}{3}$	Converts Type B film for use in daylight.
FLD	Daylight	Fluorescent	1	Converts daylight film for use with fluorescent lights: Reduces blue-green cast.
FLB	Type B	Fluorescent	1	Same as FLD, but for use with Type B film.
CC30R	Daylight	Underwater	$2\frac{1}{3}$	Helpful when using daylight color film underwater or when photographing through transparent boats (warming filter).

wipe a drop of fluid in a circular motion until it's gone. Use the tissue's torn edge and as little pressure as will do the job. If you allow fingerprints to remain on your lens or filter surface, eventually the oils will etch themselves into the coating and your image quality will deteriorate. Allowing dust or dirt to accumulate on these surfaces will likewise result in permanent damage.

Finally, if you notice small bubbles in the glass of your lenses or filters, don't be alarmed. Many fine high-refractive-index photographic glasses contain these bubbles, which will not in any way affect the image produced with them.

LENS SHADES

These are another essential, in our estimation. They reduce flare induced by having skewed or scattered rays of light entering from extreme angles. A good lens shade is designed to exclude any light trying to enter from beyond the angle of acceptance the lens is designed to encompass. Many lenses have built-in shades, but many do not and so you must

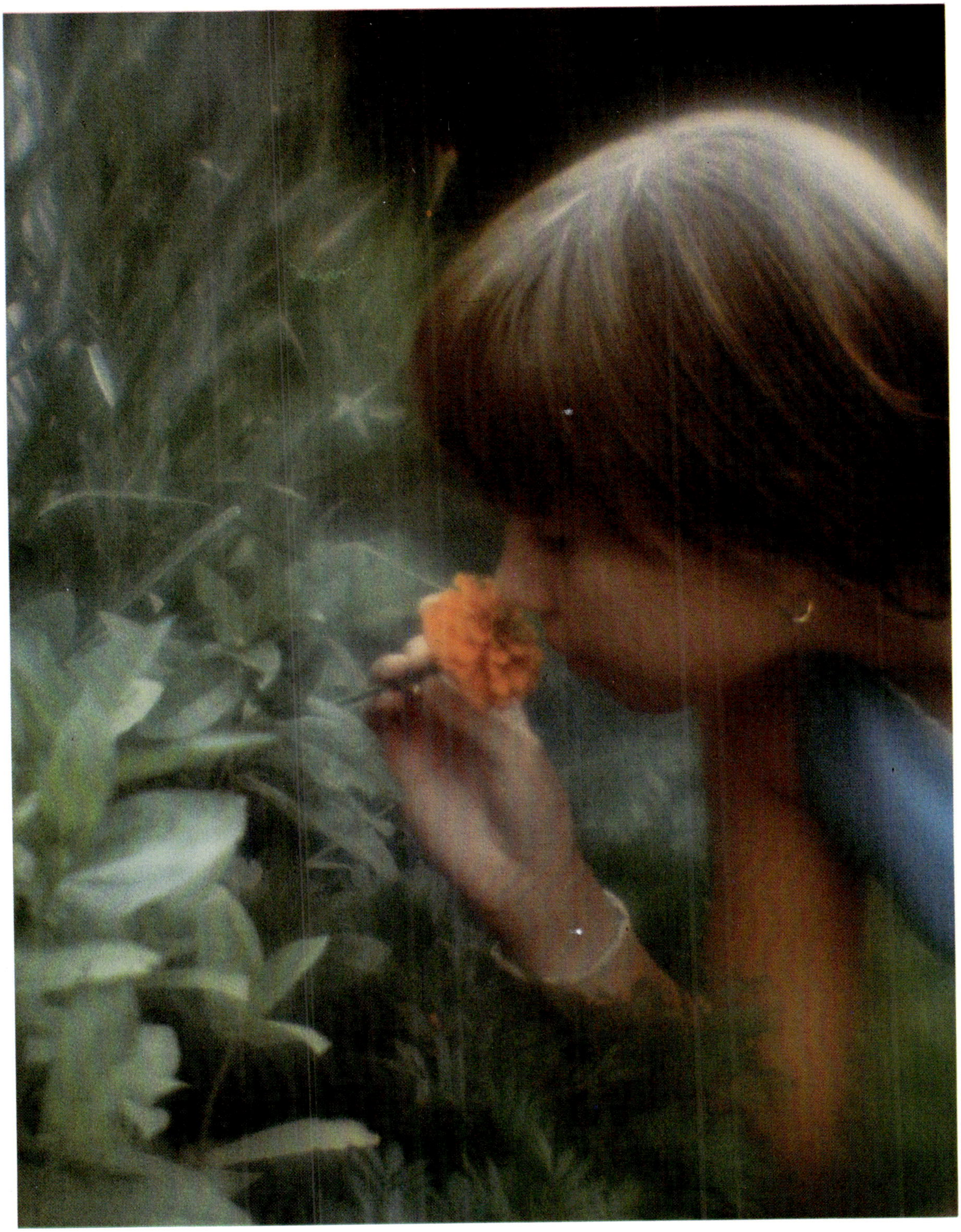

Photograph taken with a homemade soft-focus lens. All color photos by Marc Levey.

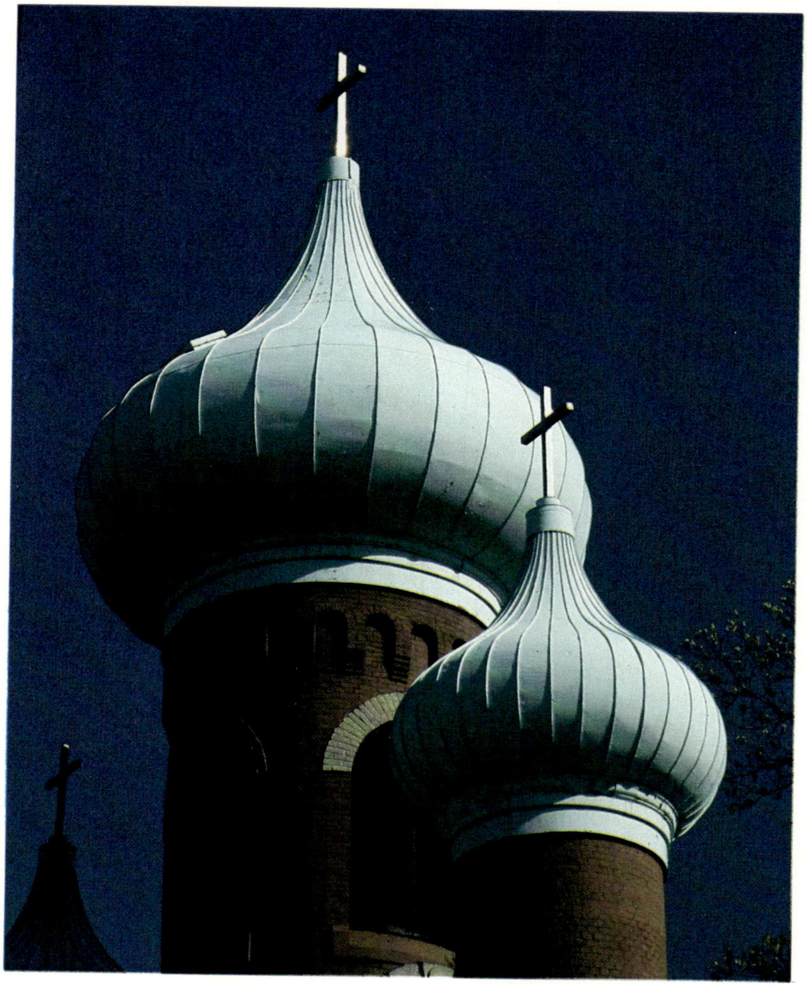

Medium-speed color slide film, Ektachrome 64 (*right*).
Vitamin B-6 (*below*).

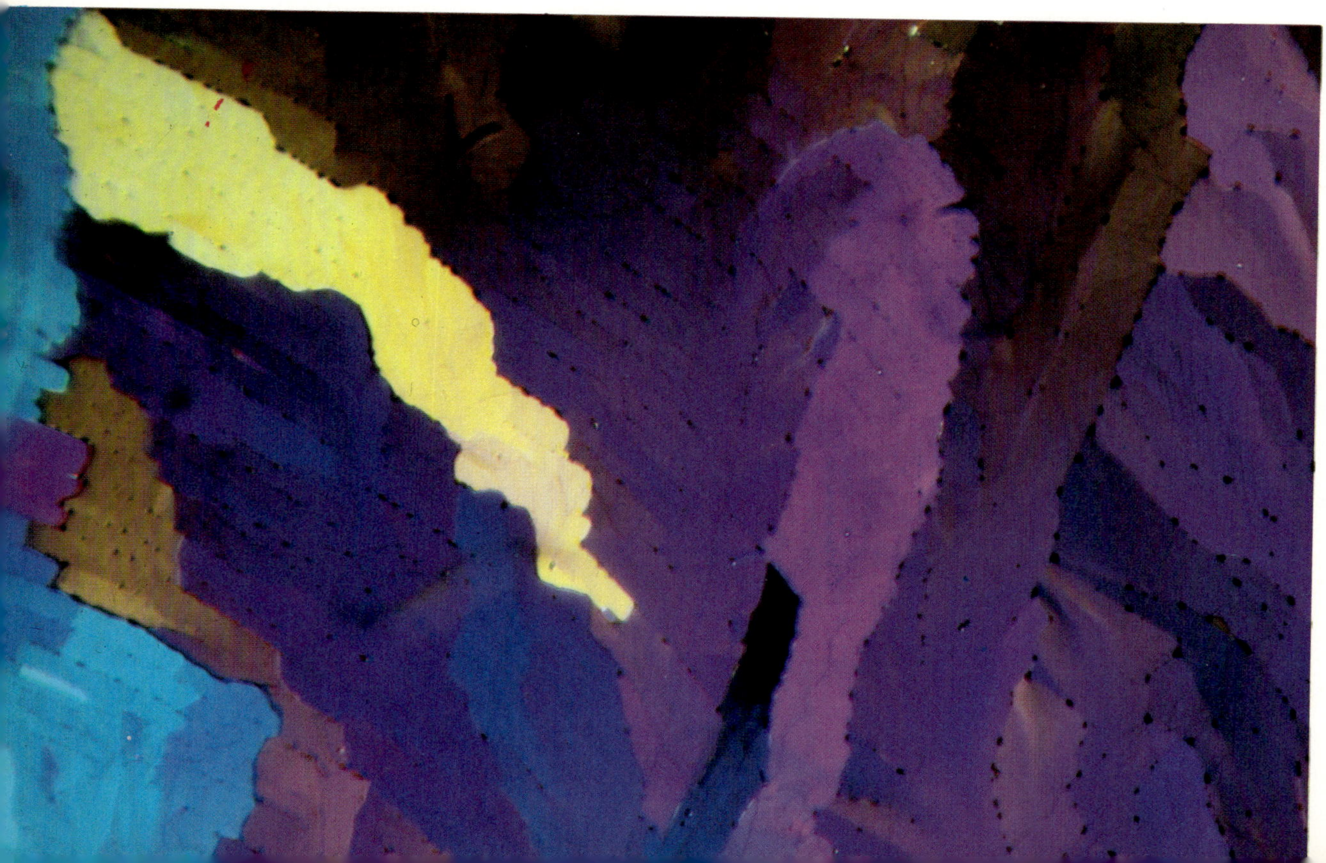

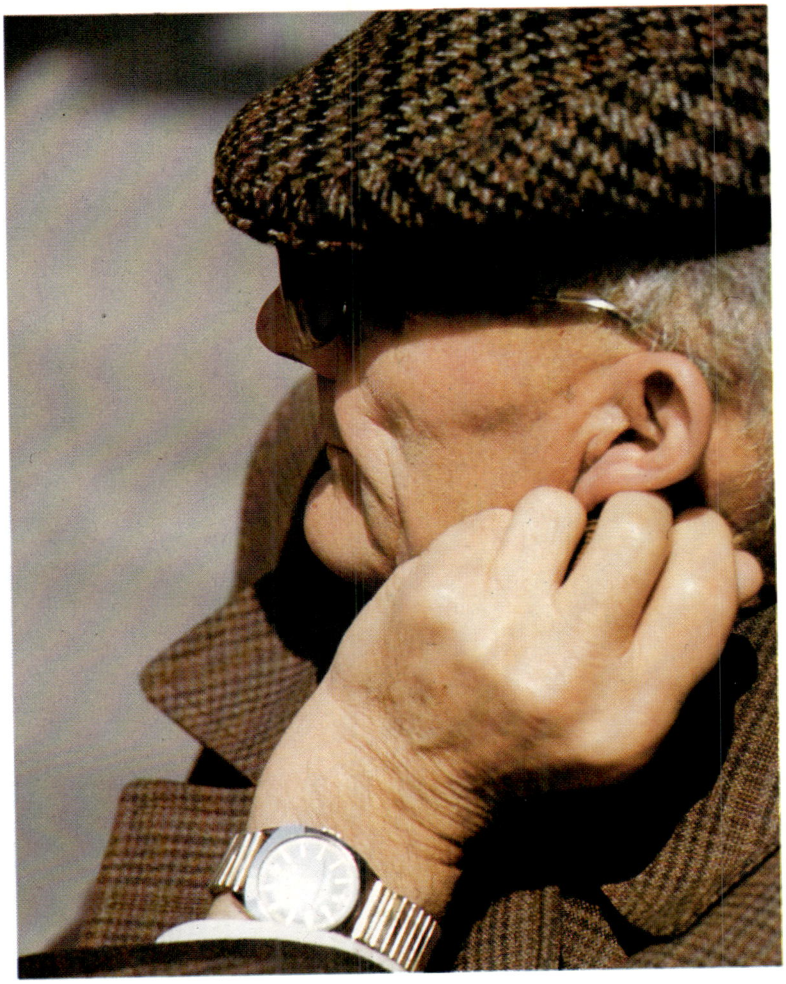

Photograph taken with high-speed Ektachrome 200 color slide film (*left*).
Photograph taken with a fail-proof close-up technique (*below*).

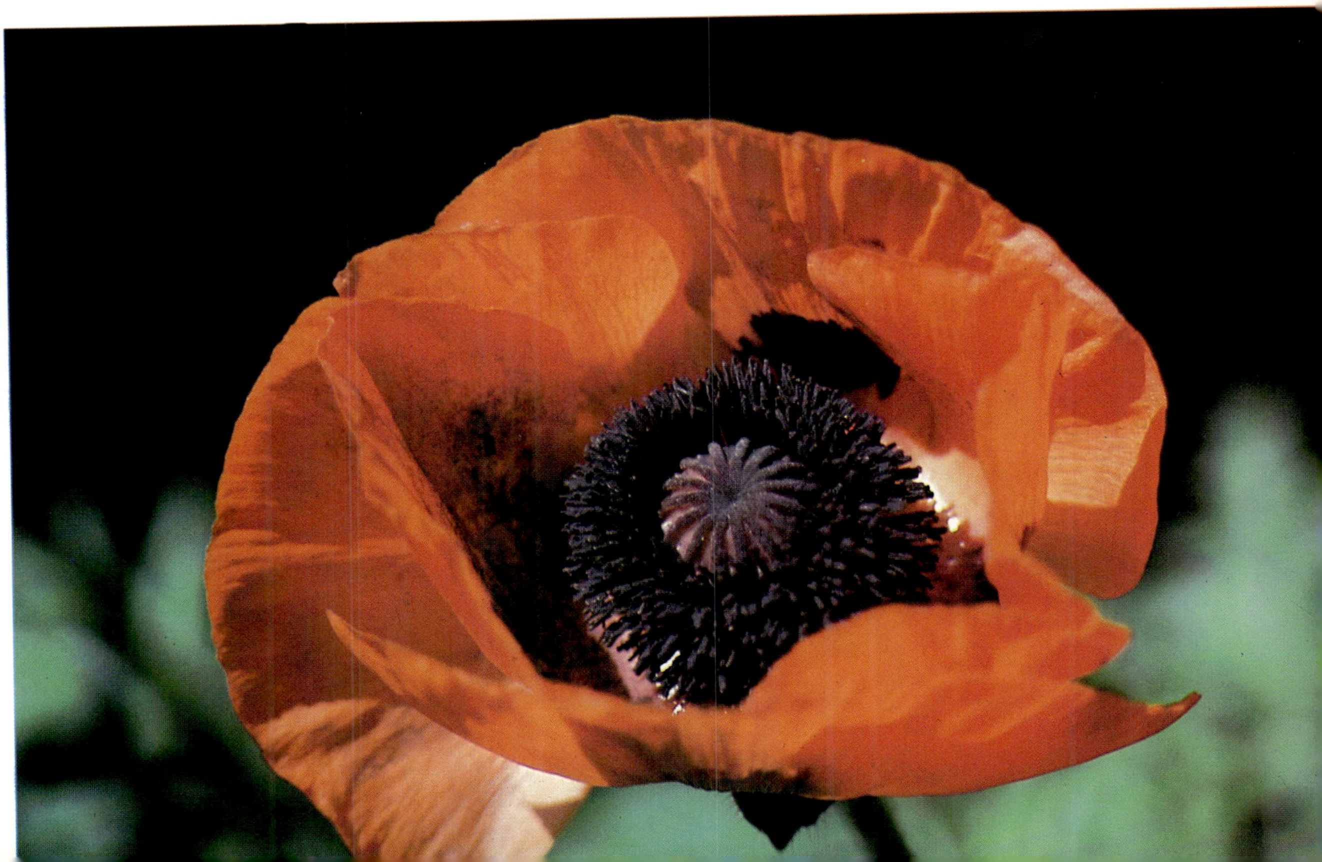

Photograph taken with Fujichrome R100 color slide film (*right*). Ektachrome Infrared Film is one of the specialty color films you may wish to experiment with (*below*).

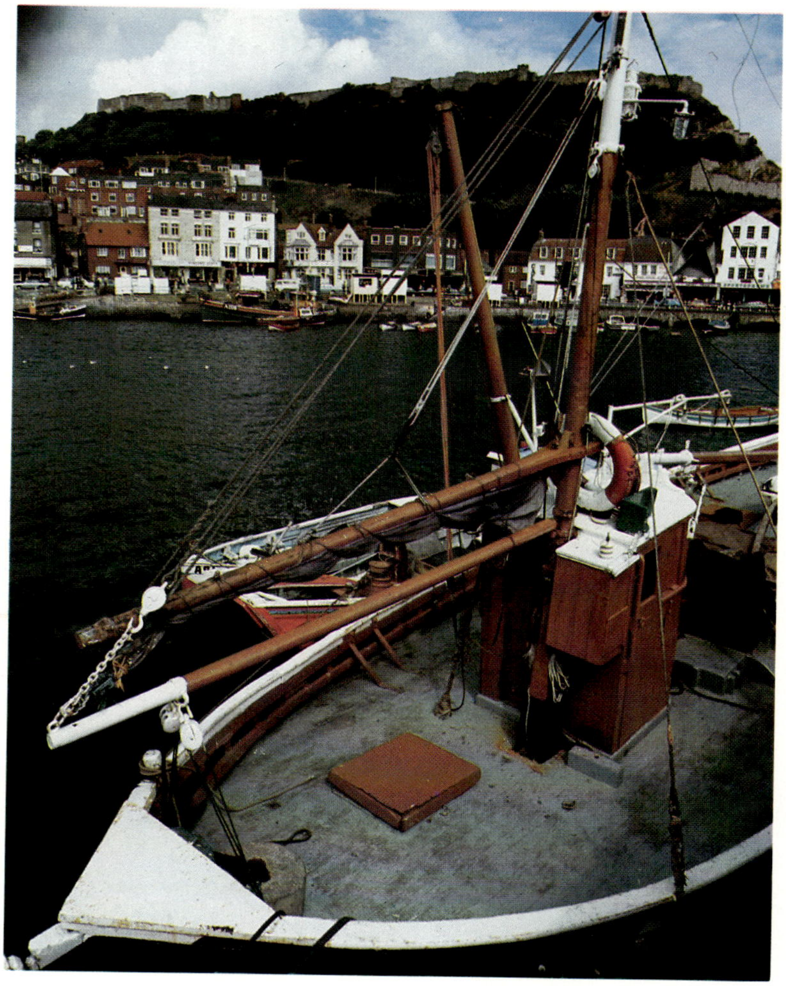

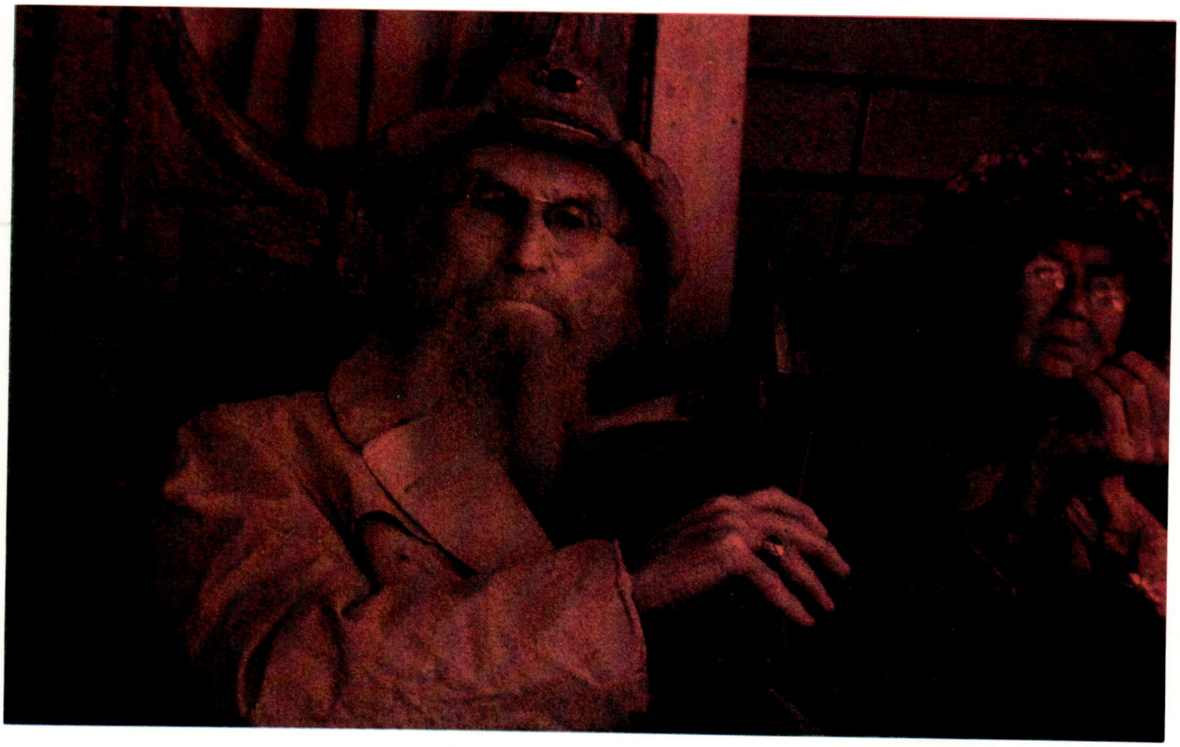

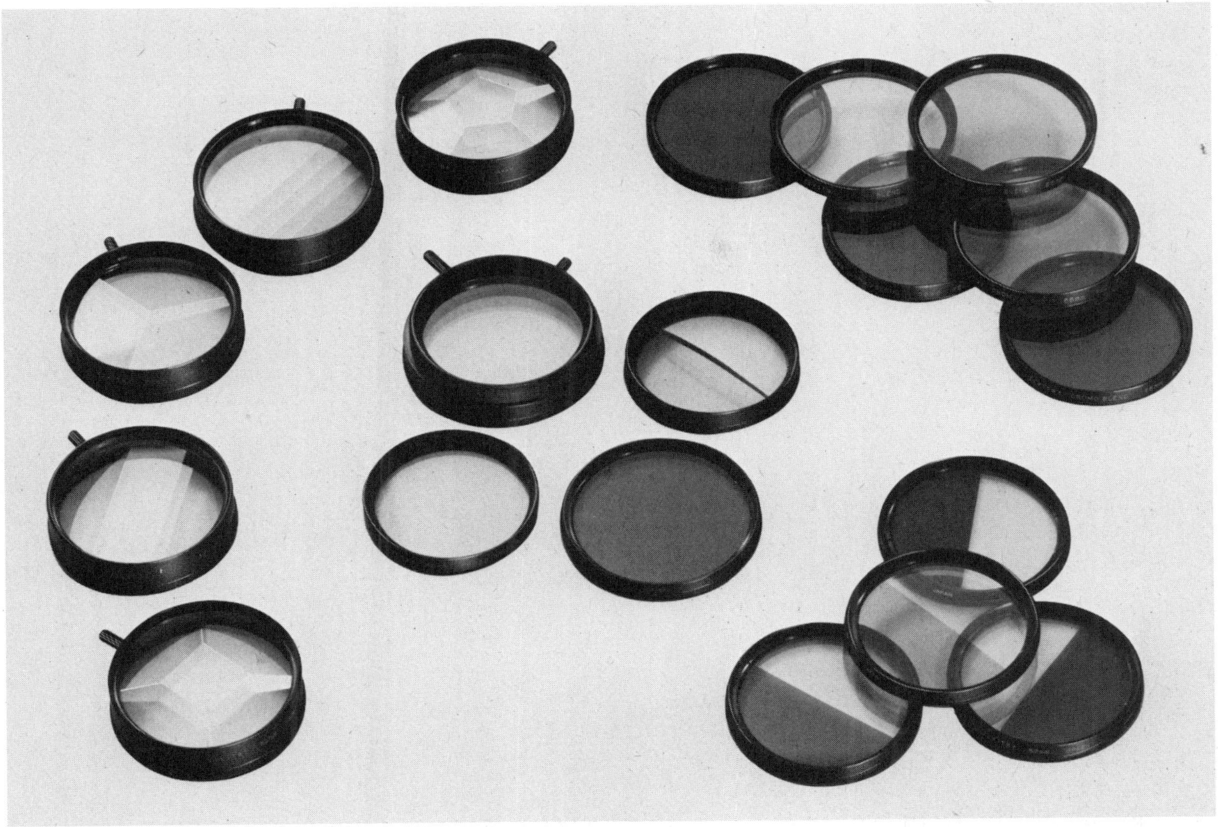

Other accessory possibilities exist in the form of prisms, diffusers, color altering filters, close-up lenses, etc. Photo courtesy Vivitar, Inc.

purchase the shade separately. Do be sure your shade will not cut off any of the picture. This is critical with lenses of 35 mm or shorter focal lengths. Check likewise to see that the lens shade is sufficiently long to do the job.

Shades come in either rigid metal or collapsible rubber. We prefer rubber only for convenience's sake, as either type will work and will provide some protection for the lens's front element, as well.

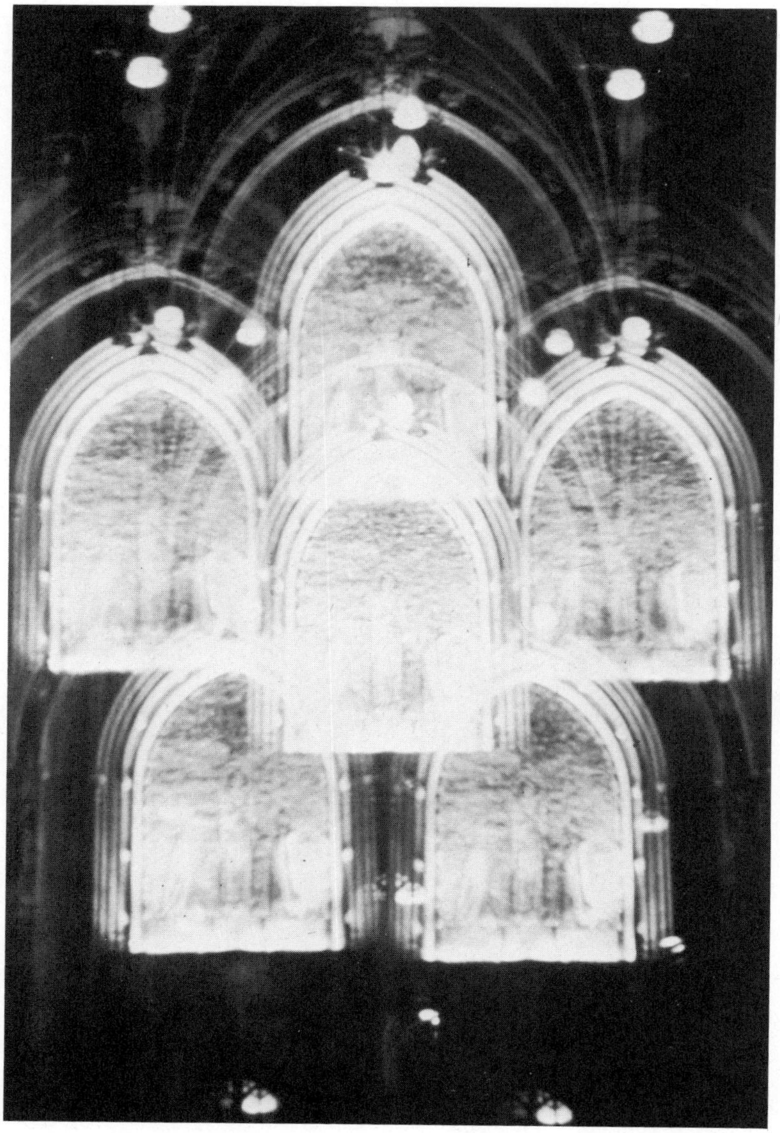

Prism shot of York Cathedral, England. Photo by Marc Levey.

OTHER ACCESSORIES

Now that we have discussed some of the "more than less" essential accessories, we'll turn to the optional items that will either help you or create havoc. All we mean is that you can become overequipped and as a result spend too much time debating about and switching your accessories. In most cases we've found accessories, once purchased, less useful than we'd thought likely. At any rate, camera shops seem to do a great business on small (not to say cheap) accessory items.

By far the most prolific accessory group includes the so-called "front-lens attachments" other than filters. There are many manufacturers of these gadgets, and consequently quality varies tremendously. Poorly manufactured F.L.A.'s will cause serious deterioration of the image, just as cheap filters will.

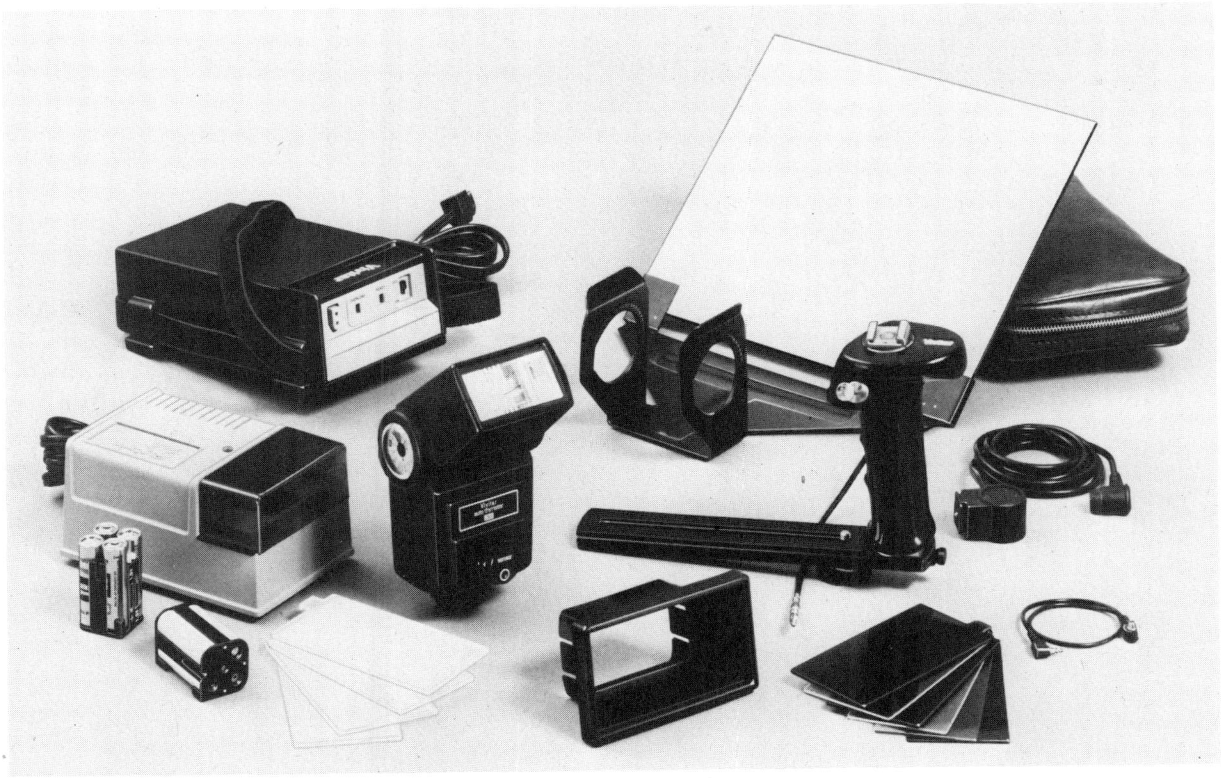

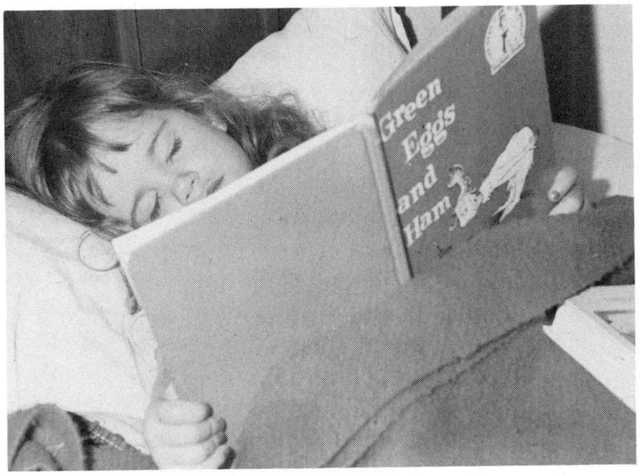

(Above) Vivitar 283 is one of the new breed of electronic flash systems. Photo courtesy Vivitar, Inc. (Left) Lighting shown here is typical of most photographs taken with a flash. Photo by James Forkner.

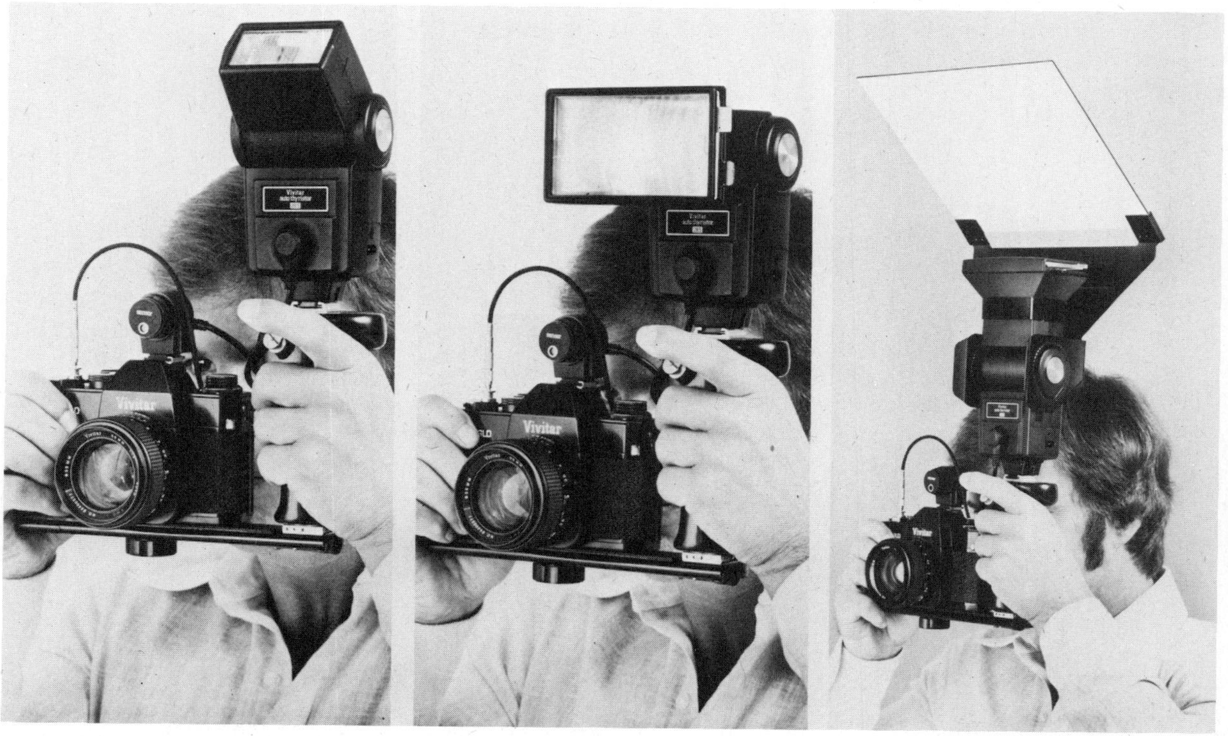

Close-up Lenses

These are simple one- or two-element optical glasses, used like filters, that permit the lens to be focused appreciably closer than is normally possible. Close-up lenses are usually numbered according to increasing strength (i.e., close-focusing ability) as 0, 1, 2, 3, 4. Zero is the weakest. Some makers suggest their close-up lenses can be used in combination; but most will, if used this way, produce disappointing results. In their favor: They are handy, relatively inexpensive, and capable of acceptable sharpness when used close up with lenses in the 85–135 mm range. The single caution we put forward is that you will find you have a very narrow focusing range—in some of these lenses, a matter of centimetres. If you plan on only a little close-up work, these attachments do work and won't break the bank.

Multi-Image and Prism Devices

You can find several attachments designed to multiply the image in series of 2, 3, 4, 5, and 6. Essentially, these are prism devices mounted in filter rings. They do produce several images on one frame; but they also create flare and reduce contrast. They don't normally alter exposure. Once again, these are like other in-front-of-the-lens attachments in that cheap ones can spell disaster.

Here are three techniques you can employ with the same flash unit. (Left) Bounce flash off ceiling. (Center) Direct, using accessory filters. (Right) Bounce flash off diffuser. Photos courtesy Vivitar, Inc.

Starbursts, Diffraction Gratings, Cross-Stars

Numerous effects, among them *spectral highlights,* can be achieved with filters like the starburst, diffraction gratings, and point-light-source attachments. They all create stars, or highlights, around points of light and reflections; but each has a specific function. Overuse of any of them can quickly produce a sense of banality. As a general rule for using them, ask yourself this question: Can my photograph stand on its own? If not, the mere insertion of highlights and auras by means of these attachments will not make it a good picture.

Variable Color Filters

New on the market is a series of variable-color filters produced by Vivitar and by a leading mail-order photographic supply house, Spiratone. These rather ingenious devices allow almost complete control of hue and intensity of single colors or combinations such as red/blue, red/green, etc. They permit nearly infinite variety in the area of the spectrum each attachment covers. Having used the red/blue combination, we can testify that dramatic results are possible. Since these filters also contain polarizing material, there will be a substantial light loss of up to 2½ *f*-stops.

Electronic Flash

To do this subject justice would require a book in itself; however, a few guidelines can be noted here with appropriate brevity.

Electronic flash units, or "strobes" as they are often called, offer the advantages of a high output of light for their weight, a low cost-per-flash when compared with bulbs or cubes, and a light output that is relatively consistent. There is also quite a choice available because electronic flash units come in all sizes, shapes, and prices from very simple units with low output to complex, expensive rigs capable of illuminating half an auditorium.

Flash units consist of a tube full of inert gas, a battery or batteries, a storage capacitor, electronic circuits to facilitate operation of the unit, and some means of attaching the whole thing to a camera. On the receiving end, cameras have built-in circuits to control the flash, in that they signal the unit when its services are required. This is known as "flash synchronization" and usually is designated *X sync.* in the case of electronic flash units. (*M-sync.* refers to mechanically-synchronized camera systems.)

We have seen three generations of flash units in the last 20 years. First came the heavy units powered by dry-cell batteries, then came miniature units powered either by penlight cells or by rechargeable nickel-cadmium (NiCd, or "nicad") batteries. A full charge from nicad batteries generally can provide power for some 40 flashes.

In the last five years or so, automatic units have become the triumph-of-the-hour. Through their own light-sensitive cells these units can sense when the subject before them has been properly illuminated and automatically shut off power. You need only program the film's ASA rating into the flash unit and set the *f*-stop indicated by the flash calculator dial. In most cases you have to set your flash unit only once per shooting session, unless you need more control over your depth of field or you need to shoot beyond the automatic flash's distance range. Automatic flash units can operate in a time frame between 1/1000 sec. and 1/50,000 sec., which makes them great for freezing action shots.

The latest automatic flash development is the energy-saving thyristor circuit. With all previous units a capacitor built up a full charge from the power source; if it was not used to light the subject, the charge was "dumped," or wasted. The power source was thus often tapped unnecessarily to fill the empty capacitor up again. Thyristor circuits permit the capacitors to store, rather than dump, the unused energy. Now the power source needs only to "top off the capacitor," that is, to restore only the portion of energy actually used. Many current units can fire as many as 700 flashes at very close range (60–90 cm; [2–3 ft]) before recharging is required. We found that at normal shooting distance of 1.8–3.6 m (6–12 ft) we got 150 to 200 flashes per charge from a thyristor unit before the recharging cycle exceeded 30 seconds.

When contemplating purchase of a flash unit, first determine the uses you'll have for it. If you only need one to light the kids in the living room it's hardly necessary to buy a unit with a 40-foot range; whereas, if you're going to use the unit heavily you might do well to consider a rechargeable flash, as opposed to one powered by throw-away batteries. Don't expect an automatic unit to be entirely foolproof: Dark objects against light backgrounds can befuddle its light sensor, and all flashes in automatic units have range limits. Neither can you expect a $15 flash to light a 6-metre (or 20-foot) living room evenly, any more than you can expect most flashes to light scenes taken with lenses covering 28 mm, 24 mm, or wider angles. Such flash units will probably do surprisingly well, but some falloff of the light may occur toward the picture's edges. Units are offered with accessories to take care of these special situations, but they cost a bundle.

Flash rating systems—with perhaps one or two notable exceptions—are notoriously overstated. The power of any flash can be measured variously as a scientific indication of footcandles emitted, as a guide number stated against the ASA rating of a particular film, or as the manufacturer's estimate. The latter can be the least reliable of the three ways to measure a flash unit's light output, since often manufacturers don't indicate what film speed they're rating the unit against. Check out any unit you're thinking of buying with a series of test pictures at different settings, noting each and comparing results.

Finally, condition your rechargeable unit by (1) recharging frequently even if not in use, (2) firing the flash three or four times before use to allow the capacitor to work up to maximum efficiency, (3) allowing about ten extra seconds after the little neon "ready" light comes on before shooting (since this mostly happens at about 70–80 percent of full charge, it's advisable to wait a few seconds more).

Flash units are rated in guide numbers that are generally keyed to film of ASA 25. The guide numbers simply tell you how much light, according to the American Standards Association, a unit will produce at a given ASA rating.

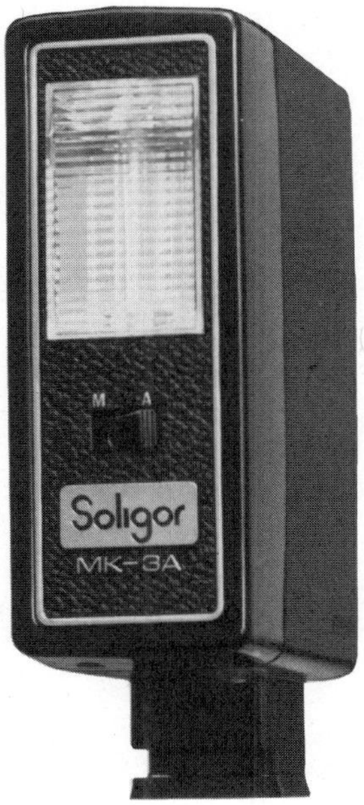

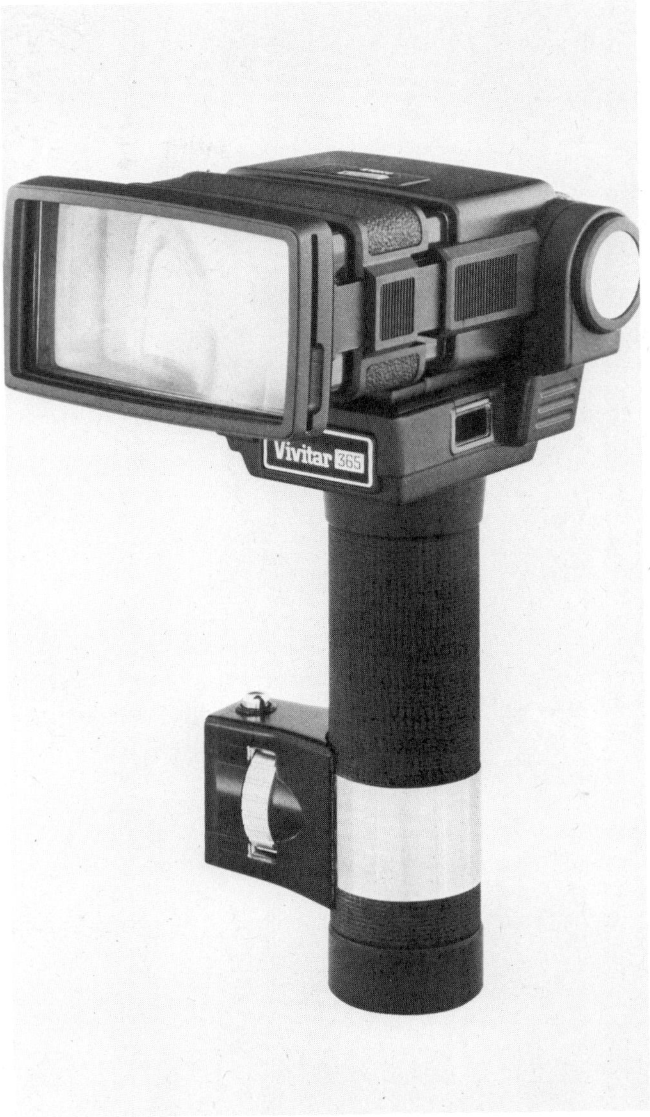

(Above) Soligor MK-3A is an example of a small, inexpensive flash unit. This one has a hot shoe mount. Photo courtesy A.I.C. (Right) This large, high-capacity handle-mount Flash (Vivitar 365) provides lots of power and versatility, but it's expensive and on the heavy side. Photo courtesy Vivitar, Inc.

For example, an ASA-25 Guide Number of 56 means that in manual operation at a ten-foot flash-to-subject distance, an *f*-stop of *f*/5.6 should be used to light the subject properly. (Cameras with focal-plane shutters are usually synchronized for electronic flash at 1/125 sec., 1/60 sec., and 1/30 sec., or somewhere between, and those with leaf shutters at any speed.) Thus, to find the proper *f*-stops for a particular flash/film combination, here's the formula:

$$\text{Manual } f\text{-stop} = \frac{\text{GN for film in use}}{\text{Film-plane-to-subject distance}}$$

Automatic *f*-stops are usually indicated on the unit.

We hope the following chart will assist you in making an intelligent flash selection.

FLASH-UNIT COMPARISON CHART

TYPE (ASA GUIDE No.)	POWER SOURCE	SHOTS/ CHARGE OR RECYCLE TIME (FRESH BATTERIES)	PRACTICAL RANGE	WEIGHT w/ BATTERIES	LIST PRICE (APPROX.)	APPLICATIONS	SPECIAL FEATURES
Miniature/ 22	Throwaway AA cells	50–150 sec.	.6– 4.6 m (2–15 ft)	142–255 g (5–9 oz)	$13–$25	Snapshots, auxiliary strobe, amateur	Most have hot-shoe connections
Miniature Auto/ 28–30	Throwaway AA cells	50–150 sec.	Auto range .6–3.9 m (2–13 ft)	227–283 g (8–10 oz)	$30	Snapshots, auxiliary strobe, amateur	Auto flash control, only one aperture
Shoe MT/ 40 Mediums	AA cells NiCd AC	150 AA 40 NiCd 5–9 sec.	6 m (20 ft)	340 g (12 oz)	$50	General flash use	High power/ weight ratio
Shoe MT/ 40 Auto Mediums	AC	150 AA 40 NiCd 5–9 sec.	6 m (20 ft) Auto	340 g (12 oz)	$60	General flash use	Same as above, plus auto capability, same *f*-stop choice.
Shoe MT Auto Thyristor/ 60	AA, NiCd AC, some 510v	Auto 50–700	Up to 13.7 m (45 ft) Auto	397–482 g (14–17 oz)	$100–$150	Flexible, portable lighting w/some professional applications	Some units have filter, bounce control, other accessories
Handle type Auto/80	NiCd, 510v	Auto 50–100 510v 500–1500	Up to 15 m (50 ft) or more	680–850 g (24–30 oz)	$125–$300	Most powerful of all hand-held flash units	Extensive accessory lists, directional accessories
Handle type Auto Thyristor/ 80	NiCd, 510v	Auto 50–700 510v 500–1000	Up to 15 m (50 ft) or more	850 g (30 oz)	$150–$300	Most powerful of all hand-held flash units	Added control of thyristors, usually multiple *f*-stop control

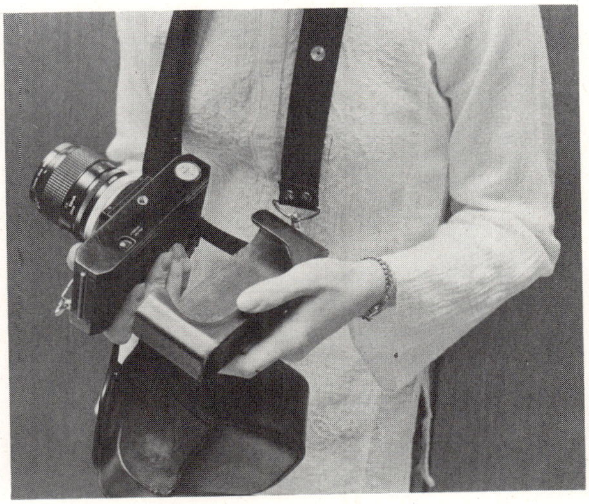

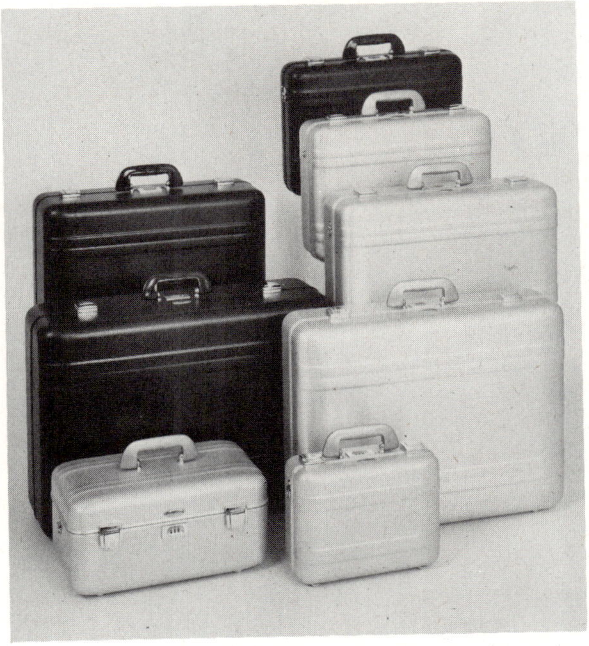

(Above) What do I do with it now? Age-old problem with camera cases. Photo by Joseph Bodkin. (Right) Zero Haliburton makes the best known line of lightweight aluminum cases. Photo courtesy Zero Haliburton Co.

Camera Cases and Bags

When you buy a good-quality camera, either it comes with a case or the salesman urges you to buy one. While camera cases are designed to protect, most of them are a pain in the neck. First, almost all cases fit properly only when a normal or wide-angle lens is mounted on the camera body. Second, the case's bottom half is secured with a tripod bushing, and you are forced to remove it for loading and unloading of film. Third, when traveling or sightseeing, keeping the case on is a nuisance and we'll guarantee you will miss shots. The problem with removing the case top is finding a place to put it—it doesn't fit in any pockets except maybe in trench coats. For storage a case is great; but in our view it would be wiser to put the extra money (and most cases are extra) toward a more convenient camera gadget bag or case.

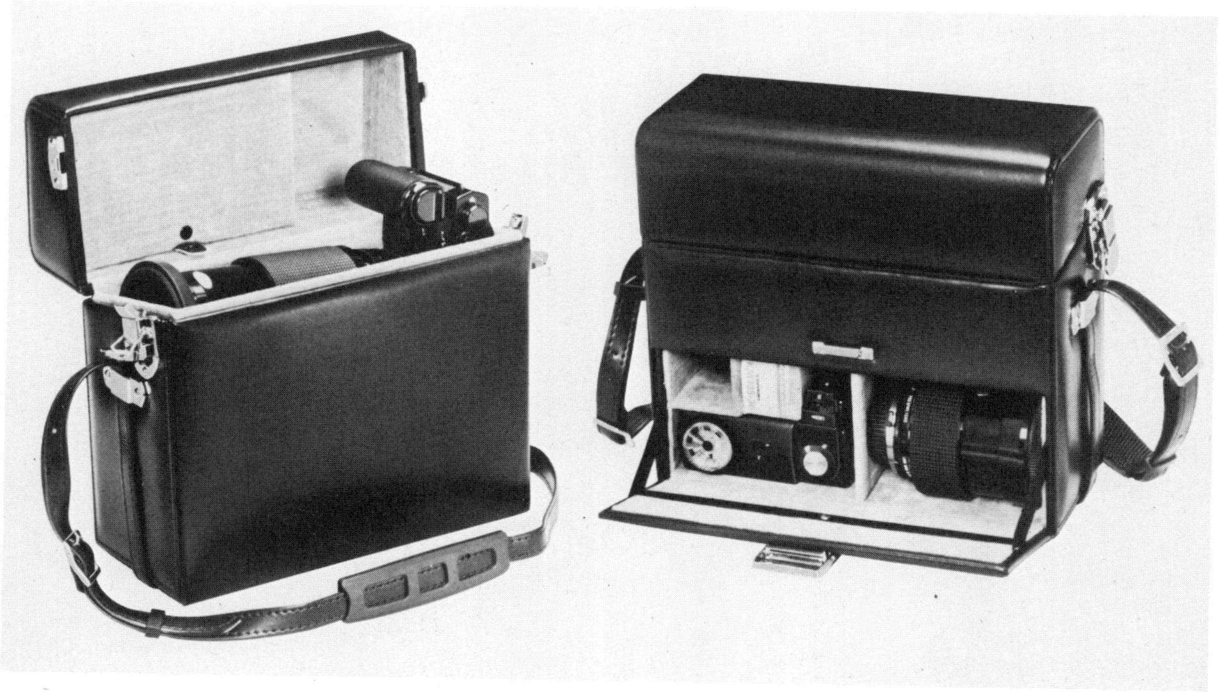

Over-the-shoulder hard case for long lenses. Photo courtesy Vivitar, Inc.

Gadget Bags. These come in such variety that choice really becomes a matter of your personal taste and the degree of protection you need for your equipment.

For example, if you have to take your equipment to the beach (sand is the great destroyer of cameras, by the way), you probably should invest in a case that is gasket-sealed against water and dirt. Other photographers may find a soft pouch or bag sufficient.

Briefcases with individual compartments are handy, too. Zero-Halliburton offers a line of aluminum attaché-style cases that are tough and lightweight, but on the expensive side.

Ultimate Experience, a California-based concern, recently introduced a backpack line for photographic gear called Shutterpacks. These carriers come in different sizes and shapes for a reasonable price, and are well constructed. They provide an alternative to conventional cases that is well worth considering.

To sum up: Gear your case purchases to how much your equipment is likely to be buffeted about. Buy a bag bigger than necessary

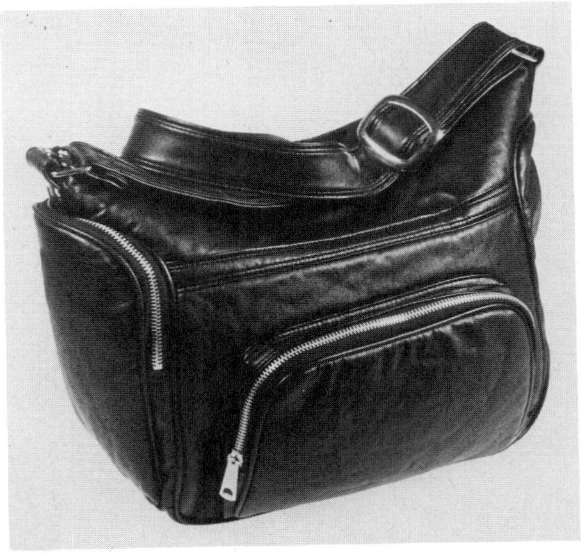

The popular tote bag provides only limited protection to your equipment from physical damage, but it is light and convenient. Photo courtesy Minolta, U.S.A.

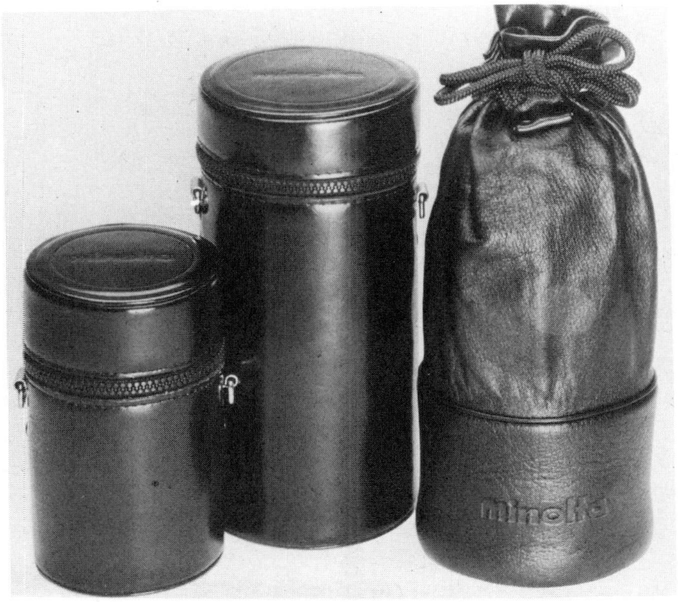

Sample lens cases and pouch. Made in sizes for virtually any lens. Photo courtesy Minolta, U.S.A.

Another view of UE-Windago Backpack showing top compartment. Note divided foam padded partitions. Photo courtesy Ultimate Experience.

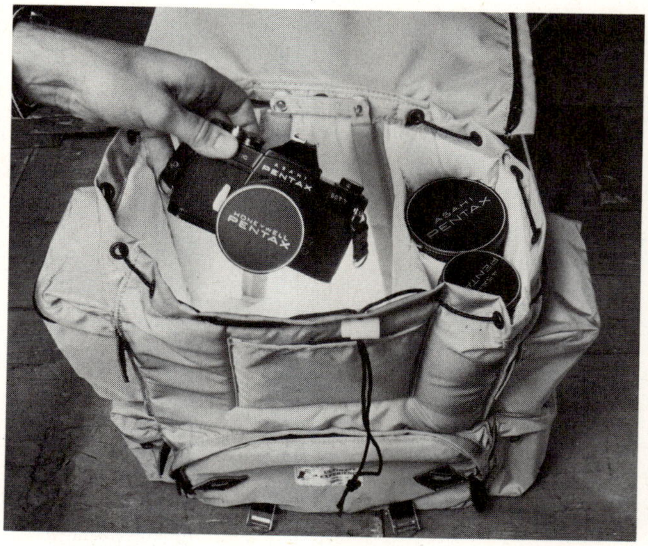

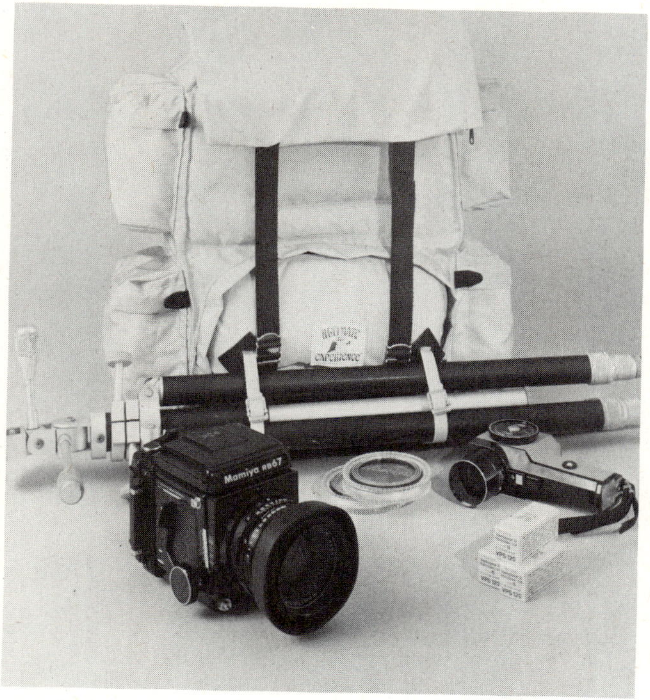

(Left) The Ultimate Experience Backpack, especially designed for photographers. Photo courtesy Ultimate Experience. (Facing page) For close-up macro or copying work, this full-bellows system is ideal. Photo courtesy A.I.C.

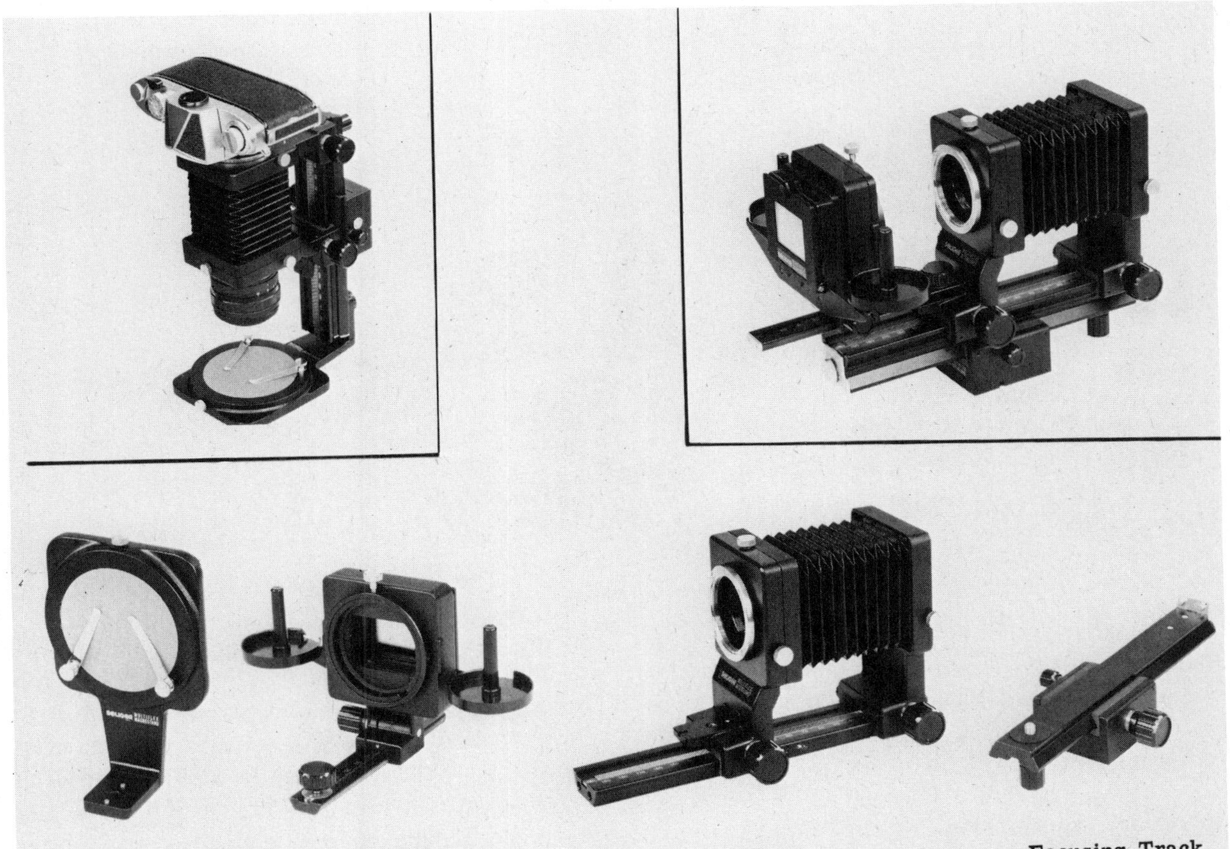

Macro Stand Slide Copier Bellows Focusing Track

for your present equipment needs—you can always throw in a lunch or a six-pack if you never purchase more extras to take up the slack.

Camera Straps. The first thing you should do when unpacking your new camera is to throw out that narrow neck strap. It's next to useless, unless you like having it cut unmercifully into your shoulder and prefer the look of cheap plastic. Actually, Canon's and Contax's nylon straps aren't too bad, but we've found them the exception, not the rule. It doesn't make any sense, as far as we can see, to hook up a $700 camera to one of these 29¢ beauties.

Instead, we recommend your buying a wide (39–50 mm [1½–2 in.]) strap, preferably made of something softer and more pliable

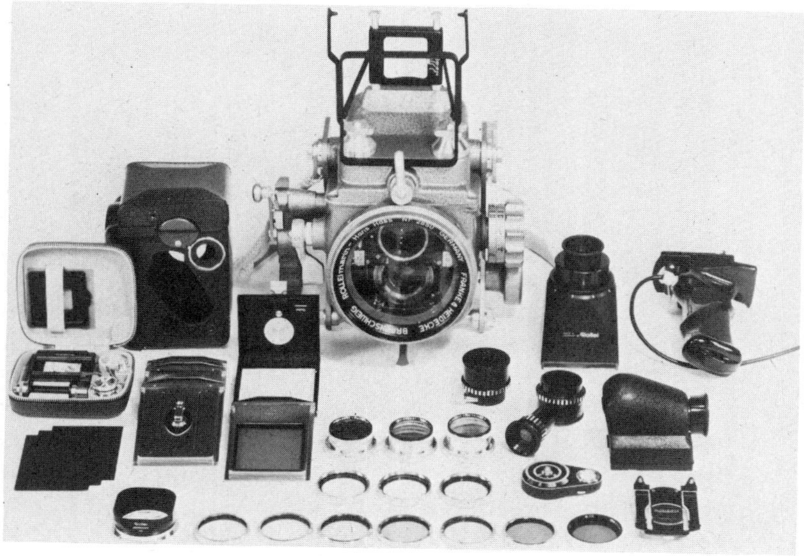

The Rollei TLR shown here is encased in an example of a professional underwater housing. Photo courtesy EPOI, Inc.

than plastic—such as leather. Then scan your dealers' shelves and the photo magazines for the kind of strap pad the mailman uses. We use them and find they distribute and cushion the camera's weight wonderfully.

Eyepiece Accessories

If you wear glasses, you may already know that many cameras offer eyepiece inserts made to your prescription needs.

Another factor for eyeglass wearers to consider is that wearing glasses can interfere with seeing all the way to the edges of some camera viewfinders. In any case, do consider a rubber eye cup. They are cheap and they effectively shield the viewfinder from undesirable light. On very bright days they are all but imperative.

Two other eyepiece accessories merit attention. The first is a magnifier that slips over the eyepiece. It magnifies the central third or so of the viewing screen and makes precise focusing much easier. Also, these magnifiers usually flip out of the way so that you can review the entire viewing screen at your convenience. The second is a device called a "right-angle viewfinder." This also fits over the eyepiece. It permits low-level or angular positioning of your camera without the need for interchangeable viewfinder prisms. It's a handy thing for copying or for photographing kids, flowers, or anything else below eye level.

While we have tried to cover accessories as thoroughly as possible, we're sure we have left out many items. If we have not mentioned a particular piece of equipment that interests you, we suggest (once again) that before you lay out the cash, first talk to people who use that particular accessory. Also, talk to your local photo dealer if you're not exactly sure what all the functions of that prospective buy may be.

III

Film

As unlikely as it seems, perhaps only one out of ten photographers could describe the characteristics of film in anything but vague generalities. Since film is basic to the photographic process, roughly fulfilling the same function as the retina in human vision, it's necessary for us to take a closer look at the properties, types, and uses of film. Remember, too, that progress in the evolution of photosensitive material is inextricably linked to other technological progress in the field, such as camera and lens design. Keep in mind that our judgments, especially with regard to the various kinds of film available, are meant as guidelines and are not intended to keep you from experimenting and testing for yourself.

A THUMBNAIL HISTORY

The first recorded mention of film comes from Aristotle in the fourth century B.C. The same principle was known to Mo Tzu in China 2500 years ago. Aristotle discusses a device for forming images in a darkened room, from which the term *camera obscura* ("darkened room") comes.

In the fifteenth century, Italian painters used this *camera obscura* to observe scenes in proper perspective. It helped them to plot out the correct diminishing of proportions necessary to realistic renderings. Leonardo da Vinci wrote about the use of these devices.

There was repeated experimentation with other alternatives, including the addition of lenses before 1550. A German by the name of Athanasius Kircher described a relatively refined, portable *camera obscura* in the form of a darkened tent surrounding a lens system, and in 1671 he wrote about a magic lantern (the prototype slide projector).

Once a method had been discovered for focusing light and thus producing an image, some way to record the image was required. Several scientists and inventors tested various chemical compounds in search of one that would prove both sensitive to light and capable of retaining its image permanently. Notable among pre-1800 pioneers in photosensitometry were Johann Heinrich Schulze in Germany, Carl Wilhelm Scheele of Sweden, and Thomas Wedgwood, son of the British potter. Each of these men made contributions to the search for photosensitive materials, but practically speaking, none succeeded. Even Humphry Davy, the celebrated British chemist, failed in the quest for a permanent image.

In 1826 a degree of success was finally

Generalized schematic of typical black- and-white film (1) Hard, protective *top layer* which prevents abrasion and scratching of the emulsion layer. (2) *Emulsion layer*. Contains light-sensitive silver halide crystals embedded in a gelatin. (3) *Subbing layer*. Holds the emulsion layer fast to the rest of the film. (4) *Bose layer*. Acetate layer which accounts for most of film's thickness, it serves to support the above layers. (5) *Subbing layer*. (6) *Anti-halation backing*. Prevents light from passing through film and then reflecting back onto reverse side of emulsion layer.

achieved by Joseph-Nicéphore Niépce, a Frenchman. He receives credit for being able to produce the first "permanent" black-and-white image (a direct positive) on a bitumen-coated pewter plate. It is of no little interest that the exposure time for this earliest surviving photograph taken from nature with a camera was a mere eight hours; so progress has considerably accelerated from Niépce's process to the present. Niépce had a young partner, Louis Daguerre. After more than ten years' effort, Daguerre discovered a means of fixing an image made in a camera. The resulting *daguerreotype* was a positive picture recorded on a silver-coated plate. It showed a reversed, or mirror, image.

Daguerre's achievement was announced in Paris January 7, 1839. Within three weeks, on January 25, William Henry Fox Talbot showed in London his "photogenic drawings" made on paper. In spite of the immediate, worldwide popularity of the daguerreotype, it was Talbot's paper prints and the negative-positive process they made possible (as he demonstrated in August 1839) that led to the photography we know today. (Talbot used paper negatives—glass plates came later, and then gelatin "films" appeared late in the century—but he showed the way.)

A major stumbling block remained: how to make the image permanent. It was Sir John F. W. Herschel who suggested (February 1839) the use of sodium thiosulfate as a fixing agent. (Until 1869 this chemical was called "hyposulphite of soda," and the misnomer "hypo" for fixer has stuck.) Herschel told Talbot about his idea and also wrote to Daguerre in France, where the latter started using it successfully. Besides his chemical discoveries, Herschel contributed the terms "negative" and "positive," as well as "snapshot" and the word "photography" itself.

Thereafter progress was rapid. Within ten years photography had become a commercially viable craft on both sides of the Atlantic. From 1850 until just before the turn of the century, though, it remained the domain of those for whom it had become a livelihood, those actively experimenting with it as a new art form, and those involved in improving materials, equipment, and techniques.

Then two amateurs, Richard Kennett and Charles Bennett, working independently, both stumbled upon a dried-emulsion process that was much more sensitive to light than earlier plates had been. This increased emulsion sensitivity freed photographers from long exposures requiring firmly mounted cameras. It now became possible to hold the cameras by hand while shooting.

This development led in turn to others, especially to ever-decreasing camera size—which brings us to George Eastman, founder of the Eastman Kodak Company. Eastman invented the box camera, and then in rapid succession invented roll film and a mass-marketing system that could reach the general public. By 1890 the amateur's fascination with photography had begun.

Around the turn of the century came another period of technological innovation as rich as that of photography's first two decades. Developments were so numerous and rapid they are difficult to sum up without going into considerable detail. Suffice it to say that reflex cameras appeared around 1900 and by 1913 Oskar Barnack had made the next breakthrough in camera design.

Others had experimented since 1900 with cameras that could use the new 35-mm-wide

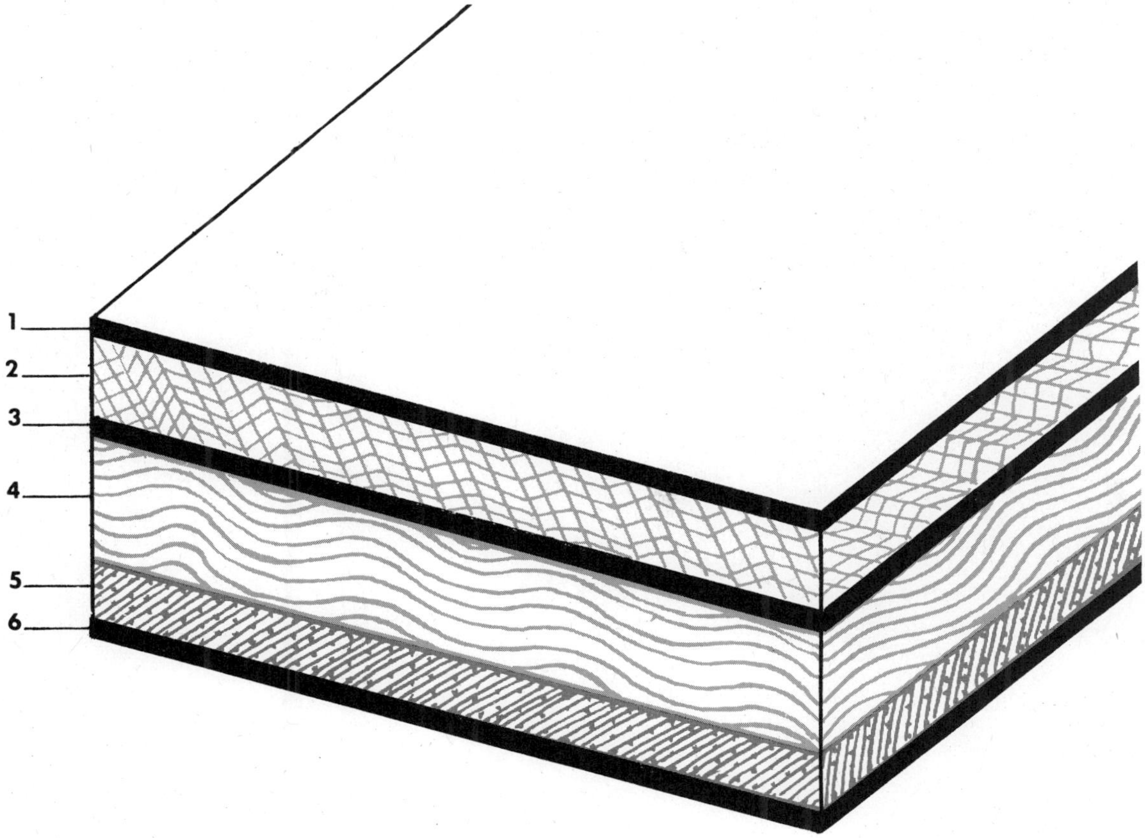

motion-picture film. What made Barnack's experimental model unique when it was marketed in 1924 by E. Leitz, the German optical concern, was the very advanced lens especially designed by Max Berek. This lens made the Leica a precision instrument rather than a miniature toy. Yet it represented a different approach from George Eastman's box camera. While Eastman sought to produce inexpensive and uncomplicated cameras for the masses, Barnack's Leica represented a sophisticated photographic instrument intended to raise the state of the art rather than simply to appeal to a mass market.

Twin-lens reflexes had been around since 1880, but the first modern one—the Rolleiflex—appeared in 1928. The small modern SLRs, using roll or 35 mm film, came on the scene in the 1930's, their development made possible by advances in lens making.

Since then, one more major revolution has occurred in black-and-white photography: the instant production of photographs inside the camera. That invention wasn't perfected until Edwin H. Land introduced his first black-and-white Polaroid camera in 1947. These cameras are now manufactured by the Polaroid Corporation.

From this point it seems entirely possible that still photography will go in several directions in the next 50 years or so. *Kirlian* lensless photography offers a vast uncharted area that has barely been explored. Another target for further investigation is the use of magnetic tape in still as well as in motion-picture photography. Finally, *holography,* or three-dimensional photography, offers unlimited potential for both development and application.

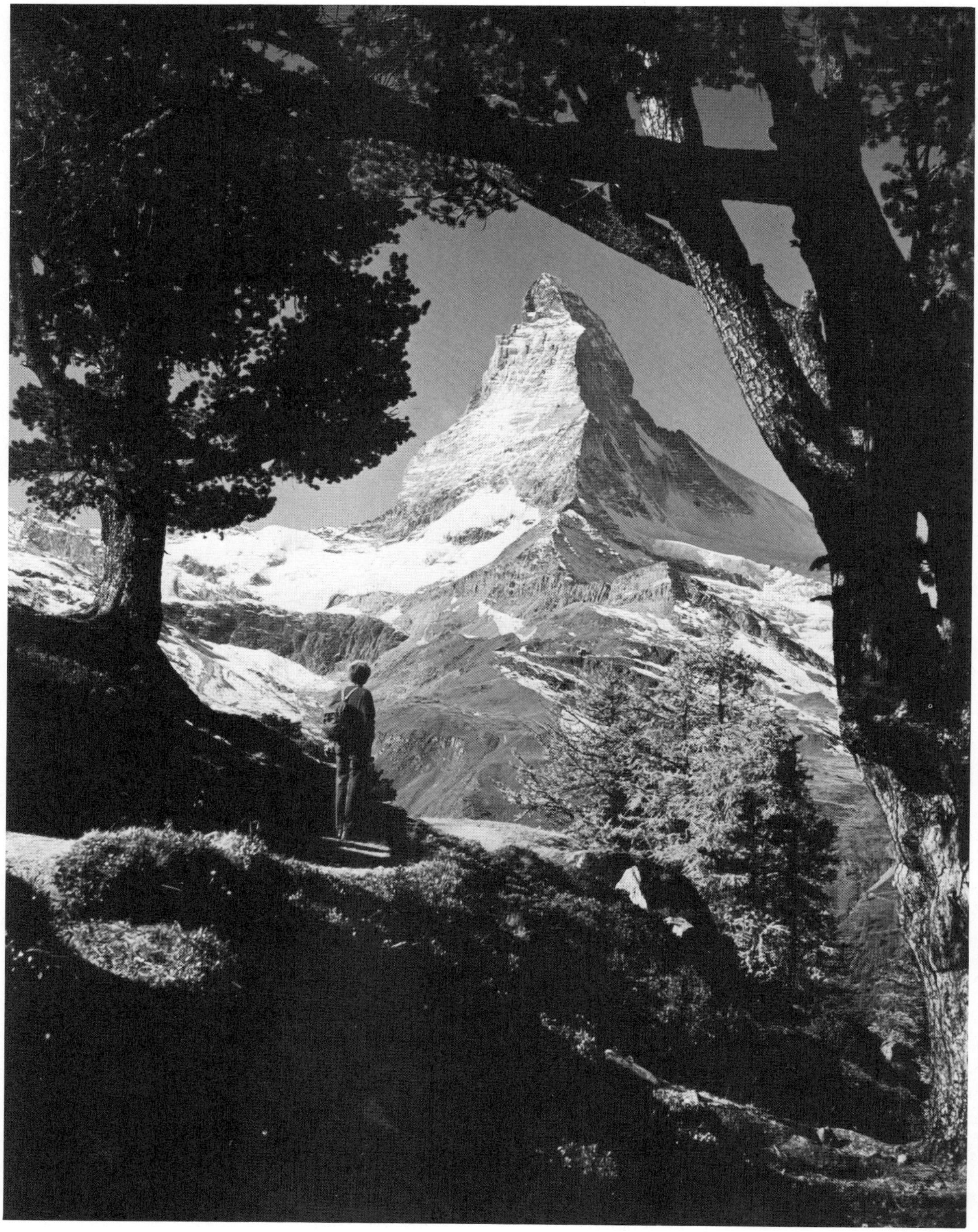

This photograph, "The Matterhorn," illustrates typical quality results attainable with modern black-and-white film. Photo by L. P. Greenhill, F.R.P.S.

WHAT IS FILM?

Simply put, film is material that can be coated with a light-sensitive chemical compound (the *emulsion*) and that will remain inert while the emulsion layer is being exposed, developed, and fixed. This base film substance can vary from the glass and metal plates used in older cameras to gelatins to Celluloid to the plastic materials currently in use.

Virtually any surface can be coated with a light-sensitive compound. The properties of light-sensitive material result in two phenomena: First, the emulsion layer (where the interaction between light and the light-sensitive coating takes place) yields an invisible, or *latent,* image when exposed to a sufficient amount of light; second, the latent image must be *chemically developed* to produce a print or photograph. With most films, the latent image, when developed, gives a negative that must then be printed to give a positive picture (an exception is the reversal-development processing of color and black-and-white transparency—"slide"—films).

We can say, then, that to achieve a finished print three steps are necessary:

1. exposure of the film to light
2. chemical development of the film to light
3. printing of the developed negative.

(The preceding refers to black-and-white negative film.)

Bear in mind that when film is exposed to light and a latent image is recorded on the emulsion layer, the stored image is *not permanent.* Depending on temperature and humidity, latent images gradually change over time—and not for the better. So, develop your exposed film promptly!

COLOR FILM AND BLACK-AND-WHITE FILM

From this admittedly oversimplified explanation of film, we now move to a consideration of the two basic film types: color and black-and-white.

Color film, in its simplest form, is black-and-white film coupled to appropriate dyes to produce a full-range color negative or transparency. Credit for the first color picture is generally given to the Scotsman James Clerk Maxwell, who with the help of Thomas Sutton first demonstrated success in 1861. Using three colored filters he produced three separate images, which he projected and superimposed on a screen to produce a color composite. As first efforts so often are, it was a cumbersome, complicated procedure that didn't result in truly natural-looking colors.

It wasn't until the 1900's that any of the many attempts to improve on Maxwell's process proved successful. In 1912 a pair of German chemists, H. Siegrist and R. Fischer, then pioneered the first commercially feasible color process. I. G. Farbenindustrie, the large German manufacturer of aniline dyes, had to wait until 1926, when Fischer's patent finally expired, to commercialize the process.

During that wait, two American musicians and amateur photographers, Leopold Mannes and Leopold Godowsky, improved on Fischer's process. They took out patents for Eastman

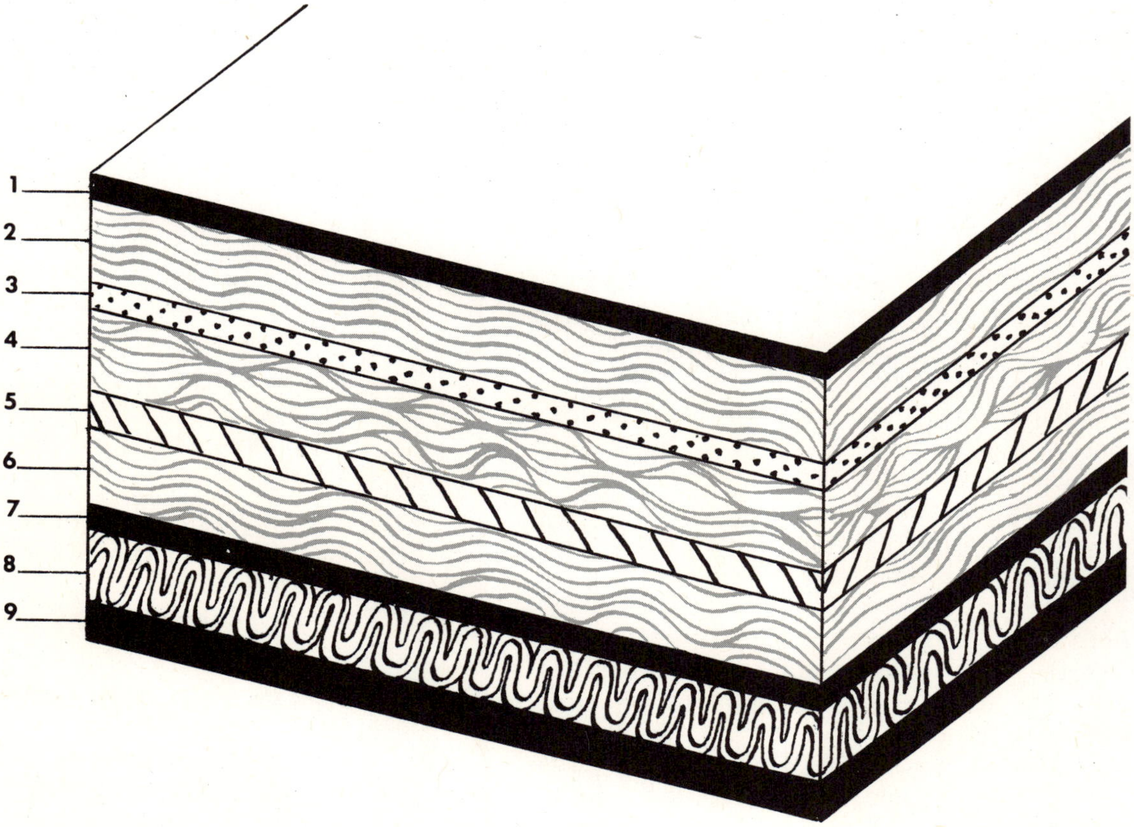

Kodak in the 1920's. From Mannes and Godowsky's work evolved Kodachrome, the first transparency material to be introduced commercially. Kodachrome uses a subtractive process (where the complementary color is taken away to achieve the desired hue in proper proportion), in which the three primary complementary colors are dye-coupled to black-and-white film layers to produce a transparent color image. In the late 1930's Agfa introduced a similar process.

After World War II many manufacturers introduced successful color processes, and the number of negative materials suited to home developing increased markedly. Kodak's transparency material for projection slides, known as Ektachrome, was introduced with the idea that it could be processed easily from a latent image to a visible color transparency in less than an hour. Today most film manufacturers market transparency color material as well as negative color film.

FILM CHARACTERISTICS

Before we get into a discussion of specific films, there are a number of film characteristics that you should familiarize yourself with from an in-use perspective. These traits are *contrast, sharpness, resolution and acutance, speed, grain,* and *exposure latitude*.

General schematic cross-section of color film. (1) Hard, protective *top layer* which prevents abrasion and scratching of the emulsion layer. (2) *Blue-sensitive layer.* Sensitive only to light waves in the blue portion of the spectrum. (3) *Yellow-filter layer.* Absorbs any excess blue not recorded by the blue-sensitive layer. (4) *Green sensitive layer.* Sensitive only to light waves in the green portion of the spectrum. (5) *Separation layer.* Separates the green from the red layer below it. (6) *Red-sensitive layer.* Sensitive only to light waves in the red portion of the spectrum. (7) *Subbing layer.* Holds the six above layers to the layer below. (8) *Support layer.* A plastic material which accounts for most of the film's bulk. (9) *Anti-halation backing.* Prevents light from reflecting back onto the emulsion layer's reverse side once it has passed through the film.

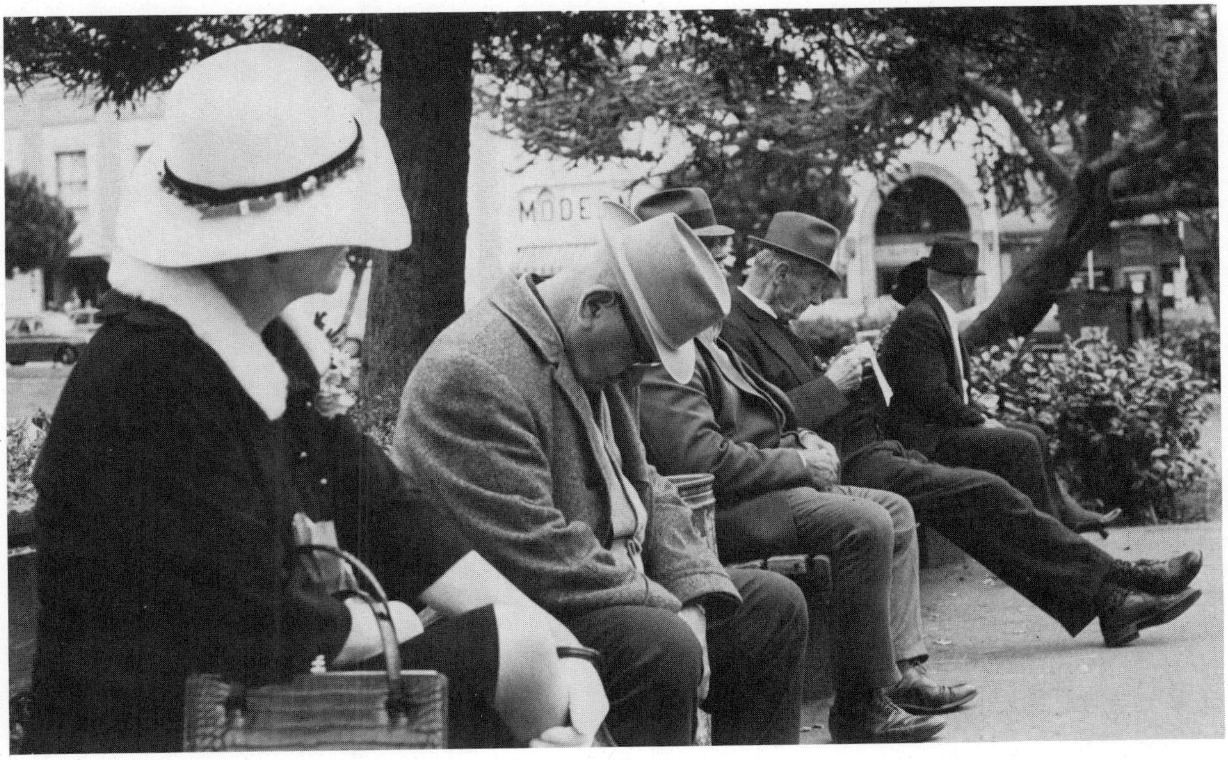

This scene shows what the term "normal" or average contrast implies. Photo by James Forkner.

Contrast. This term refers to a film's capacity to capture a range of tones from black through gray to white. Unfortunately, the word is all too often misused, in that so-called "high-contrast" film actually possesses a limited ability to render tones, whereas a "low-contrast" film can record a far greater range of tones.

Very-high-contrast film (see section on Litho Film) produces dramatically stark pictures that generally lack detail. Such pictures appear to many people to be more like pen-and-ink drawings than photographs because of the absence of any middle gray tones. To a lesser extent, general-purpose films, such as Kodak's Panatomic-X, still manage to produce

High resolution film has numerous applications. Note extremely fine detail. Photo by L. P. Greenhill, F.R.P.S.

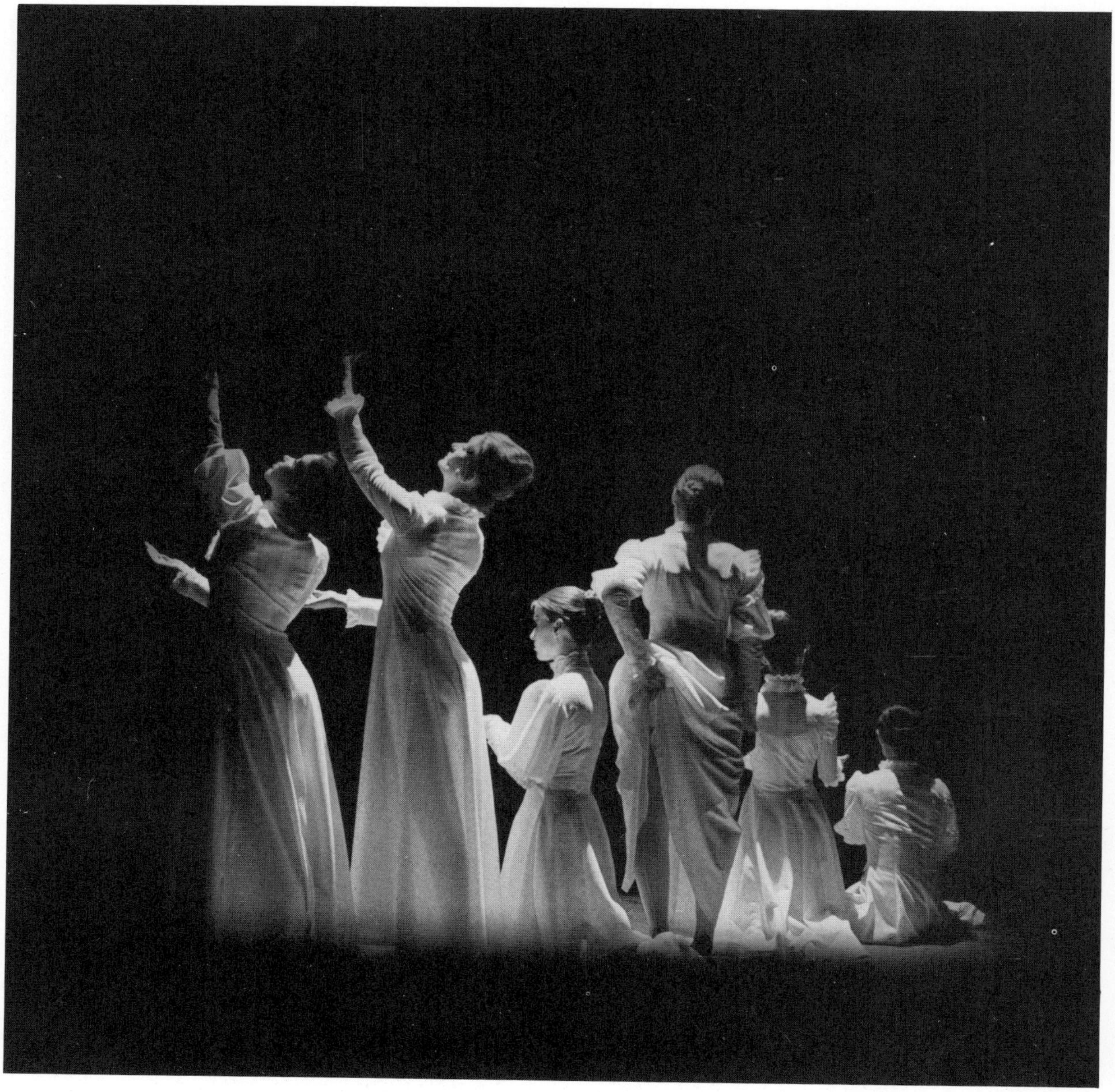

High contrast photograph. Note absence of middle tones. Photo by Bill Coleman.

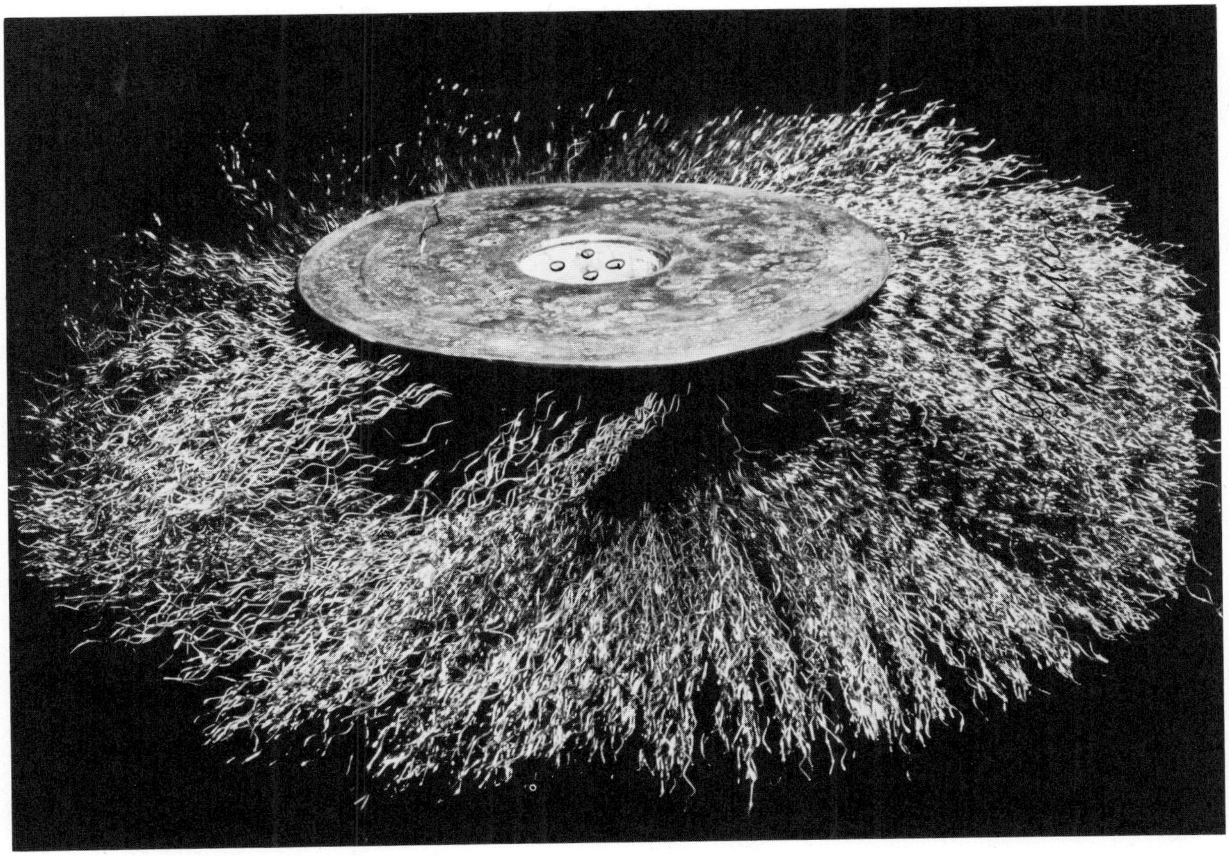

some detail in shadow areas while maintaining high contrast.

For most picture-taking situations, black-and-white films like Kodak's Plus-X or Tri-X tend to be more useful. They are medium-contrast films and can record a relatively wide range of tones.

The contrast characteristics of color films are more involved than those of their black-and-white cousins. Contrasty color material, although it creates highly saturated colors, cannot record a wide range of hues in a single scene. For example, Kodachrome KR (ASA 64), a contrasty film, usually produces pictures that are brilliant, deeply color-saturated, and detailed—provided that the scene has a relatively narrow brightness range between shadows and highlights. On the other hand, a film such as Fuji R-100 can handle a wider range of hues and so is not judged to be as contrasty as KR.

Visually, high-contrast pictures *appear* to be "sharper" than low-contrast ones by the very nature of their high visual contrast. This is a psychological phenomenon, not a physical one. Nevertheless, it can serve the photographer's needs.

Sharpness. "Sharpness" is a catch-all expression that has no technical standing. Essentially that quality of a film or photo that we term "sharpness" is really a product of two characteristics, *resolution* and *acutance.*

Resolution is a measure, usually expressed in terms of lines-per-millimetre, of how much detail a given film can reproduce; that is, how many clear lines a film can discern in each millimetre of image area under standard test con-

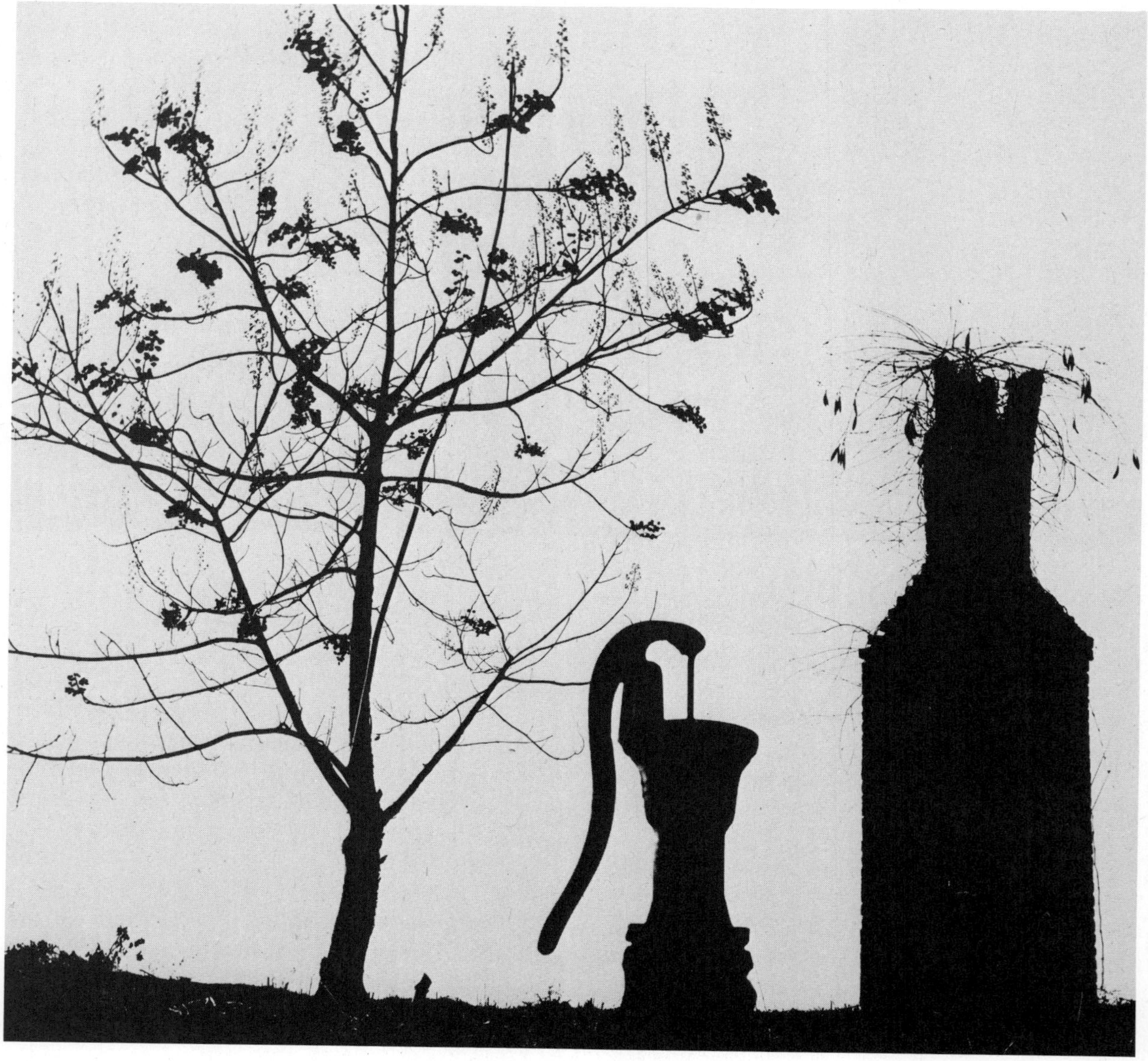

High acutance film enables the photographer to produce some rather dramatic graphic results. Photo by James Forkner.

ditions. The more lines that are visible per millimetre, the sharper the film is said to be.

The second characteristic of sharpness is *acutance.* Acutance can be defined as a film's ability to delineate clearly the boundaries between various tones contained in the latent image. The more sharply defined these boundaries are, the more sharply detailed the picture will look. A film possessing high acutance characteristics will produce clear details, while a low-acutance film will produce images with fuzzy edges between objects of different tones in the scene.

Obviously a high-resolution film without high-acutance characteristics is not generally desirable. The converse is true, too. So it's the combination of high resolution and acutance that can contribute to those razor-sharp images most of us hanker for. From a creative perspective, however, high sharpness is only desirable when the intent of the photographer is to bring about an image that shows finely detailed subjects. If you want a different mood, a "softer" film—one with lower sharpness characteristics—would be better.

Speed. Film speed is an expression of a given film's sensitivity to a fixed amount of light. It is stated as a number in one of the two scales accepted around the world to rate this characteristic: ASA (American National Standards Institute) or DIN (Deutsche Industrie Norm). These numbers also give photographers an idea of the sensitivity relationship of differently rated films to one another.

The practical importance of these numbers is that with each doubling of an ASA number or at every third DIN number, film sensitivity is doubled; thus, an ASA/DIN film rating of 125/22° is twice as sensitive as one rated at 64/19°.

Let's assume that you've loaded an ASA 25 film into your camera. The camera's meter indicates an exposure of *f*/2 at 1/60 sec. In advance you've determined that 1/125 sec. is the slowest shutter speed you can use with the telephoto lens you've mounted on the camera. Simply switch to an ASA 50 film and you can shoot at *f*/2 at 1/125 sec.: By doubling the ASA you will pick up one additional faster shutter speed or one smaller *f*-stop—your option.

Grain. Grain is the accumulation of those microscopic granules of light-sensitive material in the emulsion layer of film that actually effect the act of image production. They vary in size and shape according to the light-gathering characteristics of a specific film. So-called "fast" films have grain features that are larger than those of slow films; so that, when images made on both sorts of film are enlarged to the same diameter, the grain of the fast film is more apparent than the grain of the slower film. Although the size of grain is a primary

NUMERICAL SEQUENCE FROM LEAST SENSITIVE TO MOST SENSITIVE

ASA	12	16	20	25	32	40	50	64	80	100
DIN	12°	13°	14°	15°	16°	17°	18°	19°	20°	21°
ASA	125	160	200	250	320	400	500	640	800	
DIN	22°	23°	24°	25°	26°	27°	28°	29°	30°	

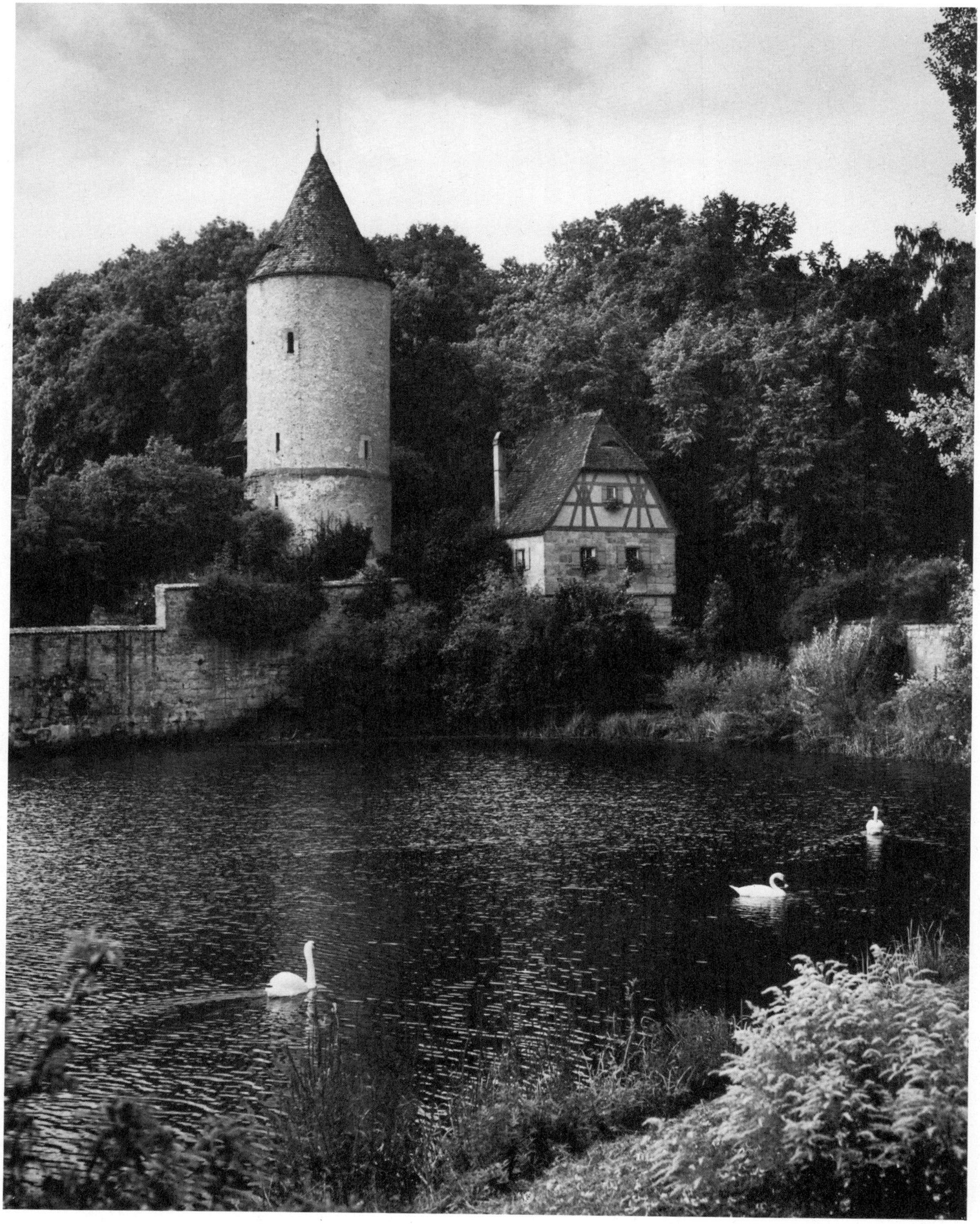

Photograph showing a very fine grain, which this scene seems almost to demand. Photo by L. P. Greenhill, F.R.P.S.

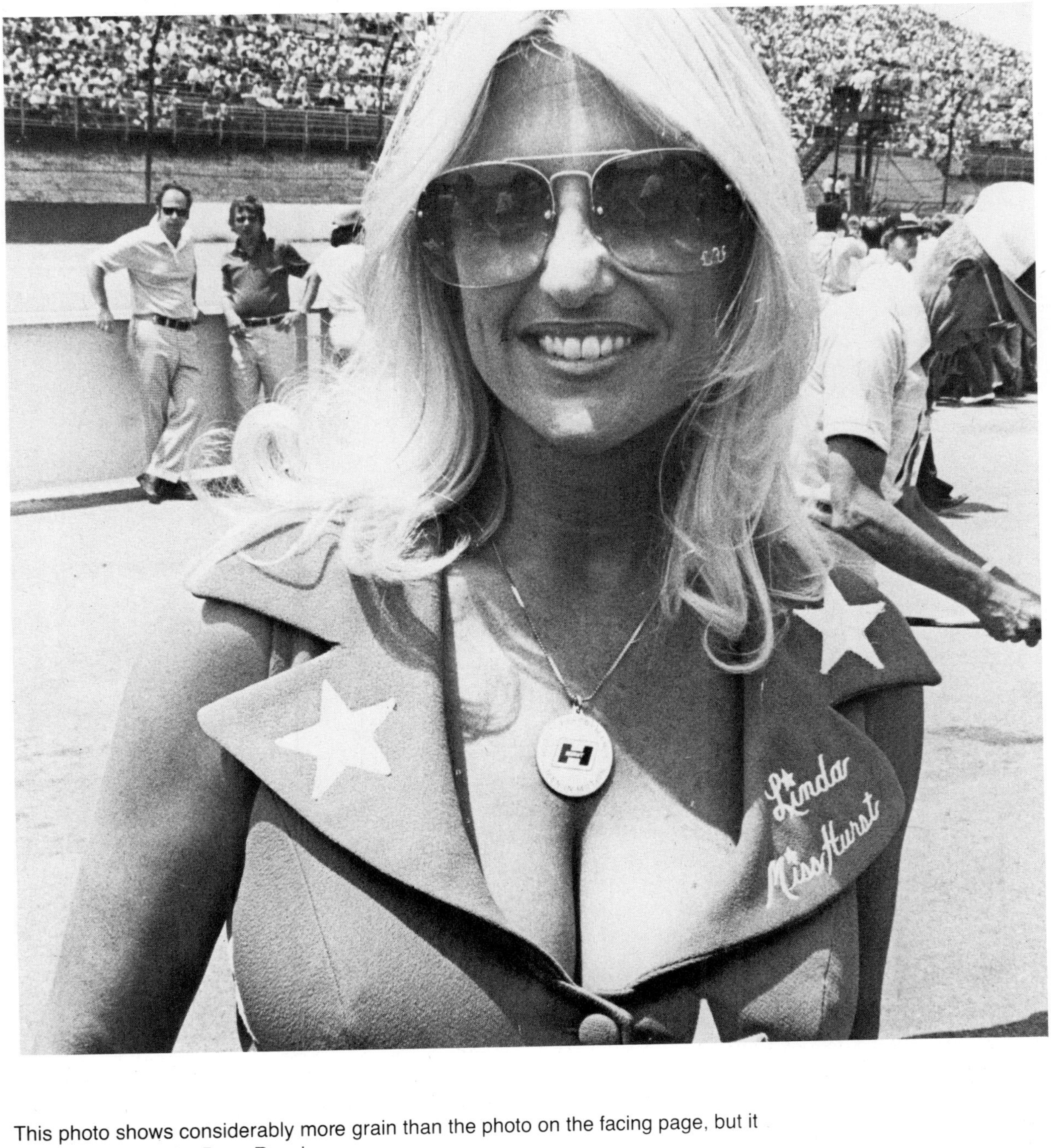

This photo shows considerably more grain than the photo on the facing page, but it still works. Photo by Dave Reasinger.

concern of photographers, its shape is also an important consideration. For example, a fast film with large but sharp-edged grains usually produces a less objectionable grain pattern (one that appears smoother and sharper) than a somewhat slower film whose grain structure is not as sharp-edged, even though smaller.

For practical purposes, grain structure is of little consequence to popular black-and-white or color material until enlargements greater than 20 × 25 cm (8 × 10 in.) are required. Then grain can become a real villain. Some people have a knee-jerk response, saying, "Simple—I'll use the finest-grained and sharpest-edged film I can find and enlarge away." As with most things in photography, it's not quite that simple.

Grain is intrinsic to film speed. The finer the grain, the slower the film will be. Conversely, the larger the grain, the faster the film. It then follows that under bright lighting conditions a slow, fine-grained film would be the proper and preferable choice. What about low-light situations when you must depend on available light? To get the picture, you must use a high-speed film with its large grain structure.

Extreme grain can make an otherwise sharp photograph appear fuzzy or mottled, and it can become so obtrusive that it destroys the visual qualities of the print or slide. On a positive note, grain can be used creatively in instances where fine detail is not desired. Grain can add an "antique" sense to a photo if used as part of an overall photographic concept.

The point at which grain becomes objectionable is mainly a matter of personal taste. Still, there are general limits that grain structure imposes on the degree of enlargement you can expect to achieve with a given film type. We have found that most 35 mm color and black-and-white film rated at ASA 25 to ASA 50 can be enlarged to 41 × 51 cm (16 × 20 in.) without objectionable grain, given that the film is properly exposed and developed. When using ASA 64–125 film in 35 mm format, 28 × 36 cm (11 × 14 in.) prints of high quality are routinely possible. High-speed films of ASA 200–500 give us satisfactory 20 × 25 cm (8 × 10 in.) prints. These are limits we feel comfortable with, and they should be viewed in that light. What *you* are willing to accept may be another matter.

Finally, while we have discussed grain characteristics in terms of the 35 mm film format, it is clear that using larger film formats, such as 6 × 6 cm (2¼ × 2¼ in.) or 6 × 6.9 cm (2¼ × 2¾ in.), will lessen the grain problem to a great extent because larger film sizes do not need as much enlargement to produce the same size print.

Exposure Latitude

Black-and-White Films. The exposure latitude of black-and-white films is generally quite broad. Since virtually all black-and-white photography is done using negative material, small exposure errors can be corrected or at the very least minimized during the printing stages. As with all negative material, black-and-white film has more tolerance for overexposure than for underexposure. For general purposes, black-and-white film from ASA 25 to ASA 400 can allow 2 to 3 *f*-stops of overexposure and still produce acceptable, if not optimum, prints. More than 1½ *f*-stops of underexposure, however, can lead to serious printing problems.

With the more exotic high-contrast and ultra-high-speed black-and-white films, exposure errors become much more critical. In some instances exposure latitude with these films is a mere ½ *f*-stop either way.

Color Films. Prints from color negatives, as from black-and-white negatives, can be altered in the printing process; but, since color rendition is also affected by exposure, critical metering is essential to preserve color fidelity. Our experience has shown that 2 stops' overexposure is tolerable, but for underexposure no more than 1 to 1½ stops should be attempted.

Color transparency (slide) material presents a more complex situation with regard to exposure latitude. We prefer well-saturated, brilliant colors in our slides. To achieve this effect we usually underexpose transparency film by about ½ *f*-stop. The easiest way to achieve this result is by increasing the film's ASA rating by 50 percent. Thus, a film normally rated at ASA 64 is increased to ASA 100. While this technique will produce well-exposed, highly saturated color in 90 percent of all shooting situations, there are times when it can be a disaster. Back-lit scenes or scenes where shadow detail is important are just two situations where "pushing" the film's speed is undesirable. Beware of contrasty light conditions.

While most color transparency films can tolerate exposure errors on the *under*exposed side—from 1 to 2½ *f*-stops, depending on the film being used—there are very few that can produce acceptable slides if they are *over*exposed by more than ¾ to 1 *f*-stop.

Photographic magazines periodically run comparisons of overexposure and underexposure on major film types—look for them and judge for yourself. Better yet, shoot a roll of the film you prefer and expose a number of different scenes in the following way, carefully noting exposure information: For the first exposure, read and follow the camera's built-in meter or a hand-held meter. For the second exposure, go ½ stop *under* (that is, give *less* exposure); for the third, 1 full stop under; for the fourth, 2 stops under. Then, for the fifth exposure go ½ stop *over;* sixth, 1 full stop over.

You can then judge results and calibrate your camera/meter combination for your personal *exposure index* for each film you normally use.

Storage and Handling

Film is delicate; so handle it with care. Here are some ideas on film storage and handling.

(1) Store film in the "crisper" drawer of your refrigerator. At room temperature or in high humidity, film will deteriorate in terms of its rated speed and/or color characteristics. This is especially true of films designated "professional."

(2) Do not load film into your camera directly from the refrigerator. Allow at least 45 minutes to an hour at normal room temperatures before using. Otherwise you risk condensation buildup on the film's surface.

(3) Never touch the film's surface with anything, especially fingers. Sweat and skin oil will adhere and could ruin a prize shot.

(4) Load film in subdued light. Even small amounts of strong light can fog high-speed film.

(5) Make sure your film is not stored in the trunk or glove compartment of your car. Heat can really do film in.

(6) Film is susceptible to breaking or cracking if used in extreme cold, as it becomes brittle; so in the winter, load and shoot carefully, don't force that last frame, and rewind slowly.

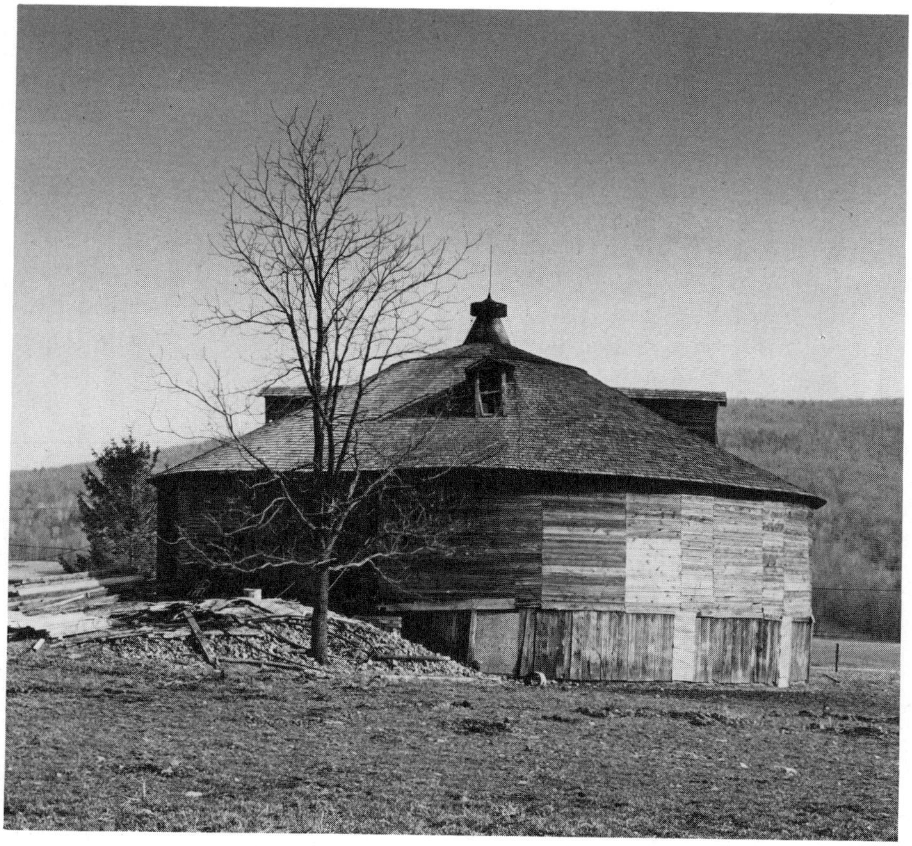

(Left) Slow, fine-grain black-and-white film makes for sharp, finely detailed and contrasty photographs. Photo by James Forkner. (Facing Page) Medium-speed film has a good grain structure and can be considered a good general-purpose film for most photographers. Photo by Bill Coleman.

(7) Make sure the film is *completely* rewound before opening the back of your camera. Even seasoned pros have sometimes opened cameras before rewinding. If in doubt as to whether the film has been rewound check the take-up knob: It will rotate without resistance if the film is rewound. If you're not sure, unload in a dark room or use a changing bag.

(8) Process your film promptly. The sooner you process exposed film, the lower the odds that you'll do something to spoil the latent images.

SPECIFIC FILMS

Let's concentrate now on films that are currently available in the United States. For your convenience we will group both black-and-white and color films according to their speed, or sensitivity to light.

Black-and-White Films

Slow Films (*ASA 20–50*). These are available in 35 mm, 120, and 220 rolls, and in larger formats in sheets. (Take note that not all films are available in all formats.) Kodak's *Panatomic-X* (*ASA 32)* is the most widely used and easiest to find of the slow films. Besides Panatomic-X, Ilford's *Pan F,* a British film (*ASA 50*), is the next most commonly available. Not nearly as accessible is Agfa's *Isopan IFF* (*ASA 25*) or *IF* (*ASA 40*).

These slow films produce extremely fine-grained negatives and possess high resolution

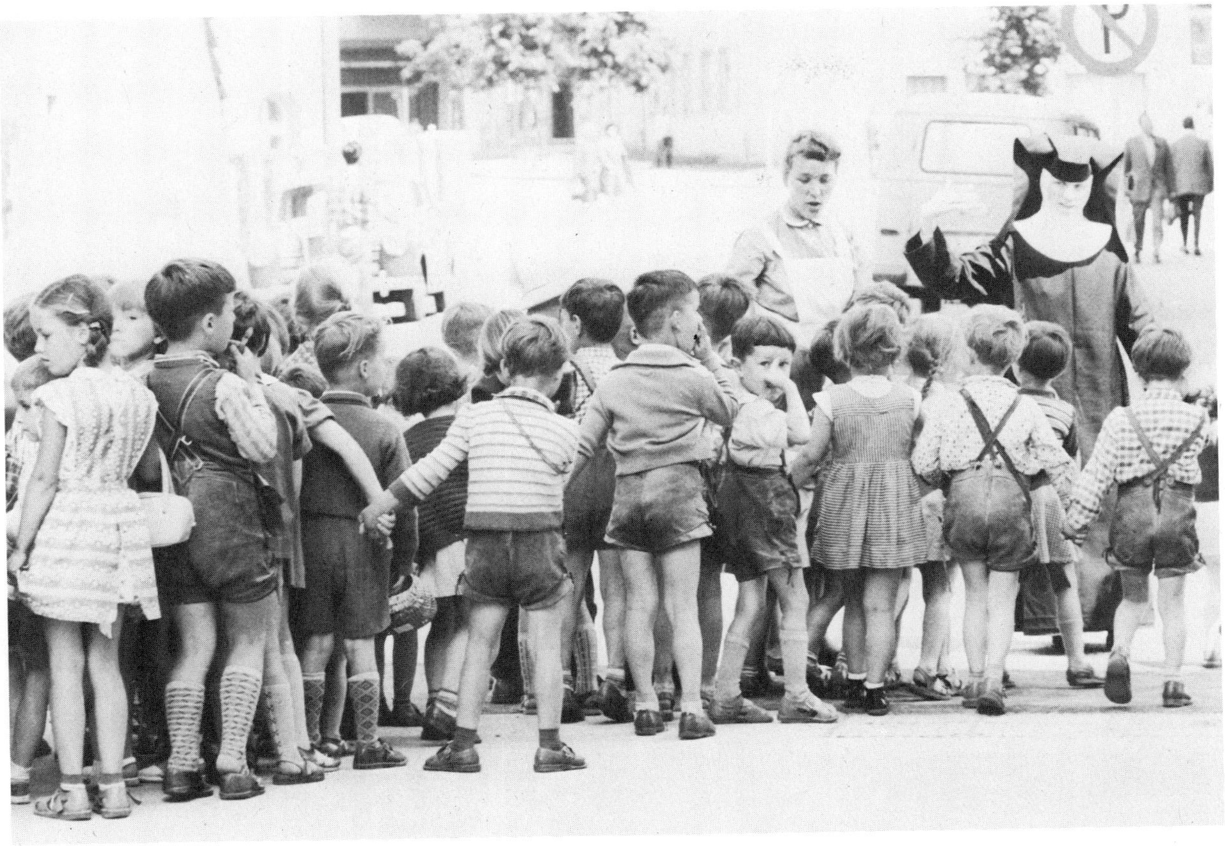

and acutance characteristics, even when we allow for variations from one manufacturer to another and for individual photographer's preferences. They are contrasty and have difficulty accurately reproducing scenes with a broad contrast range, though the high contrast inherent in these films can create dramatic portraits of male subjects and moody landscapes, just to name two applications. They are also very good for detailed copying work.

Medium-Speed Films (*ASA 50–125*). These films come in the same sizes as the slow films and in 110 or 126 drop-in cartridges. This category of black-and-white film is probably the most popular. Much of the medium-speed film is used by amateurs. Kodak markets two films in this range: *Plus-X pan* (*ASA 125*) and *Verichrome pan* (*ASA 125*). The differences between the two are slight, although Plus-X pan is a bit sharper than the Verichrome. Ilford's entry is *FP4,* rated at *ASA 125.* Agfa offers *Isopan ISS* (*ASA 100*).

Such medium-speed films produce a fine grain, though it is not as fine as that in the slower films. Further, they are less contrasty and consequently more suitable for a wide range of general photography than either the slower or the faster films.

Fast Films (*ASA 200–400*). These black-and-white materials come in 35 mm, 120, and 220 rolls, as well as in sheets, but not in drop-in cartridges. In this particular division, Kodak's *Tri-X* (*ASA 400*) must rate as the all-time favorite. It enjoys a well-earned reputation as a versatile emulsion, especially among photographers inclined toward action and sports

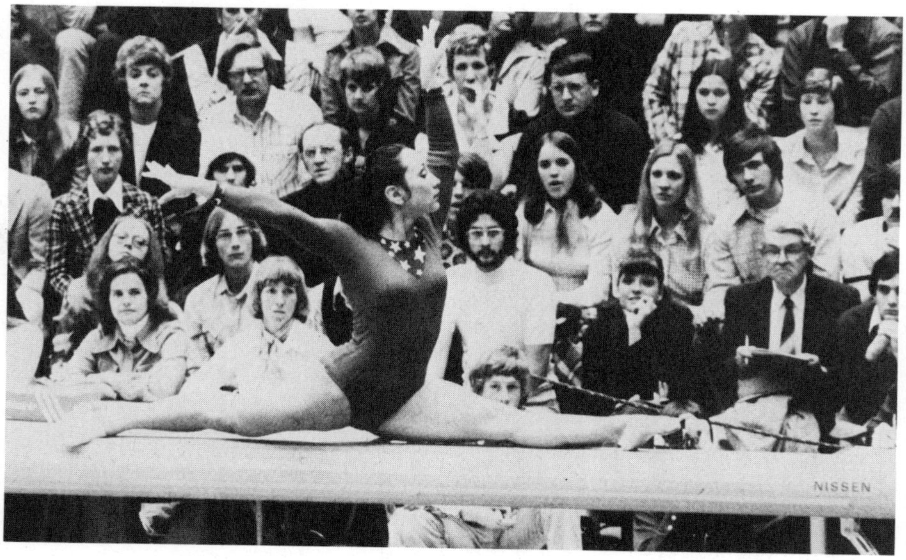

(Left) Fast black-and-white film is a natural for action photography. Photo by Dave Reasinger. (Below) super-speed film tends to produce extremely grainy results. Photo by Marc Levey.

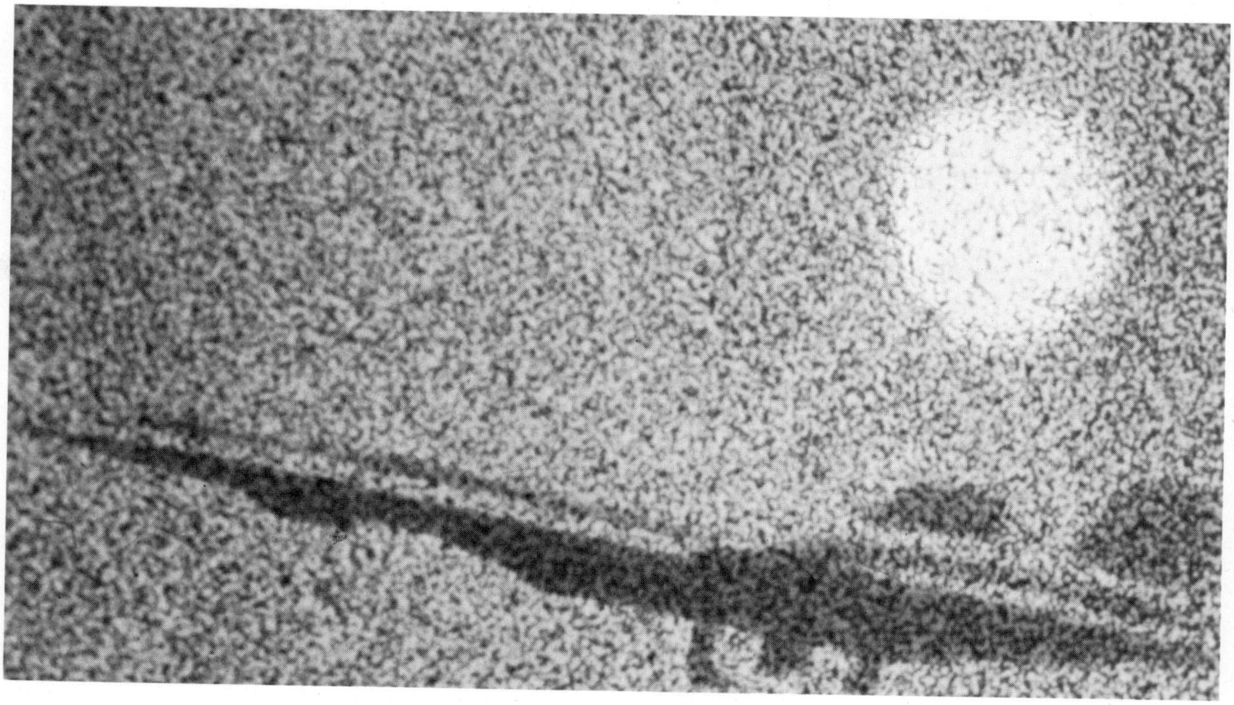

photography. Among Tri-X's competitors are Ilford's *HP4 (ASA 400)* and the new *HP5 (ASA 400)*. The small but growing group of professionals who use HP4 and HP5 say they are even better than Tri-X in exposure latitude and grain quality. Occasionally Agfa's *Isopan Ultra (ASA 200)* can be found, but it is not generally available.

These high-speed films possess moderate grain and exhibit lower contrast traits in comparison to the medium-speed or low-speed black-and-white films already discussed.

Even though Tri-X and HP4 and HP5 are rated by the manufacturers at ASA 400, many photographers use these films at considerably higher speeds. We have consistently shot HP4 at ASA 800 or even 1000, and we know of professional photojournalists who use Tri-X at ASA 1600 and even higher. Granted, there is considerably more graininess and a loss of shadow detail as you increase film speed, but no other technique works quite as well when shooting in very low ambient light. In many cases the quality of prints made by "pushing" the film to higher speeds is surprisingly good, and the fact that there is increased grain often adds to the dramatic statement the shot makes.

Super-Speed Films (ASA 500–3200+). Superfasts can be had in 35 mm format on special order, in sizes 120 and 220 roll film, and 4 × 5 in. sheets. There are three films available in this grouping: Kodak's *Royal-X pan (ASA 1250)* and *2475 recording film (ASA 1000–3200 and up)*, and Agfa's *Isopan record (ASA 400–2000 and up)*.

Characterized by coarse grain, these are specialty films with somewhat limited applications in general photography. In our experience the images produced are not detailed enough to take very much magnification in the darkroom. However, where lighting conditions are poor and the photographer is limited to what little light is available, any image might be better than no image at all.

Specialty Black-and-White Films. Because of their unusual and unique capabilities, these films are not suitable for most picture-taking situations but can be used in specific creative applications.

Black-and-White Infrared Film can be obtained from both Kodak and Agfa. Infrared film does not have an ASA rating, since it is not sensitive to the visible-light spectrum. A convenient starting point for establishing exposures might be to set your ASA dial at 125, shooting at *f*/16 and 1/125 sec. and bracketing your shots as described earlier (review Exposure Latitude). This film produces a variety of distorted effects, depending upon the amount of infrared radiation present and the color of the filter used. Filters that are often used with infrared film are red, deep green, deep yellow, and orange. Green vegetation and trees reflect a great deal of infrared radiation and so make good subjects. The film has a coarse grain to it, is very contrasty, and requires *total* darkness in processing.

Litho Film (Kodalith) probably sees more darkroom than in-camera use. It is rated at ASA 6–12 and is the most contrasty of all films, yielding images virtually free of all middle gray tones. Properly handled, litho images can produce dramatic line-drawing effects by reducing most subjects to basic forms. Strong linear subjects like buildings are most appealing for use with this film. Litho film can also be

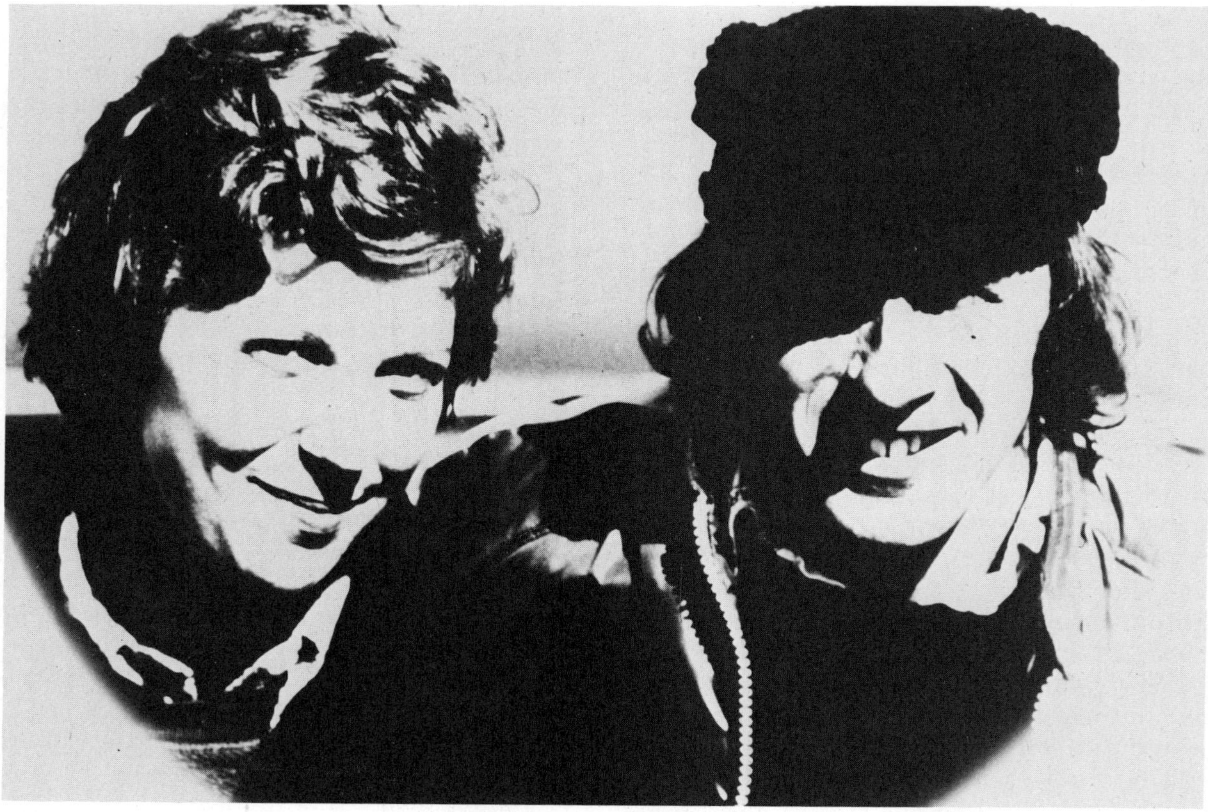

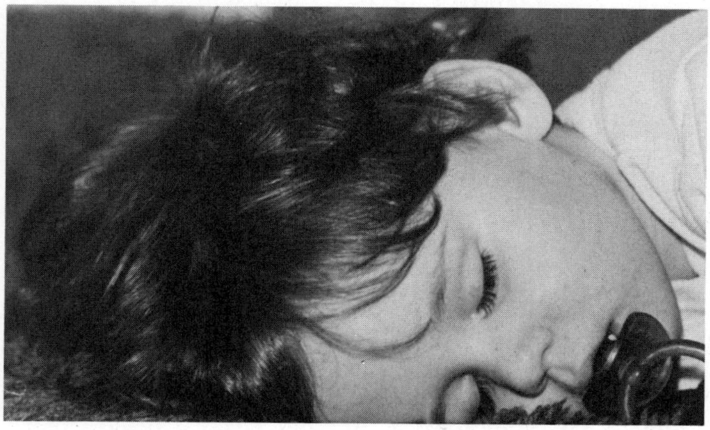

(Above) This solarized portrait of racing driver Jackie Stewart and the photographer's wife, Jan, was shot with lith film. Photo by Dave Reasinger. (Left) H + W Control film yields ultra fine grain results. Photo by Marc Levey.

used in combination with *color separations* to bring about *posterizations*.

Ultra-Fine-Grain Films such as Kodak *line-copy film* (*ASA 6*) will reproduce almost unlimited detail but will not show middle tones very well. However, another film, H + W *Control Pan* (*ASA 50–64*), is much more manageable. The H + W film is a German data-recording film, respooled in this country and distributed by the H + W Company; it is found in the larger camera stores. This ultra-fine-grain film can sustain extreme enlargement with little or no grain at all. We've seen 100× enlargements with no visible grain and full tonal scale present. Although H + W is somewhat contrasty, you can control this by rating it at about ASA 50. Be aware that H + W needs its own special developer. For detailed or macro work, this film is hard to match.

All fine-grain films are available in 35 mm; some come in other formats, availability depending partly on geographic location.

Color Negative Films

There are medium-speed and high-speed films available that produce negatives from which to make color prints. Falling into the category of *medium-speed color negative films* are Kodak's *Kodacolor II* and *Vericolor S, Fujicolor II,* and *Agfacolor*. All produce negatives ready for printing and are rated between ASA 80 and ASA 100. They are available in 35 mm cassettes, 120 and 220 roll film, 110 and 126 cartridges, and some sheet-film sizes.

Since much of the final result when using color negatives depends upon the skill of the printer, it's difficult to talk of these films' specific characteristics. However, Vericolor S and Fujicolor II yield the finest-grained results and appear to be able to handle a wider range of lighting conditions than the others. For critical applications, our vote goes to Vericolor S. You should be able to get quality prints up to 41 × 51 cm (16 × 20 in.) using this film in its 35 mm format.

Not long ago two manufacturers, Fuji and Kodak, introduced *high-speed color negative films* rated at ASA 400. Presently these two films, *Fujicolor 400* and *Kodacolor 400,* are available in 35 mm cassette and 110 cartridge sizes only. While admittedly more grainy than the slower films, they open up new possibilities for available-light color photography. Tri-X fans now have two color films rated at ASA 400 against which they can compare their standard fast-rated black-and-white film. Color action and sports shots should now be easier, since higher shutter speeds can be used with smaller *f*-stops. Sharp, clear prints should be possible up to at least 20 × 25 cm (8 × 10 in.) with these films.

Color Transparency Films

Not unlike black-and-white film, color transparency films are offered in a bewildering array. To help you out we'll divide them up according to their ASA ratings.

Kodachromes. The one *slow color transparency film* that all others are judged by is *Kodachrome KM,* formerly called Kodachrome 25 (only in 35 mm), which replaced Kodachrome II. This film is extremely fine grained and capable of withstanding great enlargement. The colors tend toward the warm end of the spectrum and are brilliantly saturated. With an exposure latitude of 1 to 1½ stops over and 2 stops under, KM, at ASA 25, is an excellent film to use under good lighting conditions.

However, the film is a high-contrast emulsion and so can be a problem in scenes that exhibit a wide brightness range.

As with the black-and-white films, the majority of color transparency films are found in the *medium-speed category,* with speeds ranging from *ASA 64* (35 mm cassettes) to *ASA 100* (both 120 and 35 mm formats). These films are a good compromise in terms of speed, grain, and contrast, having a latitude of 1 stop over and 1½ to 2 stops under. One of Kodak's most popular entries in the medium-speed range is *Kodachrome KR,* formerly called Kodachrome 64, sibling to Kodachrome KM and successor to Kodachrome X. The KR is almost as sharp and more than 1 stop faster than the KM. Initial problems with a greenish cast have been overcome and it now appears to be a fine performer.

You should realize that both Kodachromes must be processed by professional labs because the color dye couplers are contained in the processing chemicals and not in the film itself. In other words, it's impossible for you to develop these films at home unless you have around $25,000 to invest in the equipment.

Ektachrome 64 (*ASA 64*). This film replaces Ektachrome X. It answers the complaints many of us have voiced for years about Ektachrome; namely, that its color balance was overly blue, particularly in shadows (often referred to as the "Ektachrome Blues"). While the earlier "X" emulsion was not very sharp and produced low contrast, the new 64 appears to be quite a bit sharper and to have a warmer, more pleasing color balance. The advantage of this film is that it can be processed by virtually any lab or at home.

Honeywell 64 (*ASA 64*)/*Agfachrome 64* (*ASA 64*). These are one and the same film though they come from different distributors. The successor to Agfa CT-18, Agfachrome 64 is a warm film that is particularly good to use with people whose skin is dark. It has no purple cast to it, and it emphasizes natural browns and yellows. Even though it is a medium-speed film, Agfa shows more grain than the Kodak films in this category.

Also available now is *Agfachrome 100* (*ASA 100*). It is essentially the same film as Agfachrome 64, but with higher film sensitivity and a bit finer grain structure.

Fujichrome R-100 (*ASA 100*). With its combination of good, crisp grain patterns, excellent color rendition, and relatively high speed (two stops faster than Kodachrome 25), it allows photographers to make hand-held shots in a wide range of lighting situations and still achieve quality results. Further, Fujichrome can be purchased for a good deal less than either Agfa or Kodak films (including film and processing). It is a favorite with many.

Just introduced is Fuji RD-100, an improved version of R-100 that is compatible with the E-6 developing process. Initial tests indicate that Fuji has improved the grain characteristics and color rendition of this film.

You should be able to obtain good-quality prints up to and including 28 × 36 cm (11 × 14 in.) using any of these films.

Special Color Transparency Films

High-Speed Color Transparency Films. Ektachrome 200 (*ASA 200*) is the new replacement for high-speed Ektachrome. The 200 is surprisingly sharp for such a fast film and produces a natural color balance that is a definite improvement over the old High-Speed's heavy blue cast. Like the Ektachrome 64, 200 can be processed at a lab or at home with the new E-6 processing kits. An additional advantage of this film is that it can be pushed beyond its normal ASA rating of 200. Although there will be grain buildup and some loss of shadow detail, exposing and processing at ASA 400—or even ASA 800—should give you acceptable reproduction.

The new *Ektachrome 400* (*ASA 400*) is winning praise. Grain patterns are sharp and crisp despite the film's high speed. Colors are rich and well saturated, and the film can withstand increased ASA ratings with more-than-acceptable results. (Note that just arriving in this country is Fujichrome 400, which is intended to compete directly with Ektachrome 400.)

For travel, we recommend that you choose a medium-speed film such as Kodachrome 64, Ektachrome 64, or Fujichrome R-100. But have at least one or two rolls of Ektachrome 200 with you, too. Kodachrome 25 is just too slow in providing needed film flexibility when traveling. In picture-taking situations where you can control the lighting or at least choose when to shoot, though, Kodachrome 25 is a good choice.

Color Transparency Film for Artificial Lighting. Thus far we have discussed films that are color-balanced to produce normal color rendition in daylight. There are several films that are specifically designed to meet the needs of those who wish to shoot under artificial lights, whether room lighting or studio photoflood lamps.

No film can exactly match colors under artificial room-lighting conditions. *Ektachrome 50* and *160,* two new Kodak films balanced for tungsten (ordinary incandescent) light, do come close, though. While most room lights are about 2800 K—that is, 2800 degrees in the Kelvin scale of color temperature—Ektachrome 50 and 160 are balanced for 3400 K.

Another more specialized film used for artificial lighting is *Kodachrome 40* (*ASA 40*), balanced for the 3200 K temperature of studio lights. This film is sometimes used indoors under ordinary lighting conditions.

Remember that you also have the option of using an 80-series A or B filter to convert daylight film to match the color temperature of indoor lighting.

Ektachrome Infrared Film. This has no ASA rating for the same reasons we mentioned when discussing black-and-white infrared film. While results can only be described as unpredictable, this film can produce some very exotic results. Start with an ASA rating of 125 and an exposure of *f*/16–22 at 1/125 sec., making sure that you bracket your shots. Try the 25A red, orange, green, and yellow filters with the film. Be sure to focus using your lens's infrared focusing mark (often colored red), since infrared is on a different wavelength from that to which your camera's focusing is adjusted. For every great infrared shot you can expect 20 losers; so be prepared for great pictorial disasters. This is especially true when photographing people, as skin tones can range from plain awful to the grotesque.

Photomicrography Film (*ASA 6–12*). Designed by Kodak for microscope work, this can be used to produce interesting images in general picture-taking situations, as well. Like infrared film, micrography film can do extraordinary things to normal color balance. It is a very slow film, with high contrast; you should try at least one roll and simply experiment with it. It is recommended that you use a CC20 (color correction) or 30R filter with this film.

PROCESSING SLIDES

As with most things in the marketplace, film processing prices are variable and subject to competition. We looked into process pricing and found some illuminating results. Below is a comparison of prices from different sources, accurate as we go to press. Bear in mind that this chart serves only as an approximate guide, also that push-processing is always extra.

USING EKTACHROME 64 (20 EXPOSURES)

PROCESSOR	PROCESSING	SHIPPING OR TAX	PRICE PER SLIDE
Discount House (K-Mart)	$1.79	$.11	9½o
Camera Store (Local Processing)	2.45	.16	13o
Camera Store (Send to Kodak)	3.35	.20	17½o
Kodak Mailers	3.55	.47	20o
Process at Home (Unichrome) Prorate Equipment to 50 Rolls	1.90	0	9½o

If you are cost-conscious and have the time, home processing and discount processing are your best bets. However, some discount processors do not take the care with your film that either Kodak would or you would at home. To us, home-processing is a chore; but with the new E-6 chemistry the processing times have been reduced to less than half an hour. You can get consistently good results at home, and you can push-process film for no additional cost. When you find a lab that gives good service, delivers in a reasonable time, and is quality-conscious, you will want to stick to it for most of your processing. However, you should try home processing; if it turns you on, you can save money!

SOME BLACK-AND-WHITE FILMS

TYPE	SPEED (ASA)	CONTRAST	GRAIN	USES	SIZES
Kodak Panatomic-X	32	High	Extremely fine	Detail copying; High magnification enlargements; Architectural	35 mm 120, 220
Ilford Pan F	50	High Medium	Extremely fine	Same as above	35 mm 120, 220 Some Sheets
Agfa Isopan IFF	25	High	Extremely fine	Same as above	35 mm
Kodak Plus-X Pan	125	Medium	Fine	General purpose	35 mm 120, 220, 620 Sheets
Kodak Veri-chrome Pan	125	Medium	Fine	General purpose; Amateur applications	110, 126
Ilford FP4	125	Medium	Fine	General purpose	35 mm 120
Agfa Isopan ISS	100	Medium	Fine	General purpose	35 mm 120, 220
Kodak Tri-X Pan	400	Medium Low	Medium	Action; Sports; General purpose	35 mm 120, 220 Sheets
Ilford HP4, HP5	400	Medium Low	Medium	Action; Sports; General purpose	35 mm 120, 220
Kodak Infrared	—	High	Coarse	Experimental and creative work	35 mm 120 Sheets
Kodak Kodalith	12	Extremely high No middle grays	Medium	Experimental and creative work	35 mm 120 Sheets
H + W Control VTE Pan	50–64	Medium	Extremely fine	Pan film for large enlargement work	35 mm only

SOME COLOR SLIDE FILMS

TYPE	SPEED (ASA)	CONTRAST	GRAIN	COLOR RENDITION	EXPOSURE LATITUDE	SIZES
Kodak Photo-micrography	16	Very high	Super fine	Does not record colors accurately	½ stop under; ½ over	35 mm 120
Kodachrome KM	25	High	Very fine	Whites a bit yellow; Others brilliant and saturated	2 stops under; 1–1½ over	35 mm
Kodachrome KR	64	Moderate	Fine	About the same as Kodak 25	1½ stops under; 1 over	35 mm 110
Ektachrome 64	64	Moderate	Fine	Traditional problem with overall bluish cast solved; not as saturated as Kodachrome	1 stop under; 1 over	35 mm 120, 220 Sheets
Agfachrome 64	64	Moderate	Fine Medium	Good reds; warm cast—toward yellows	1 stop under; 1 over	35 mm 120
Fujichrome R-100	100	Moderate	Fine	Good overall saturation; Accurate warm colors	1½ stops under; 1 over	35 mm 120
Ektachrome 200	200	Moderate	Fine Medium	Accurate colors; a bit cool but not nearly like high speed Ektachrome	1½ stops under to 1 over	35 mm 120, 220
Ektachrome Infrared	—	High	Coarse	Unpredictable	½ stop under to ½ over	35 mm 120 Sheets
Ektachrome 50 (Tungsten)	50	Medium	Fine	In tungsten light relatively normal color balance	1½ stops under to 1 over	35 mm 120
Ektachrome 160 (Tungsten)	160	Medium	Medium	In tungsten light relatively normal color balance	1½ stops under to 1 over	35 mm 120

IV

Photoequipment Buying

The one question asked of us more than any other is: What kind of equipment should I buy? Unfortunately, there are as many answers as inquiries. To solve this dilemma, you as a potential buyer have to be armed, not only with all the facts about the equipment being considered, but also with some knowledge of current marketing practices.

The initial step you should take is in determining what you are interested in photographing. For example, if action shots are your main concern, a 50 mm macro lens is not a sensible choice as a first accessory lens, while if nature, stamp, or coin photography is what you want to pursue, the 50 mm macro is a natural.

Once you have determined your photographic priorities, think about how often you plan to use that additional piece of equipment. As was suggested in the chapter on lenses, an inexpensive lens is perfectly acceptable if used infrequently. If you shoot an average of one roll of film per week, though, consider yourself an above-average film user. In that case you will probably find you need something more reliable, and in most cases that translates into more expensive equipment.

THE TRICKS OF THE TRADE

Assuming you have made these two determinations, what next? First, read all the literature available to you about the class of equipment you're thinking of investing in. After all, you wouldn't buy a new car without checking the mileage, features, and performance records. Photo magazines such as *Modern Photography, Popular Photography, Camera 35,* and *PhotoGraphic* offer abundant information, especially in regard to equipment features and test reports. Advertising in these magazines is informative but, as elsewhere, must be taken with that proverbial grain of salt. In case you haven't noticed, camera promotions are full of "hype" and use more glowing superlatives than just about any other commodity line. If taken at face value, nearly any ad will leave you with a burning desire to own that new "Fitzmo 2000" or "Snapaflex 100" or die.

We have been witness to several other practices that manufacturers and their advertising agencies indulge in to entice buyers.

The first we call the "tickle." When they decide to introduce a new product or series, equipment makers herald it many months in advance by trickling information and specifications to leading publications. Magazines often

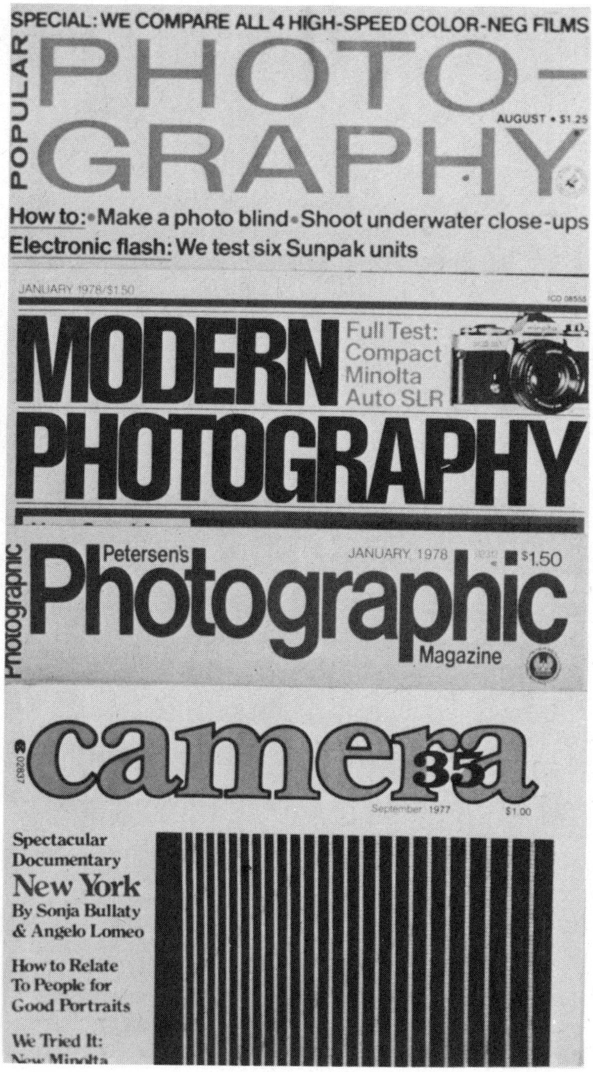

There are a number of monthly references for the photography buff. Photo by Marc Levey.

print these "rumors" about the new product. The next phase begins when prototypes are shown to photography commentators, who are allowed to handle and experiment with them. If all goes according to schedule, the equipment makers then run lavish full-color ads in the magazines to "officially introduce" their new product. The verbiage really begins to get fanciful at this point.

The "tickle" process is intrinsic to advertising as a genre. But exaggerated claims often appear, many times worded to overemphasize the new product's virtues without actually guaranteeing specific performance. Phrases such as ". . . *designed* to equal or outperform any comparable product on the market" are the norm, apparently. The operational word, of course, which we have italicized, is "designed." The term implies performance—but only states goals and intentions, not actual performance. In terms of the residual message left with the reader, "designed" translates into fact and a real expectation of actual results.

Some ads are much more blatant in their assertions because advertising, through the subtle use of language, creates an imposing demand in the prospective buyer's mind. Be careful when you read photography literature for words such as "incomparable," "incredible," "precise," "uncompromising," "professional," "revolutionary," and so on. Rarely are any of these adjectives accurate. They are part of the hype and intended to stimulate an acute emotional need (not a pragmatic one) for the equipment shown.

After the promotion, drum-beating, and trumpeting have heralded a product's introduction, a series of "sustaining ads" appear. These are run to keep your interest piqued. At this point the campaign is some four-to-nine months in progress. And you're sold! You'll buy it. You tramp off to your local store or call your mail-order crony, and what do you get? Mostly, nothing. The bitter truth is that in most instances the product has not even reached the dealers yet. Often *they* don't know when to expect its arrival. If the product has been shipped at all, it's probably in such small numbers that you'll end up on a waiting list. Now you might think to yourself, "It must be terrific if people are willing to wait just to purchase it." It's all by design, dear friends: The design is to create and then tickle the demand, because people often assume scarcity equals rarity and thus the product acquires an inherent quality, a desirability in the mind of the consumer-to-be.

If it is a major manufacturer's product and a significant new one (such as a camera model, a line of lenses, or a lens with seemingly revolutionary performance promise), be prepared *not* to see it in the flesh for six months to a year from first publicity. We know that several products widely advertised for months never made it to the dealers at all. Vivitar once advertised an automatic camera that never materialized; it even had a name and designation. In all fairness, products don't always work out. But premature introduction is worse in such a case than none at all.

Speaking of premature introductions, let's take a hard look at them. Sometimes the photoequipment introduced is not ready to justify claims made about it. The first close-focusing zoom lens came out in the early 1970's. This Vivitar bombshell sold as fast as it could be crated and shipped from Japan. And while the first 70–210 Series I zoom performed well, it was hardly spectacular and far from what ad men alleged ("a quantum jump in the state of the art"). Some months later Vivitar quietly presented a second model with an improved design that considerably upgraded the lens's performance. Finally, the company brought out the definitive model, an excellent optic with multicoating. Certainly, the buyers of the first model weren't cheated; but they would have done better to wait, in this case.

Another instance of premature introduction is Soligor's 70–220 C/D zoom lens. The barrage of advertising promised outstanding performance, but as the importer, A.I.C., Inc., later conceded, major flaws made the lens undeliverable at the time. Yet several mail-order houses continued to accept orders, fully aware that the lens would not be available for months.

The lesson in all this is to be cautious about advertising claims. They aren't objective or independent opinions; so don't rush out and order equipment the moment you see it advertised. Later, we'll map out a specific buying strategy.

THE BEST DEAL—FROM WHOM?

After sifting through the literature supplied by various manufacturers you will find that several decisions you need to make will keep cropping up, for example:

1. Whom should I buy from?
2. What should I expect to pay?
3. How can I determine performance, beyond what I read in advertisements?

Whom Should I Buy From?

There are four choices in the new-equipment category: local dealer, chain store or discount house, mail-order dealer, or foreign sources. Each has its advantages and its drawbacks.

The Local Dealer. Camera dealers in this category sell service, as well as hardware. Prices at local sources usually go higher than

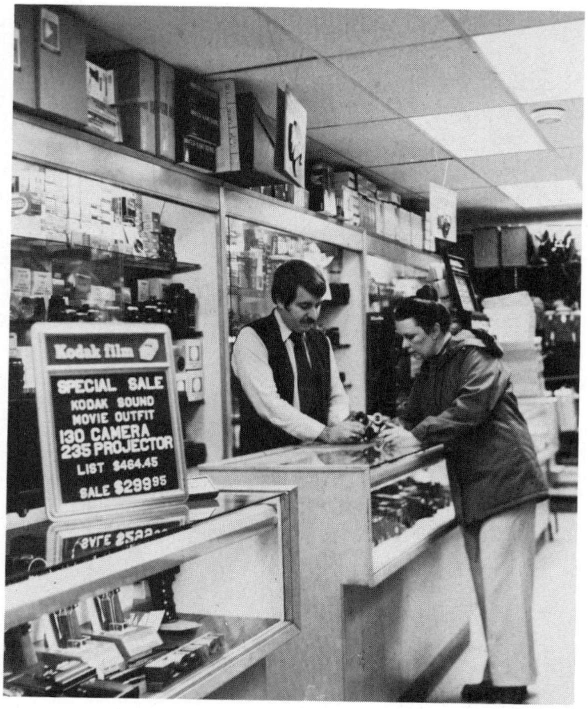

Local camera stores can afford the personal attention some of us require. Photo by Marc Levey.

at other sources, but your dealer probably believes that you also want advice, counsel, and personal consideration. By that line of reasoning, the extra dollars spent for ready access to these benefits at your dealer's are dollars well spent. This is only true if the area dealer offers knowledgeable and personal service, however. Several retailers we have encountered hire salespeople on straight commission, so that their prime concern, naturally, is volume rather than "quality" sales. Local dealers commonly say they have facilities and a sufficient expertise to make general repairs. This may be true for some kinds of repair work; but the equipment's manufacturer has facilities and repair specialists your local dealer cannot match. Most local dealers will merely forward your inoperative equipment back to the distributor, anyway.

The greatest advantage to local purchase is "hands-on" selection. You can handle the equipment and, in many cases, actually use it before buying. Equipment you've never seen or held may look enticing on the printed page, but it will not necessarily feel or perform as advertised. The choices you make will be subjective and individual; so being able to get the feel of new equipment and to test it prior to purchase may be invaluable to you. One final consideration in favor of local purchase is the chance of special consideration or terms of payment that the dealer may offer to well-established customers.

Discount Houses. Many carry a variety of photo products, although most aren't likely to carry the top lines. Most frequently, discounters stock Minolta, Ricoh, and some Eastman Kodak and Bell & Howell products. There are always exceptions, but the major problems with discount purchasing are the poorly informed salespeople. You cannot rely on the clerk behind the counter for insight into your purchase. If you do find just what you want at an attractive price, fine. Go ahead and buy it—but don't count on much service.

Mail Order. The last 20 years have seen this method grow faster than any other means of purchase. Mail-order firms reason that their prices are unbeatable: Because of their low overhead and the large volume of merchandise they can turn over, they can work on a relatively small profit margin. A local dealer must maintain a 20 percent or more profit on each camera sold, whereas a large mail-order house might do just as well on 5 percent or perhaps even less. So, if you're willing to shop around, you should be able to save some money buying equipment through the mail. This is usually, but not always, the case.

Mail order can prove tricky because:

1. you don't know whom you're really dealing with;
2. you can't examine your purchase in advance;
3. there are some less-than-honorable characters in the mail-order trade;
4. you must know precisely what you want before you order;
5. it's difficult to tell whether you really get new merchandise or a sample or "demo" (demonstration model).

Recent years have seen both the photographic mail-order industry and the government tighten up regulations on the business. But be advised that abuses still exist. Our extensive dealings with photo mail-order houses in various parts of the nation have for the most part been uneventful. We saved money and usually received our orders in less than three weeks. The thing to remember is that mail-order houses rely on quick turnover and huge volume. You're not likely to get personalized service. But if you're looking for the best price, you can do your shopping in the photography magazines.

There are many markets in this group, all competing for your dollar. The competition gets pretty wicked, too. This is a multimillion-dollar business, after all. A quick count in recent issues of *Popular Photography* and *Modern Photography* reveals some interesting statistics. Some 60 percent of the space contains advertising. Of that, almost half is occupied by shop-by-mail ads.

Magazines are the primary advertising source for mail orders, and it behooves you to read the ads very, very carefully. Typical mail-order houses only honor prices advertised in the *current* issues. Even then, most ads appear with disclaimers such as "Prices subject to change." The other fine print to peruse with care relates to the terms of sale: return privileges, premiums offered for specific purchases, etc. Send a copy of the ad with your order after underlining the particular item you want.

Be especially wary of "package deals." In reading the ads, keep in mind that ordering by mail is a business transaction, and you're not likely to get what you don't pay for. Often the same combinations are offered by your local dealer and by nearby discount houses, but don't allow that similarity to strip you of all caution—mail orders don't give you the advantage of prepurchase inspection. The appeal of these combination offers is obvious: They seem to offer lots of equipment at a bargain. Phrases such as "famous-make telephotos" or "135 mm tele included at no extra cost" become added inducements to the unwary buyer. But does the ad list brand names for anything but the *major* purchase? In most cases it doesn't, and the fact remains that you can't count on getting all-top-quality merchandise in any of these deals. We've taken a typical package (shown here) from a recent issue of a major photography

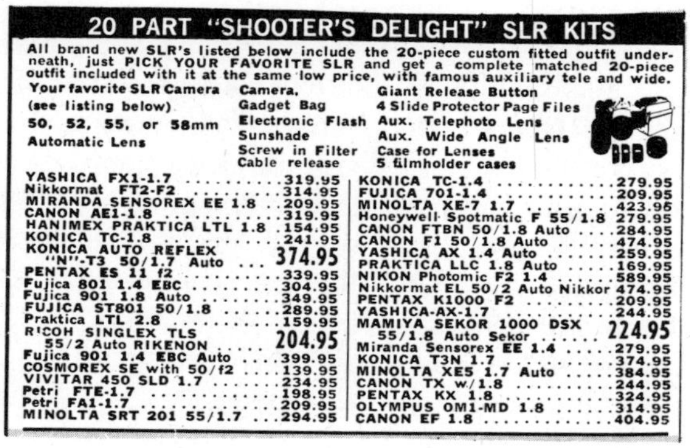

Ads like these should be subjected to more than a passing scrutiny if you're in the market for equipment.

magazine to see how it compares with well-known components, item for item.

Here is how the same package breaks down, using well-known brands and prices taken from the same issue of the same magazine.

Canon FTBn *f*/1.8 with case	$224.00
Low-powered flash (Vivitar, Honeywell, etc.)	12.95
Sunshade (Telstar)	3.50
Cable release (Rowi)	1.95
Giant release button	1.00
Cambron auxiliary tele, wide-angle lenses, with cases	39.95
4 slide protectors	1.20
5 film holders	2.50
TOTAL PRICE:	$282.00

The above comparison illustrates one hazard inherent in taking advertising copy at face value. Most "package" ads imply that all you pay for is the camera, the rest is free—as in this example: "All brand-new SLRs listed below include the 20-piece custom-fitted outfit underneath; just pick out your favorite SLR and get a complete matched 20-piece outfit included with it at the same low price with famous auxiliary tele and wide." The operational phrase is ". . . included with it at the same low price . . ." It may not be illegal, but it most certainly seems deceptive to us. So read the ads carefully and analyze what they *really* say, as opposed to what they seem to say—it's a good consumer reflex to develop in any purchasing situation.

As mentioned earlier in the discussion about introduction of new cameras and lenses, you might have to wait a long time. Some companies will take your money and then sit on it, knowing they can't deliver for quite some time. Recent legislation now requires mail-order houses to either deliver the merchandise or return your money within 30 days. Many offer a refund if they are out of stock, or ask you if you would rather wait—but not all of them do.

There is no sure way of telling whether you have received brand-new merchandise. But new, unhandled cameras do have a smell and appearance much like a fresh-from-the-showroom car. If you suspect the camera or the lens is not new, return it promptly. Most ads will state what your return privileges are.

The following nine steps ought to precede your ordering through the mail and help you check out your new equipment when it arrives.

(1) When considering a particular camera or major accessory, read all you can about it. Talk with people who have used it or a similar piece. If you can, handle the equipment and shoot a test roll. No one piece is perfectly designed just for you, and you'll probably find each has its drawbacks.

(2) Check out all the ads in major photography magazines for several months to see what the price trend has been.

(3) Be sure the quoted prices are for the exact piece you want. If your heart's set on a Primoflex 70–200 zoom, Model II, multicoated lens, make certain the ad isn't quoting a price (especially when it appears to be a super bargain) for the Primoflex 70–200 zoom, Model I. That one roman numeral might have enormous significance in terms of new or improved features. For example, Canon added the letter "n" to its FTB designation when it redesigned that camera; Konica did the same with its T3, as did Nikon with the Nikkormat. The changes involved in these new designations ranged from minor ones for the T3 and Nikkormat to a rather extensive redesign for the FTB.

(4) Before you place your order, spend the extra dollar or so necessary to call and confirm (a) that the price is as quoted, (b) that the equipment is currently in stock, (c) an estimated delivery date, and (d) name of the person to whom you are speaking and his or her title or position. If the firm stalls or refuses to reply to any one of these questions, hang up and try another company. Otherwise you might find yourself being urged to consider a make other than the one you had decided was for you.

(5) Send a registered check, money order, or bank draft. Personal checks will not be honored until they clear the bank, and this will slow up your order one to two weeks. By all means send your order by registered or certified mail and request a return receipt.

(6) If you do not receive your order in a reasonable time (three weeks is a good average), pick up the phone again and call the person you talked with before you made the order. Be factual but firm. If you feel you're being stalled, *demand* to speak to the sales manager. If that is no help, you can always call the Better Business Bureau in the company's home territory. If you still receive no satisfaction, write to the editors of the magazines in which the concern advertises and outline your complaint. Send a copy to the mail-order house itself. If a mail-order house is refused space in a major magazine it is likely to suffer where it will hurt most—in the pocketbook. (Deserving mention here is *Modern Photography*. This magazine has established a code of ethics that offers some additional protection in the mail-order marketplace. Inquire of the firm you choose to deal with whether it advertises in *Modern Photography*. It might help you.)

(7) Check your order when it arrives, starting from the outside. (a) Inspect the package before opening it. If it looks battered, open it only in the presence of a UPS or United States Postal Service employee. Save the packaging, for the moment (see item #10 below). (b) Once you've opened the parcel, carefully check the appearance, the packaging, and even the smell of the contents. Make sure instructions and guarantee cards are there. If not, be alert to the chance that you might not

have received new equipment. (It has been known to happen that a package supposedly containing a "new" camera contained a note from a previous customer explaining why he was returning it.) (c) Closer inspection should include checks of the outside of the camera, or whatever, for nicks, dust, and signs of wear; loose parts, screws backed out or sheared off; dust or dirt in the viewfinder; fingerprints on the front lens element; unusual noises apparently unrelated to normal operation. (d) Check all control operations—shutter-speed dial, aperture ring, switches, etc. None of them should bind, but they should be tight.

(8) Once you're satisfied with external appearance and function, open the camera back, checking the back-release mechanism as you do so. (a) Check the focal-plane shutter for fingerprints. (b) Run your fingers lightly over the film guide rails (shiny chrome strips running horizontally most of the camera's length), noting any irregularities. You should then wipe them clean again with lens-cleaning tissue and fluid. (c) Click the shutter and observe its operation closely. You can usually detect visible and audible differences between at least every other shutter speed. There will be more noise below 1/15 sec. from mechanical shutters, because of their timing mechanisms. (d) Finally, check the interior for any debris (dirt, fingerprints, film scraps) that might indicate previous use. If you find any of these signs, send the camera back: It's more than likely been used. (e) Also, you should check the condition of any accessories (case, strap, batteries) you might have ordered. Batteries often do not work, and there's no way of knowing how long they may have been sitting around.

(9) Before mailing in the warranty card, shoot a roll of film and inspect the results. Use a variety of subjects, some at the closest focusing limit, some at infinity; try different shutter speeds and apertures. Check for proper operation of the battery, self-timer, rewind mechanism and other controls.

(10) *Be aware* that many mail-order houses will not accept returned equipment unless *all* the cards, especially the warranty, and the *original packing* are included. If you do find it necessary to return your purchase, be certain to enclose a letter explaining in all possible detail what's wrong with it. Mail the package back by insured registered mail and ask for a return receipt.

Foreign Purchase. Inevitably everyone has a friend with international connections. Fanciful stories of huge savings from buying direct in Hong Kong, Japan, Singapore, or Taiwan are abundant—and probably exaggerated. There is considerable risk involved in this sort of transaction, whatever the savings.

First, you risk trouble with U.S. Customs officials. Many camera products are U.S.-trademarked and therefore can be imported legally only by the trademark owner. Customs may levy a fine or duty, or even impound, any illegally imported merchandise bearing trademarks registered in the United States.

Second, the warranties of several camera makers are valid only when the equipment is imported and distributed by them. Minolta has a one-year worldwide guarantee, but the special "M-Tag" designates a two-year warranty for American-sold Minolta products. A.I.C., Miranda's distributor, places its own three-year guarantee on any Miranda product sold in this country. Several other manufacturers will not honor guarantees on foreign-purchased camera equipment.

Third, several cameras appear in other parts of the world under designations different from those of their mechanically and optically identical U.S.-imported cousins. While a Topcon might appear as a DM in the United States, it might be an RE Super in the rest of the world. In fact, Honeywell imported Pentax products for years and designated them "Honeywell Pentax," while abroad they were "Asahi Pentax" (the parent manufacturer's name). The risks you take in foreign purchase may not be worth the 10–15 percent you save over discounted prices in the United States. Sending your money 8,000 miles, with no legal protection and a long delivery wait, is a questionable practice, at best.

The following chart may help you weigh the purchasing variables already discussed.

SOURCE COMPARISON CHART

A. MAJOR PURCHASE (Camera, Lens, Enlarger, etc.)

SOURCE	PRICING	PROS	CONS
Local Retail Shop	List to 20% discount	• handling/testing of product in advance • service, advice • personal treatment	• higher priced than others, local sales taxes applicable • value of service a subjective judgment
Discount or Chain Store	Between retail and mail-order discounts	• cheaper local purchase	• little advice • limited selection • possible trouble with defective equipment
Mail-Order House	Lowest domestic prices	• vast selection • lowest prices (usually)	• delayed acquisition of new products • impersonal • some questionable marketing practices
Foreign Purchase	Lowest prices anywhere	• low cost	• customs problems • questionable guarantees • no legal protection to consumer

B. MINOR PURCHASE (Small Accessories, Film, etc.)

SOURCE	PRICING	PROS	CONS
Local Retail Shop	Most discount 10–20%	• large selection • advice/recommendations • special order products	• prices higher than other possible sources
Discount Department Store	Greater discount than local retail	• cheaper local purchase	• generally limited selection
Mail-Order House	Lowest domestic prices (in bulk)	• low prices for bulk purchases	• time-delay on small orders • no savings on product when paying freight on small orders

The Minolta "X" series pictured here share the same lens line, basic body design, and exposure system. Photo courtesy Minolta, U.S.A.

Photo Industry Pricing

Let's begin by saying there's no such thing as "list price." That term applies loosely to whatever price suits advertising and promotional purposes. List prices are intentionally high to create buyer appeal. Most of us would admit to equating "expensive" with "excellent"—the most expensive must be the best, right? And when we see equipment, especially the most costly, offered at less than list price, we can't help feeling we've found ourselves a steal. It seems so transparent it's hard to believe this practice is so effective—and it certainly is that.

Essentially, what you pay for are the extra frills and/or features differentiating one model from the next. Most major camera makers produce a standard camera body, or perhaps two, then add or delete features. For example, Minolta markets an "X" series (XE5, XE7, XK) that share the same lens line but have relatively minor differences in other features. We say "relatively" because to one photographer a certain feature could be absolutely essential, whereas to another it might seem unnecessary. It's important to remember that the insides of a camera are pretty much the same from one model to another, but the cost often is not. Canon's TX and FTBn share the same body and lenses, as do their AE-1 and AT-1. If you want a good basic picture taker and don't need the added convenience of battery checker, shutter-speed display, and 1/1000 sec. top speed, you'll save $50 to $75 in buying the TX instead of an FTBn.

Certainly such maneuvering sounds like the auto industry strategies we hear about. In many ways, the pricing of camera equipment reflects such tactics. General Motors makes only three basic car bodies but manages to fit all their "models" into those three body styles. Manufacturers such as G.M. try to convince us there are *significant* differences, even though it should be obvious there really aren't any in terms of use and function. However, psychological factors do come into play and ultimately sway the public into going to a Buick from a Chevy, which could do just as good a job but possibly at a lower price than the Buick. The photographic equipment industry plays the market in the same manner.

Be advised that several features touted in the top-price-line cameras are rarely, if ever, used. One such extra is the self-timer. We have used it less than half-a-dozen times in the last ten years. Another is a mirror lockup, to be used in critical, slow-shutter-speed photography. Many premium-priced cameras sport shutter speeds of 1/1000 sec. or 1/2000 sec. You'll probably be disappointed to find these speeds are notoriously inaccurate, and unnecessary in all but a few applications. In fact, most surveys indicate that more than 90 percent of all professionally taken photographs are exposed at between 1/30 sec. and 1/250 sec.

Now, if you can afford to go first class, that's fine. The extra features are really a comfort to have—if and when you need them. But they alone will not make you any better a photographer.

We recommend the following approach when looking for a new camera: Start at the bottom. If the least expensive or lower-priced models will do the job and your ego will not suffer dreadfully, then buy one of those. Perhaps doing without some of today's wizardry will prod you into more inventive and creative thinking. Someone once said that the best photographer in the world is not as good as the worst camera.

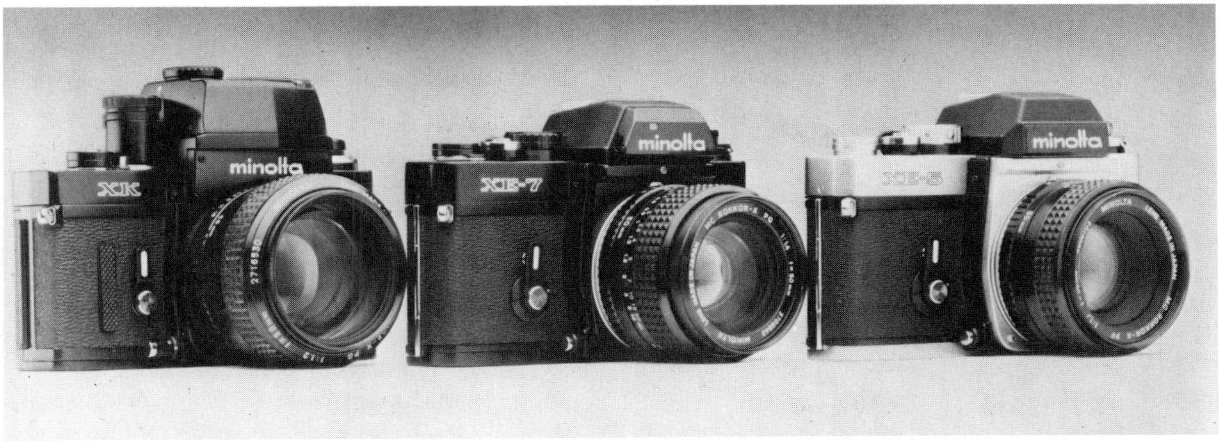

Back to pricing. Most manufacturers try to cover the whole market by presenting low-end no-frill cameras, middle-line feature-laden products (the real bulk of their sales), and top-of-the line "prestige" models. While there's no doubt that the best camera systems do provide added versatility with huge accessory selection, we question the wisdom of becoming burdened with gadgets. Most good photographers keep their equipment simple in terms of both features and accessories. Probably the best cost/benefit ratio comes from the middle-line camera.

When the suggested list price of a middle-line camera with a 50 mm lens is around $500, you can expect to purchase it from your local dealer for between $300 and $375. The same combination can usually be purchased for $225 to $275 from a mail-order house. Obviously the discounts from the mythical list price go all the way up to 45 percent, and even over in some instances. The actual selling price of our $400 camera, then, is really anywhere in the $215–$300 range. There is one additional factor to consider. Unless you are a resident of the state where the mail-order house does business, you need not pay any state sales tax. This fact can save you an additional three-to-seven percent.

You can anticipate, then, spending roughly up to $100 more for the service and personal attention gained in purchasing your medium-priced camera and lens locally. Usually top-of-the-line cameras, because they do not sell as fast, are discounted at a lower rate. This is not always true, since large-volume dealers can cut their costs more; but it is almost always so when buying from a local camera store. The most prestigious lines, such as Hasselblad and Leica, are rarely discounted more than 25 percent, the average discount on them falling in the 10–25 percent range.

If you are considering a new product you should know something about the pricing of introductions. Our study of the industry press and retail advertising revealed a pattern repeated far too often to be mere coincidence. Let's say a new product is listed at $470. With the first introduction there is a lot of advertising, but no mention of price. A month or two later ads show up in the national photography media quoting $340 or so. This price holds until the first customer rush appears; then the competition between mail-order houses begins, so that the price lines finally break. Nine months to a year after introduction the price again drops, this time to about $275–$300. Probably the price will continue to fluctuate then between $260 and $275, depending on demand and on production efficiency. At this price, given a high enough sales volume, the retailer, wholesaler or distributor, and manufacturer all make a reasonable profit. If the product does not sell well, the price naturally remains relatively high. It is only fair that manufacturers regain their research and development costs as rapidly as possible.

The lesson in all of this is: You can save a bundle if you are willing to wait a year or so. Of course, most of us are not. Our enthusiasm may be exceeded only by the money we willingly spend. The photography industry counts on that enthusiasm and prices its newest merchandise accordingly.

A final word about pricing. The introduction of a new model in an established equipment line often sends the prices of the older models to an all-time low. Then you can pick up a perfectly good piece of equipment at an excellent price. Unfortunately, that advantage also has a flip side: If you have an older model and want to trade it in on the newest one, don't expect much for it. Established "blue-book" prices for used cameras do not pertain to trade-ins. Take a $450 Nikon Photomic FTN with standard lens, in top condition, purchased five years ago. Selling it outright might net you $200 or more, whereas trading it in is likely to bring only about $120. Quite a difference, wouldn't you say? If your camera is functioning well, you might think twice before trading it for a new model.

Warranties

Virtually all photographic equipment is covered by a *limited warranty*. The "limited" part refers to such obvious abuses as dropping, floods, fires, etc. Other limits usually are spelled out in terms of time and shipping obligations, product registration, etc. We are glad to report that the vast majority of the warranties we've had to test were honored by manufacturers or their distributors.

Most new camera warranties are for one year. A few extend over two or even three years. For lenses it's a different story. While most original-equipment lenses (camera makers' brand names) are covered for one year, many independent lens manufacturers warrant their products for longer periods (Soligor, three years; Vivitar, five years). Duration and conditions of the warranty offered should be considered before choosing the brand to buy.

When you buy from a retailer, whether by mail order or from a local shop or department store, he has a legally binding obligation to you. If your equipment fails within a very few days, or even weeks, you should get a replacement unless the problem can be repaired quickly. Inquire as to the individual store's policy and if possible get it in writing.

Warranties generally are *not* transferable from one owner to the next without specific written permission from the manufacturer or its representative in this country. In some cases you cannot make such a transfer at all. Be advised that a distributor or manufacturer of photoequipment might require proof of purchase (bill of sale) in registering your equipment for warranty purposes. Save the bill of sale or your cancelled check on any major purchase.

Many people expect equipment makers to repair or adjust merchandise that obviously has been mistreated. Things such as chipped lens elements, bent lens mounts, crooked prisms, and dust in the viewfinder or prism are not covered by limited warranties. If you are in doubt, call or write the parent company.

In sum, although warranties do not offer blanket protection, they do lend some measure of confidence in the product and are usually honored.

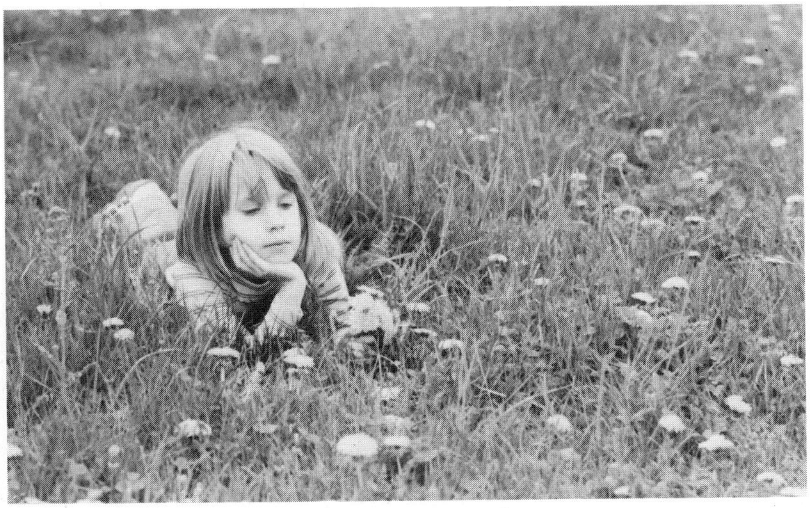

"Robin's Dream." Photo by Marc Levey.

Out-of-Warranty Repairs. Camera repairs do not come cheap. Back in 1975 the average repair charge at a leading New York facility ran about $40. The recent repair bill for a bent lens mount on a zoom lens came to $55. Not only was the relatively inexpensive mounting ring replaced, but the lens repairman also insisted on a thorough optical check for proper realignment of the lens.

One factor in repair costs is the scarcity of competent people in this country to perform such tasks. Consequently, the available repair people have more work than time. Charges of $30 an hour are not uncommon. Extensive repair and adjustment on quality equipment inevitably require specialized training and expensive repair tools, and someone has to pay for it. That someone is us.

Another point about repairs is the necessity of retraining repair personnel to keep up with the increasingly complicated new electronic designs. The burden on repair technicians is now threefold. Not only must they have a thorough understanding of *mechanical* and *optical* systems, but they must also have an expertise in *electronics.* Many cameras are designed in modules to avoid complete disassembly when repairing specific components or subsystems. But even so, a typical 35 mm SLR may contain upwards of 1000 separate parts. With 30 or 40 different cameras on the market, the job of keeping up to date on such complex technology is nearly impossible.

At one point the repairs your equipment demands may become economically unjustifiable. Going beyond routine repairs often becomes a time-consuming and costly venture, possibly beyond the actual value of the equipment.

When estimating camera maintenance costs, count on a thorough cleaning and adjustment every two or three years. Right now, that runs between $25 and $50. If you don't know a trustworthy local repairman, your best bet would be the manufacturer of the camera or lens. Describe in detail the problem or the work required, and ask the company for an estimate first. Then package your equipment securely and ship it by insured registered mail or UPS. There are several independent repair facilities around the country. Two of the most reliable and best-known are the Professional Camera Repair Service (37 West 47th St., New York, N.Y. 10036) and Strauss Photo-Technical Service (1240 Mount Olivet Rd., N.E., Washington, D.C.). When in doubt, consult the yellow pages and then check the outfit with your Better Business Bureau. Your local camera dealer also may be able to make some recommendations.

Arashiyama, Kyoto. Photo by L. P. Greenhill, F.R.P.S.

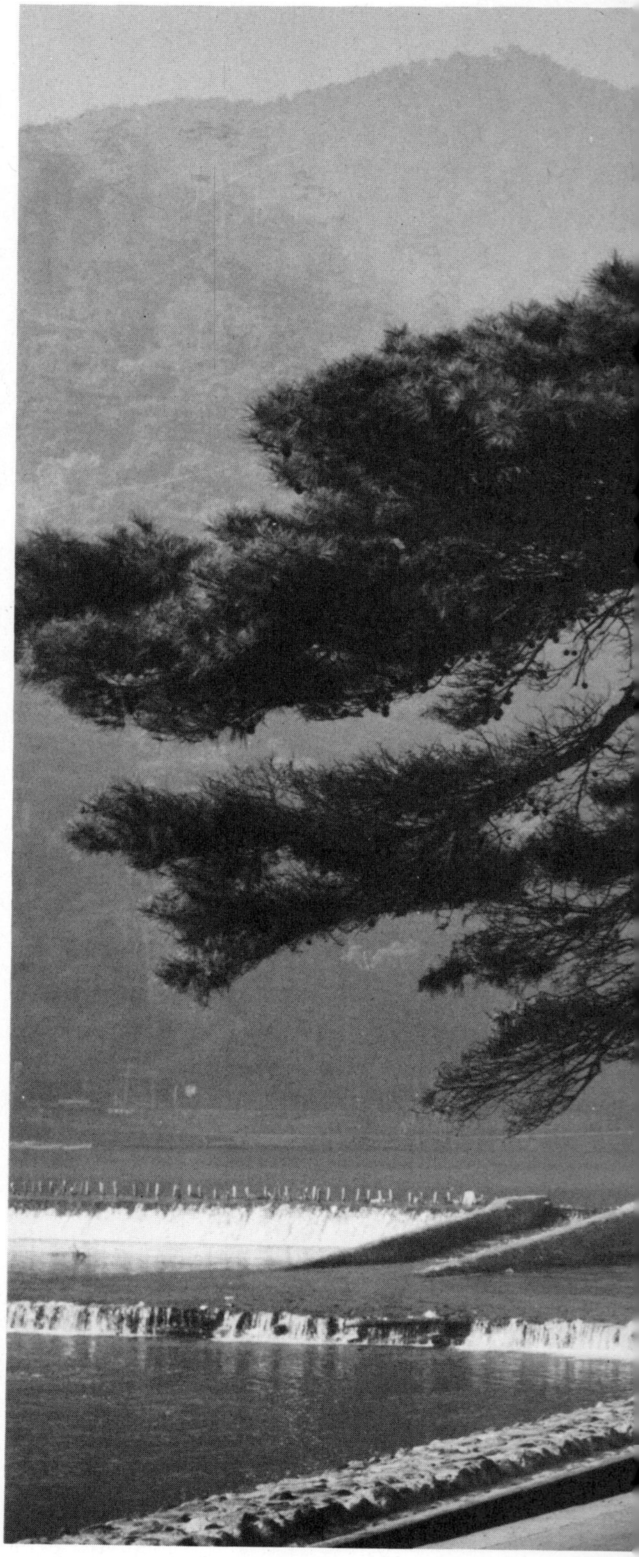

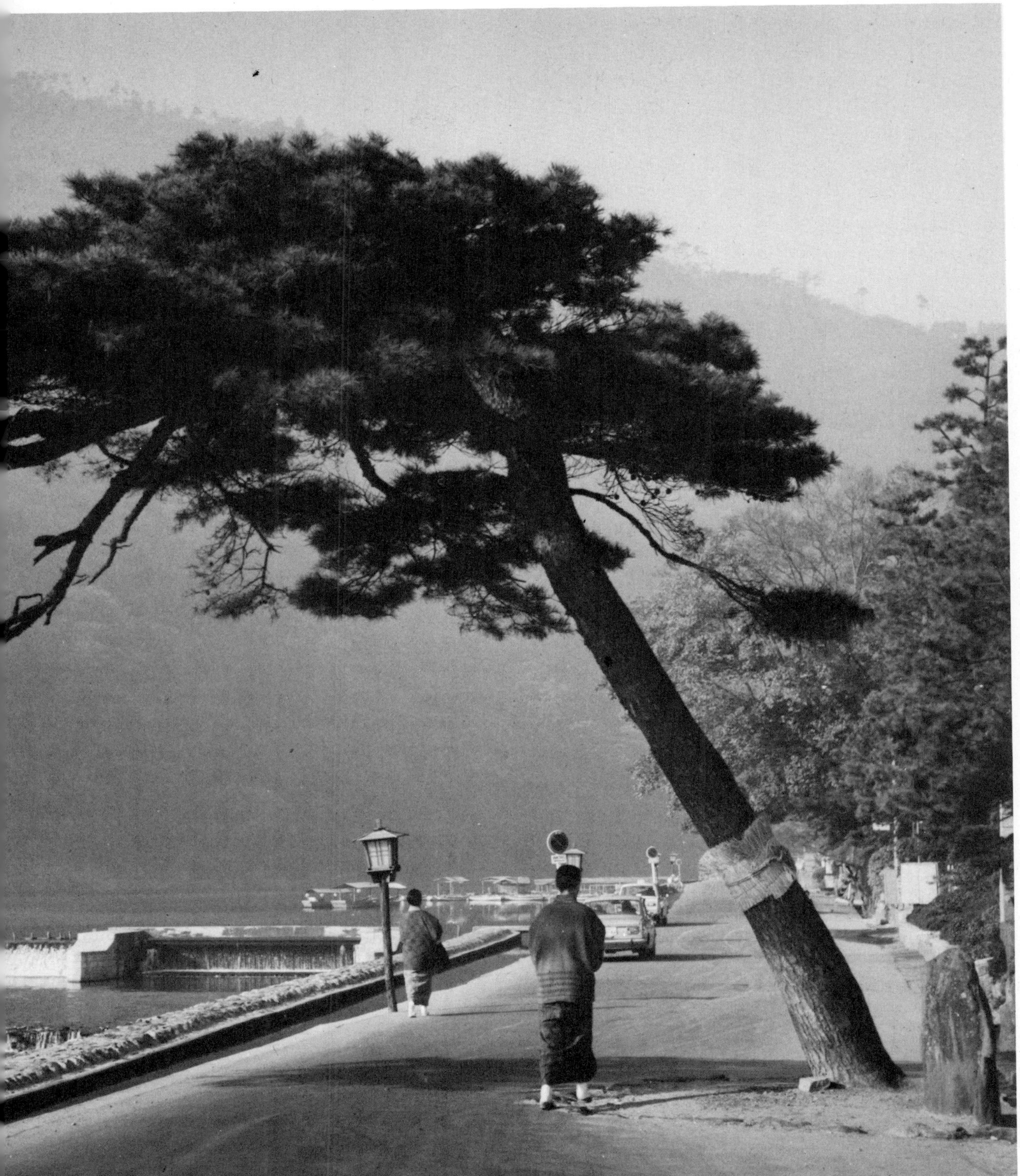

"It's Late." Photo by John Mertz.

Before committing yourself to extensive repairs, by all means ask questions and make it perfectly clear what you want done. Otherwise you could easily wind up with a repair bill that includes a complete adjustment and cleaning when your camera didn't need such work.

On any repair, you should expect a guarantee for a period of one month to one year on the work performed. Also, ask for the old parts that needed replacement.

Used Equipment

There is a large market in good used equipment, and if you are sharp you can pick up used gear at very reasonable prices. First, you ought to know precisely what you want. Consult the magazines, your local dealer, and/or a publication called *Shutterbug Ads* (P.O. Box 730, Titusville, Fla. 32780) to establish fair market value. *Shutterbug Ads* is particularly rich in that kind of information, since serious traders advertise in it and their prices are a good reflection of the used-photo-equipment market in general. You'll find every type of photography gear imaginable advertised on a monthly basis, so *Shutterbug Ads* gives you the latest, *most current* selling prices.

Once in firm possession of a fair price you can launch your search. Some of the places to look for used camera equipment are auctions, garage sales, pawn shops, or second-hand stores. You can also look through the classified sections of newspapers and *Shutterbug Ads* as well as advertising, yourself, or inquiring at your local camera dealer or photography club. If you live in or near a major city, such as New York, Chicago, or Los Angeles, make the rounds of the camera stores. Keep in mind that the smaller merchants tend to ask lower prices for used equipment than the larger ones.

Beware. Urban camera stores are the dumping grounds for professionals, many of whom have thoroughly beaten up their equipment. Brands and cameras to be wary of in this regard are Hasselblad, Nikon, Canon (especially the F1), Linhof, Mamiya RB67, Bronica, Pentax 6×7, and most large-format view cameras. We don't mean you cannot find good buys among these models; just advise caution.

When selling your equipment, follow the same procedure in establishing a price by looking through the ads, then advertise through local camera clubs, newspapers, etc. If you feel your used gear would appeal to a lot of camera collectors, you might consider placing an ad in *Shutterbug Ads*. That publication reaches some 25,000 camera buffs each month.

We've included the following guide for selection of used cameras and lenses, to reduce your chances of getting stung.

(1) Look at the overall exterior condition of the camera, paying particular attention to dents, gouges, or bent components.

(2) Look for file marks, burred screw heads, and any out-of-alignment parts that might indicate an amateur repairman at work.

(3) Take the steps suggested in the new-camera purchase checklist, but be more critical of binding or "rasping" gears or moving parts. Make sure the lens focuses smoothly and that the aperture ring turns without excessive play.

(4) Remove the lens; then, viewing it from front to back, manually operate the diaphragm and see if it opens and closes precisely. Do the blades seem loose? If so, look for another lens.

(5) Are there any chips or cracks greater than 1.6 mm ($^1/_{16}$ in.) in diameter visible on the lens surface? Yes? Then don't buy it.

(6) Make sure the camera's viewfinder presentation is free of dust and scratches.

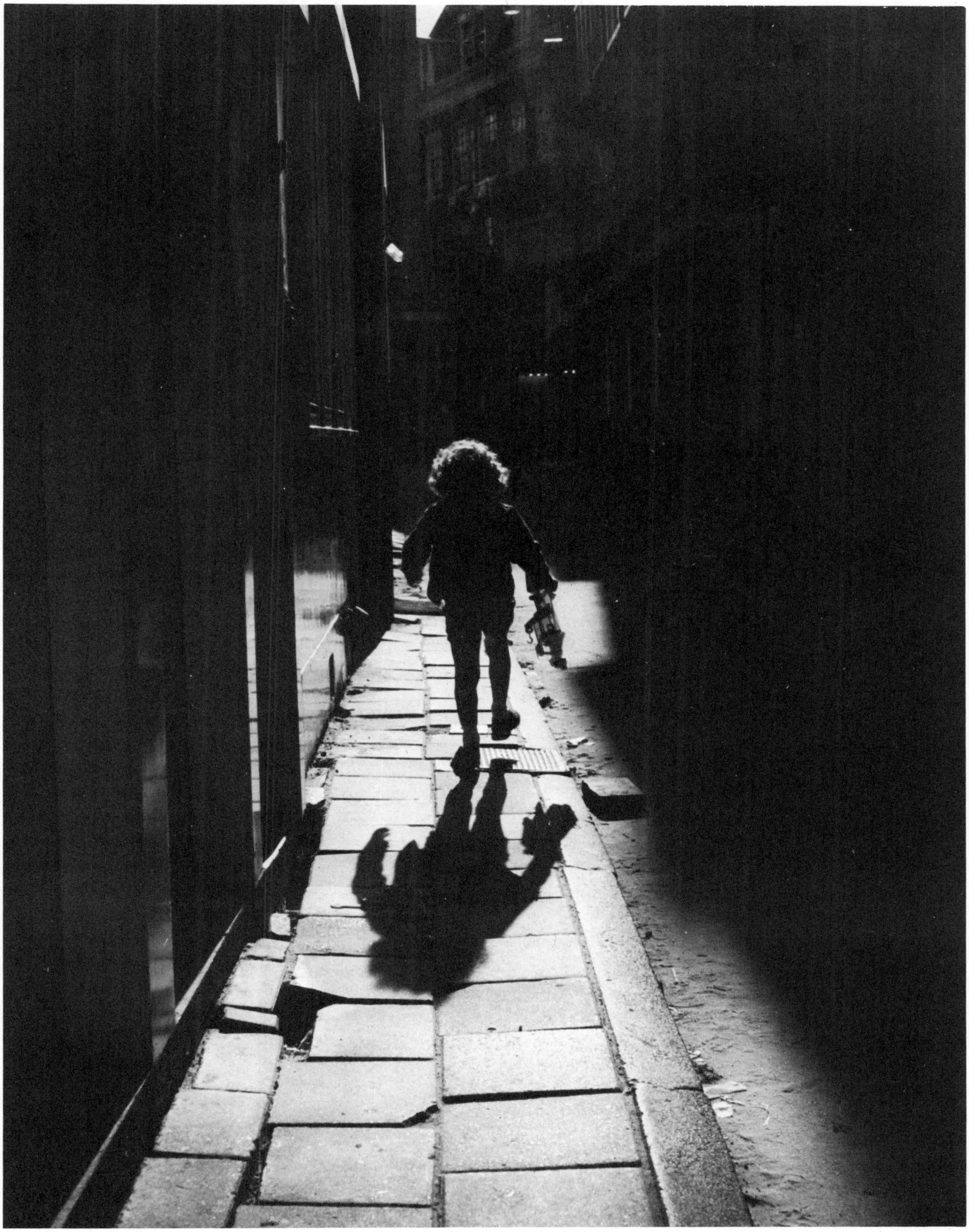

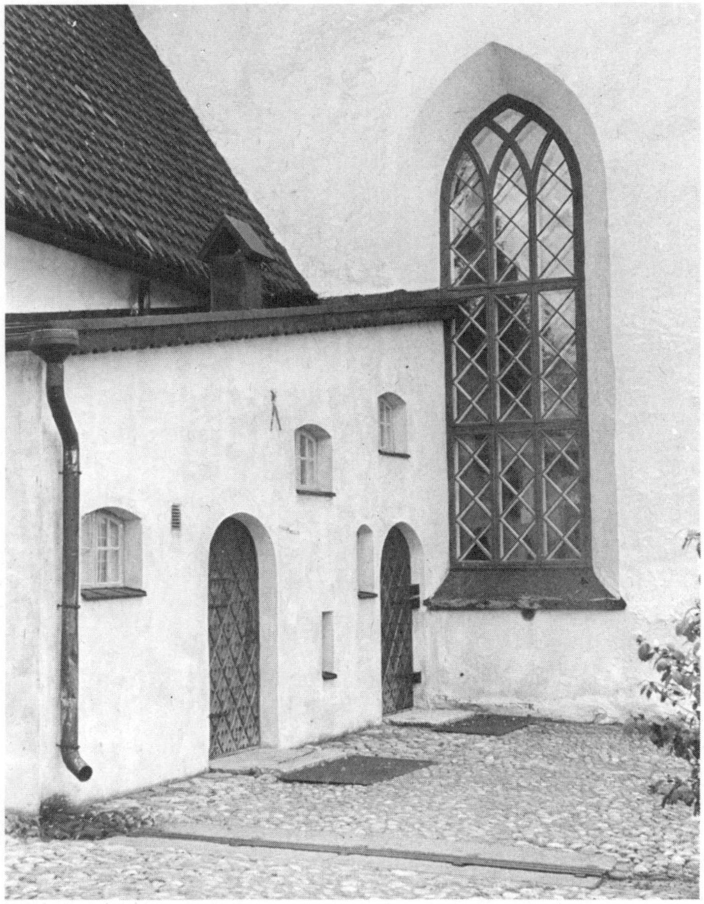

(Left) "Texture and Angles." Photo by Bill Coleman. (Facing page) "Scheckter," taken at the 1974 Grand Prix, printed directly from a color slide. Photo by Bob Baumbach.
Celestron 1250 mm photograph taken by Marc Levey.

(7) Check the focus by directing your view to something at least 23 m (75 ft) away and focusing on it slowly. Repeat the process, checking each time to see that the focusing index mark lines up with "infinity" on the rotating collar of the lens.

(8) Investigate all camera functions by running a roll of outdated or exposed film through the camera just as if it were fresh.

(9) Shake the camera body, then the lens. Listen for loose glass or small metal parts bouncing around inside. *Note:* Some noise is to be expected, so compare the used equipment against a new camera or lens.

(10) Look for excessive wear on the film guide rails and the pressure plate. Does bare metal show through on the latter? If so, the camera has been used extensively.

(11) Check the carrying-strap lugs for excessive wear. Thin, almost-worn-through lugs can indicate heavy or long use.

(12) Look for damage to the shutter curtain or blades, especially in rangefinders with cloth focal-plane shutters. Check the evenness of shutter operation at all marked shutter speeds. Look for uneven or sticking shutter blades or curtains.

(13) Check battery operation and look out for possible damage from leaks in the battery compartment.

(14) Place a flash unit on the camera to check for flash synchronization.

(15) Ask the dealer about a guarantee, and get it in writing.

(16) As soon as possible, run a roll of *narrow latitude* film through the camera. Vary

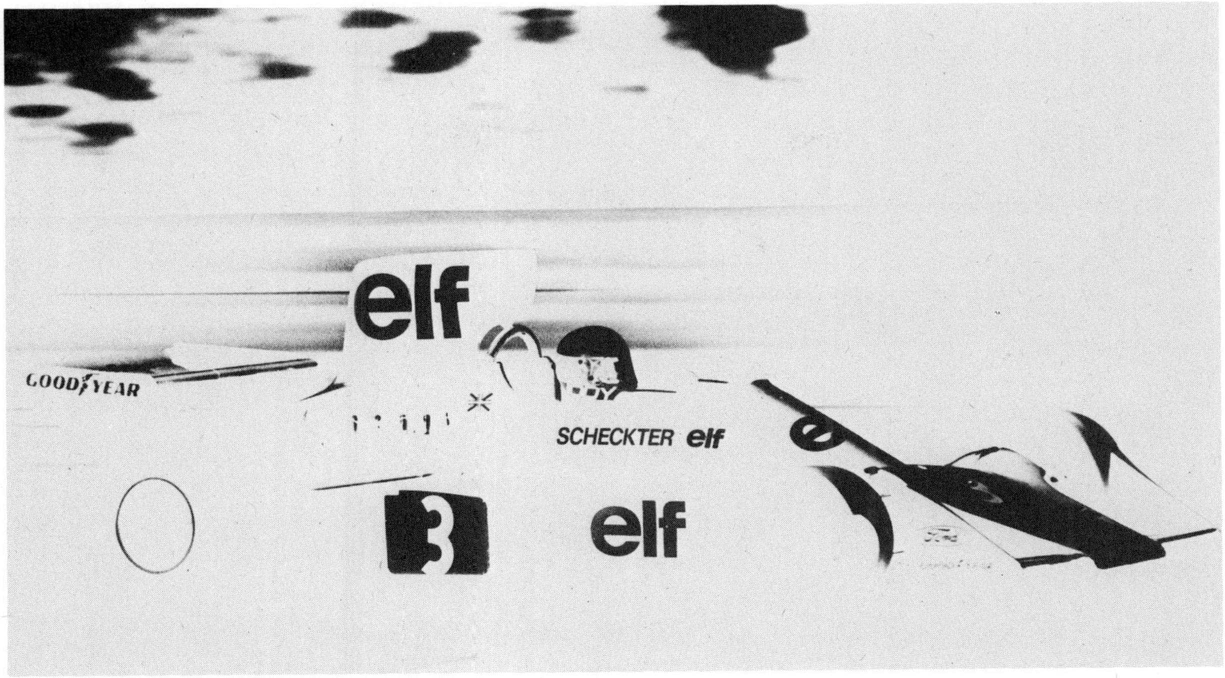
elf
GOODYEAR
SCHECKTER elf
3
elf

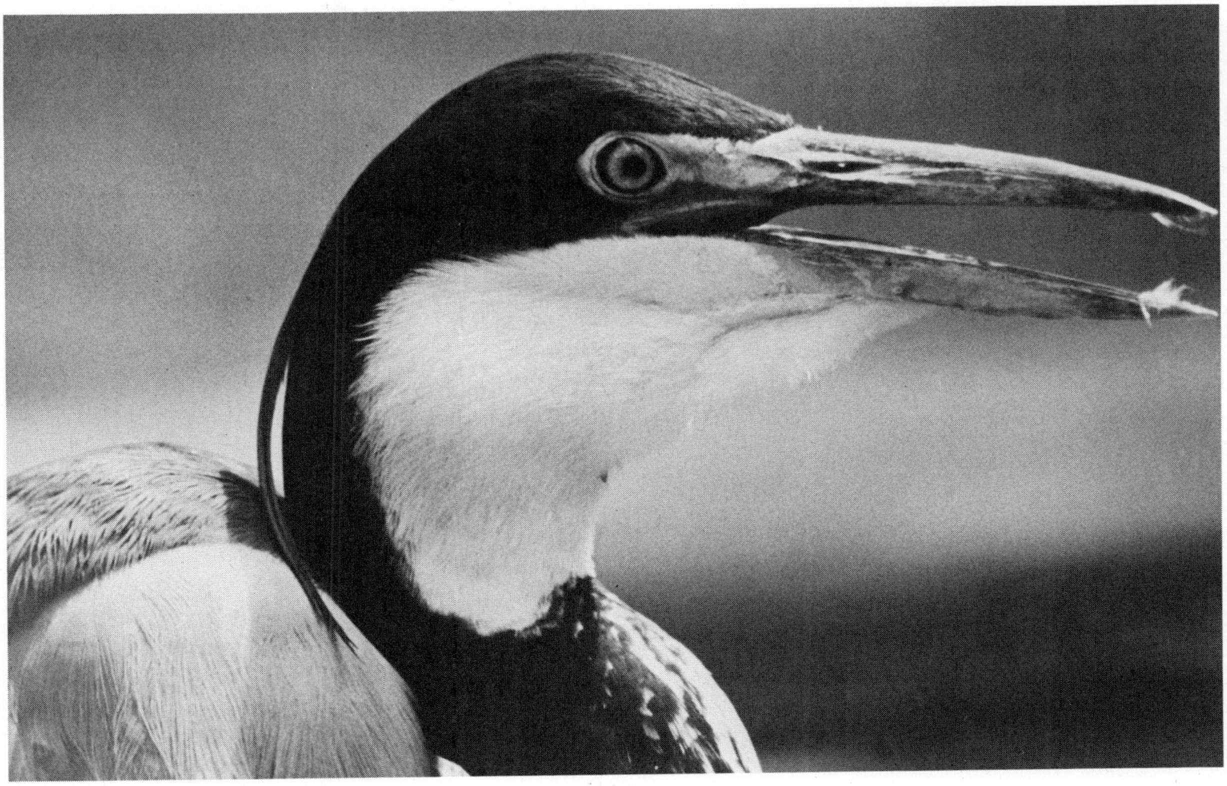

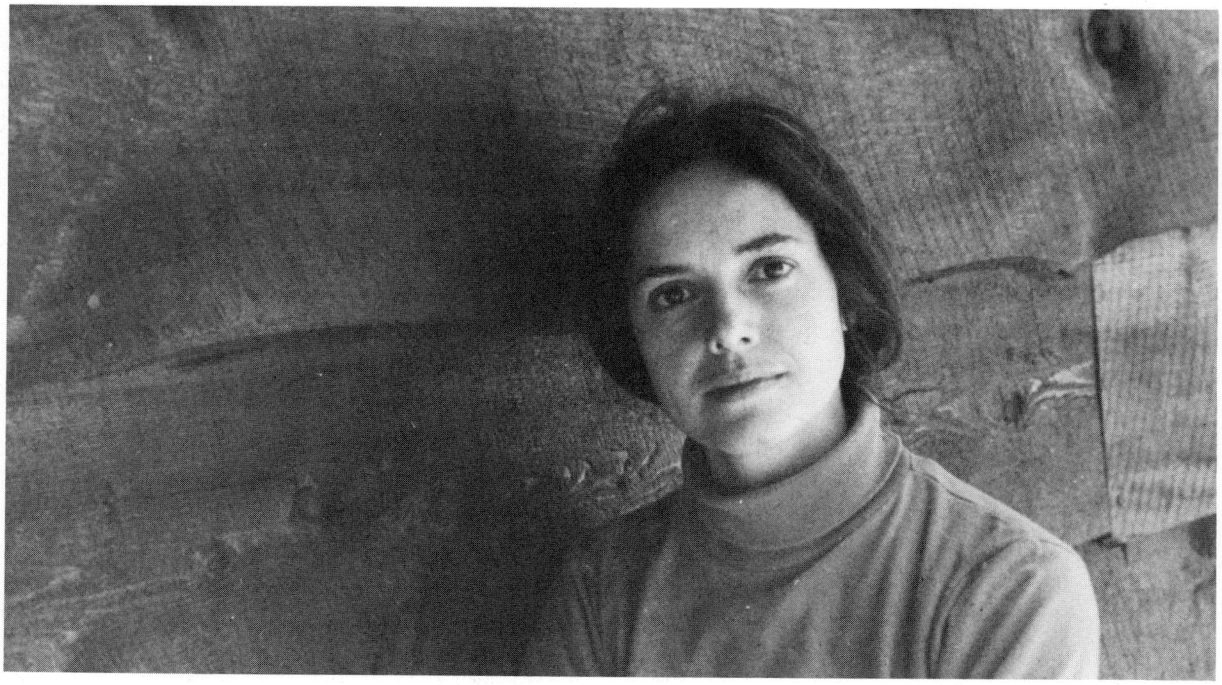

"Winter Dreams." Photo by Guy Pilato.

your shutter speeds and *f*-stops and try focusing at different distances. Note each frame and jot down focused distances, *f*-stop, shutter speed; include a few flash shots indoors to check synchronization while you're about it. If you're not happy, take the results and the equipment back. In some cases you'll find the dealer able to arrange minor repairs or adjustments.

(17) If you decide you wish to purchase the equipment and the investment merits it, take it to an independent camera technician for a thorough check. The $5–$10 you spend may be well worth it.

(18) Finally, be prepared to haggle over price. Dealers usually have a substantial profit margin in used equipment and you often can get the price down—especially if you know the piece has been on the shelf for a while. He *wants* to sell it, perhaps even more than you want to buy it.

The watchword, as we have attempted to show you, is *care;* care in cautiously interpreting Madison Avenue camera jargon, in establishing the truth of advertising, in choosing equipment from a dealer who will give you the best combination of price and service that you desire, and lastly in seeking repair work.

If you do your homework carefully, reading the ads and talking to as many people as you can about the advantages and drawbacks of a particular piece of merchandise, the chances are that your purchase will last you for many years and give you great enjoyment, too. On the other hand, a snap decision to buy a new or used lens or camera, based on little or no consumer research or handling of the prospective equipment, is an invitation to bitter disappointment. Most dealers feel a legal and moral obligation to keep their customers satisfied because these customers are or could become "repeaters," coming in for film, another lens, a tripod. Some sellers, however, are not so generous in their appreciation of the consumer. In the final analysis, the responsibility for any purchase, whether good or bad, lies with you; so know your rights!

V

The Parting Shot

We urge you to investigate all the possibilities that exist in your community to improve your picture-taking skill. If you have a local camera club, by all means try it. If not, perhaps you could organize one with a few friends.

Most communities have adult-education programs, virtually all of which offer photography courses. We recommend you take them. In addition to adult education, there are a few respected correspondence courses in photography you may wish to investigate. Among the more well-known and established are:

1. School of Modern Photography (not to be confused with the magazine), Little Falls, N.J. 07424.
2. New York Institute of Photography, Dept. P57J, 263 9th Avenue, New York, N.Y. 10001.

Beyond formal long courses either in residence or by correspondence, you might wish to take advantage of workshops or seminars.

If the Nikon school comes to your area, the admission fee is well worth it. It's an excellent learning experience, even if you do not use Nikons.

Beyond formal learning, one more source is open to you: P.S.A. (the Photographic Society of America). This organization offers local meetings; a national magazine; circulating slide/cassette study material on a number of subjects; critique on a traveling basis of your pictures; many, many contests; and a number of other services to its photographic members. Ask your local camera-store owner for information. He should be able to point you toward a P.S.A. member.

Finally, do take a lot of pictures. Study them and don't be surprised if you find yourself becoming your own worst critic—the best photographers we know are rarely if ever satisfied with their work.

In the meantime, here are some suggestions about sources of information. The next section lists books and other publications you will enjoy, and after that is a glossary explaining commonly used photographic terms.

SOURCES OF CONSUMER INFORMATION

From the producers of Public Broadcasting's *Consumer Survival Kit* comes an excellent booklet, *Photo Equipment,* which details some of the pitfalls in selecting and purchasing photographic equipment. For a copy write to: Photo Equipment Consumer Survival Kit, Maryland Center for Public Broadcasting, Owings Mills, Md. 21117. Enclose $1.00 to cover shipping and handling.

Before purchasing through the mails, consult *Modern Photography*'s "Limited Warranty Policy" in each issue of that magazine. It details some additional protection afforded its readers when they purchase equipment advertised in the magazine.

Annotated Bibliography

Books

There are a number of books we can recommend that should serve as a basic photo library. Our criterion for selection is based on educational function. Information presented in these books is useful to serious photographers and they are the best in their field as of this writing.

Boyd, Harry, Jr. *A Creative Approach to Controlling Photography.* Austin: Heideberg Publishers, Inc., 1974. Boyd's approach is no-nonsense but emphasizes the creative aspects of photography. Lots of line drawings and illustrations. Good section on creative techniques. Heavy emphasis on darkroom manipulation.

Eastman Kodak Co. *Adventures in Color Slide Photography.* Rochester: Eastman Kodak Co., 1976. An excellent survey of the use of color transparency material and a good idea-book for creative color work. Illustrated entirely in color, the book is a good teaching or learning tool.

Eastman Kodak Co. *Encyclopedia of Practical Photography.* Garden City, NY: Eastman Kodak Co. and Amphoto, 1977. 14 volumes. This series will prove invaluable to both beginning and advanced photographers as a continuing reference work. Very well-executed illustrations and lucid explanations. Highly recommended.

Eastman Kodak Co. *Kodak Professional Photoguide.* Rochester: Eastman Kodak Co., 1975. This small spiral-bound guide is loaded with information, charts, computers, and tables that should prove essential to serious photographers. Information on films, exposure, filters, flash, cameras, and lenses is included. Of special merit are several circular computers for such things as existing-light exposure calculations, color temperature, depth of field.

Eastman Kodak Co. *Professional Portrait Techniques.* Rochester: Eastman Kodak Co., 1974. Softbound. A superior, inexpensive book on portraiture. Especially helpful is the section dealing with types of lighting. Another noteworthy section is on makeup for portraiture. A must for those interested in "people" pictures.

Frechen, Wolfgang. *Modern Photographic Techniques.* New York: Crescent Books, 1976. A well-thought-out book of general photographic interest.

Hedgecoe, John. *The Book of Photography.* New York: Random House, 1976. A large-format book, lavishly illustrated. A soup-to-nuts survey of photographic equipment, techniques, processes, and art. The book is an excellent guide for the beginner, as well as a ready-reference for the experienced professional. Curiously lacking in detailed description of color applications.

Isert, G. *The Art of Color Photography.* New York: Van Nostrand Reinhold Co., 1971. Currently out of print, but still available in some areas, this book covers a broad scope. Isert discusses color photography in all aspects. You'll probably find the book somewhat curiously arranged and a bit cutesy (attempts at humor in illustration are sometimes a bit overdone), but the content is solid stuff. Heavily illustrated, it can serve as an excellent introduction to color.

Mante, Harold. *Color Design in Photography.* New York: Van Nostrand Reinhold Co., 1972. Outstanding in both subject matter and manner of presentation. Mante explains and illustrates the use of color, contrasts, and the impact of color in photography. The best source available to learn about the use of color as an artistic tool. A "must" book.

Morgan, Douglas O., David Vestal, and William Broecker. 15th ed. Dobbs Ferry, NY: Morgan & Morgan, 1973. A complete book of 35 mm photography, covering both rangefinder and SLR cameras.

Nibbelink, Don. *Picturing People.* Rochester: Eastman Kodak Co., 1976. A solid base of information on formal and informal portraiture, lighting, posing, and effects. Heavily illustrated.

Purves, Frederick, ed. *The Focal Encyclopedia of Photography.* London: Focal Press, 1972. 2 volumes. Desk Edition (single volume, 1699 pages) published in the U.S. and Canada by The McGraw-Hill Book Co. The bible of photography. From simple to complex, every subject is explained clearly and concisely. An absolute must. If you own no other photo books, get these.

Q, Pat and Mike. *The Manual of Slide Duplicating.* Garden City, New York: Amphoto, 1978. The most up-to-date book on the subject. Information presented is based on years of professional experience. Black-and-white and color illustrations abound.

Rothschild, Norman. *Making Slides, Duplicates and Filmstrips.* 3rd ed. Garden City, NY: Amphoto, 1977. A thorough work on duplicating. Although a bit dated now, still a source of sound advice on a tricky process.

Snyder, Norman, ed. *The Photography Catalog.* New York: Harper & Row, 1976. This catalog is more than a mere compilation of facts and figures. It's an entertaining and informative book that debunks a lot of the myths of photography, such as the supposed difference in quality among major lens lines. Well worth reading.

Swedlund, Charles. *Photography.* New York: Van Nostrand Reinhold Co., 1974. A basic college text, well illustrated, but dry reading. Lots of technical explanations and illustrations for those so inclined. Very good section on darkroom work for beginners.

Magazines

Camera 35. This magazine is devoted to 35 mm photography, with heavy emphasis placed on the esthetic aspects. It is written for serious amateurs. Little advertising included. Gets a bit pretentious at times by indulging in artistic excess, but its valuable interviews with well-known personalities in the photo industry are interesting and illuminating. Not particularly oriented to technique or how-to-do-it. Equipment tests are not as elaborate as those of either *Popular Photography* or *Modern Photography,* but are more commonsensical and practical. Subscriptions are available at discounts.

Modern Photography. The greatest strength of this mass-audience monthly is its detailed testing of photo products, especially cameras and lenses. *Modern* contains a high percentage of advertisements, but not quite as high as that of *Popular Photography.* Does not print equipment reports on products that fail its tests. Places heavy emphasis on tests of color films. Editorial copy is somewhat limited, but monthly columns do contain a good deal of useful information. Little copy devoted to composition, esthetics, and the like. Subscriptions are available at considerable discounts.

Petersen's PhotoGraphic Magazine. The newest of the major photo periodicals, *PhotoGraphic* blends features of the three other publications listed here. Little emphasis placed on test reports of new equipment, but much on projects, how-to-do-it techniques, and creative darkroom work. Aimed at serious amateurs. Good color reproductions and little advertising. Back issues are of particular merit, for they contain a host of articles suggesting creative techniques to photographers. Petersen's actively solicits work and articles from amateurs. Subscriptions are now becoming available at discounts.

Popular Photography. This weighty monthly magazine is probably the best-read photo journal in the U.S. Its strong points are in-depth technical features on new equipment, films, and accessories. Color reproduction is outstanding. Nearly half of all copy in any typical issue is comprised of ads from major photoequipment mail-order firms or photo products distributors. Editorial copy and monthly columns are skimpy and somewhat variable in the utility of material presented; nevertheless, contributing editors are top-flight. All in all, worth reading; but don't expect how-to-do-it articles or much copy concerning itself with composition, theory, or esthetics. Subscriptions are available at substantial discounts.

Specialty Photo Publications

Recent years have seen a proliferation of specialized photo publications in soft covers selling for $2 to $6 or so. Some of these booklets are general in nature, others concentrate on one subject. Many are published by the major photo magazines. They may appear as quarterlies, semiannuals, annuals, or title releases at various times during the year. While most contain at least some useful information, many merely reprint articles that appeared in past issues of major magazines.

Notably among these publications has been a series of specialty guides published by the Petersen Publishing Company. Of particular merit are *Petersen's Basic Series* and *How-To PhotoGraphic Library,* covering such subjects as lighting, creative darkroom techniques, a how-to book, special in-camera effects, and so on.

Another publication that contains useful information is *35 mm Photography.*

A wealth of ideas about print display is contained in *Book X-6* (1973) by Royal Dossett. This thin (60-page) book is a goldmine of information on mounting and framing. If you want a copy, write to Mr. Dossett at 2793 Pheasant Ave., Excelsior, MN 55331. The cost will be around $3.

We suspect that softbound magazinelike speciality books will increase in number in the near future. How well they will serve the educational needs of photographers is yet to be seen.

Free or Inexpensive Photo Information That Has Proven Useful to Us

Edmund Scientific Company Catalog. 222 Edscorp Bldg., Dept. PG, Barrington, NJ 08007. This catalog is packed with all sorts of science-and-technology gadgets, surplus, and items of Edmund's own design. One section is devoted exclusively to photography. It's free for the asking.

Guide to Electronic Flash. Honeywell Photographic Products, 5501 S. Broadway, P.O. Box 1010, Littleton, CO 80120. While this free booklet mainly describes Honeywell flash systems, several pages are devoted to electronic flash theory and practice. Well worth reading.

Hasselblad Booklets. Braun North America, Cambridge Parkway, Cambridge, MA 02142. Hasselblad, makers of prestige 2¼″ × 2½″ cameras, has prepared a series of booklets on a variety of photo topics. Each booklet is handsomely printed and contains much good information. Of particular interest are the booklets covering child photography, nature, composition, and close-up and macro work.

Index to Kodak Information. Eastman Kodak Co., 343 State St., Rochester, NY 14650. Here are listed the hundreds of Kodak publications available, priced from 5¢ to $15 or so, from the well-known *Here's How* series to books on supertechnical data.

International Photographic Books Catalog. International Photographic Books, 393 Seventh Ave., New York, NY 10001. This catalog, which lists virtually every photo book in print, fills the gap left when Laurel Photographic Books closed. It is a handy reference index.

McDonald Photo Products, Inc., 1121 Gemini Lane, Dallas, TX 75201. Write for free catalog of things useful to print mounting and framing.

Picturing America—A Student's Guide to Traveling With a Camera. Minolta Corp., 101 Williams Drive, Ramsey, NJ 07406. This informative booklet describes the techniques that turn travel photography into a pleasure rather than a pain. The authors make film and equipment recommendations.

Porter's Catalog. Porter's Camera Store, Inc., P.O. Box 628, Cedar Falls, IA 50613. In approximately 110 pages of a newspaper format, this free catalog illustrates and describes virtually all the accessories currently on the market. Many items are unique to Porter's. Prices are reasonable—not the cheapest, not the most expensive—but Porter's service is first-rate and they've always been helpful.

Shutterbug Ads. P.O. Box 730, Titusville, FL 32780. Monthly, by subscription. The 40–50 pages of this newspaper format are crammed with every type of camera, lens, and accessory. It is fascinating reading even if you are not a collector. Since most advertisers are private parties who are collectors or swappers, the condition stated for most equipment is very likely accurate and the dollar value reliable. Some excellent buys can be had in used quality.

Spiratone Catalog. Spiratone, Inc., 135-06 Northern Blvd., Flushing, NY 11354. Spiratone markets a wide variety of lenses, accessories, and filters, as well as darkroom and general photoequipment. Their catalog is full of gadgets and is fun to look through, even if you don't intend to buy.

Vivitar Booklets. Vivitar, Inc. (formerly Ponder & Best), 1630 Stewart St., Santa Monica, CA 11377. Vivitar offers three booklets that should be of interest. Just write and ask for them.

How to Photograph Auto Racing is a well-written booklet, with some detailed information to make your auto racing pictures come alive.

How to Photograph Sports is an informative publication, written by pros, giving tips on photographing a number of sports.

How to Use Multiple Flash, by Peter Gowland, is a study of multiflash by a master.

In addition to the industry sources listed above, most monthly photo magazines list a page or so of photographic equipment companies who offer free or inexpensive information.

Glossary

Accent color—a secondary color of objects in a scene that highlights or goes well with the color of main subjects.

Acutance—a measure of image sharpness. In essence it is a measure of the sharpness of the edges or boundaries between different hues or intensities of gray contained in a print or negative.

Ambient light, also **available light**—existing light not supplemented by artificial means.

Angle of coverage, also **angle of view, angular field**—an angle expressed in degrees of the coverage of a specific lens across the film diagonal. Therefore, a wide-angle lens of 28 mm in 35 mm film size will cover approximately 74 percent across the diagonal. A so-called "normal" lens of 50 mm will cover 46 degrees across the diagonal.

ANSI. See **ASA.**

Aperture-priority metering—an automatic exposure system in which the user selects the aperture and the camera system selects the appropriate shutter speed. Usually shutter speeds are infinitely variable in this type of system, which is used in most automatic cameras. See also **Automatic camera.**

ASA—American Standards Association, the old name of the American National Standards Institute (ANSI). "ASA" followed by a number designates U.S. standard rating of the light sensitivity of films and photographic papers. See **DIN.**

Automatic camera—a camera whose functions are controlled either mechanically or electrically to a point where the camera performs most, and in some cases all of the functions of exposure control. Decisions on proper exposure are made by programs built into the camera system; the photographer merely focuses and presses the shutter. Some cameras called "automatic" are in reality semiautomatic, for the photographer must select either the *f*-stop or the shutter speed, while the camera selects the other function to achieve proper exposure. See also **Aperture-priority metering** and **Shutter-priority metering.**

Automatic diaphragm—a diaphragm, built into the lens, that remains wide open to focus and set the exposure meter. As the photographer presses down on the shutter release, a mechanical pin is depressed or an electrical contact is made to close the diaphragm opening to the preselected size (*f*-stop). As soon as the film has been exposed, the mechanical or electrical contact is disengaged and the diaphragm returned to the fully open position. In most cameras this all happens in a fraction of a second and is hardly noticeable to the human eye.

Available light. See **Ambient light.**

Barrel distortion—an aberration characterized by outward curvature of vertical lines near the edges of film or of a print.

Brightness range. See **Lighting ratio.**

Camera shake—the movement inherent in hand-holding a camera which can have an adverse effect on the photographs. Slower shutter speeds record more shake than high shutter speeds. A rule of thumb is to try to use a shutter speed equal to the reciprocal of the focal length of the lens in use. For example: 50 mm lens—1/60 sec. or faster; 135 mm lens—1/125 sec. or faster.

Cassette, also **cartridge**—a lighttight metal or plastic container for film. Film for 35 mm cameras generally comes in cassettes. Some cassettes are reusable, some are not. The term "cartridge" is mostly used for the drop-in film container used with instant-load cameras.

CdS (Cadmium Sulfide) light meter—a photoelectric device employed on many modern exposure-metering systems, either built-in or separate. Compact and sensitive to all but very low light levels, it has replaced earlier types of meters that used other power sources.

Chroma—the intensity of a specific color. It is also defined as the combination of saturation and hue.

Coatings of lenses—microscopically thin layers of chemical compounds affixed to the surfaces of modern lenses to increase the amount of light transmitted through the lens to the film. For example: An uncoated 100 mm *f*/2.8 lens might transmit 60 percent of the light striking it to the film, while a 100 mm *f*/2.8 coated lens might transmit nearly 90 percent to the film. Coatings come in single- or multiple-layer varieties (see *Multicoating*). Coatings impart magenta or amber color casts to the lens glass, but the apparent color in no way affects the color rendition in the picture.

Color balance—a term usually applied to color printing. It refers to the use of filters to achieve a natural or, in some cases, desired balance of hues in a print. In transparency films, the term refers to the slight differences in color rendition between one type or brand of color film and another, which are especially noticeable in projected slides.

Color cast—an overall bias toward one particular color in a picture. Taking photographs at certain times of the day induces color casts naturally: Late afternoon tends to produce yellowish or gold casts in pictures, while overcast days produce bluish tones. Strong reflections from colored surfaces can produce color casts in the picture, too. Slight differences in color rendition between one type of color film and another is very evident in projection slides.

Color harmony—pleasing balance of color in which various hues are not fighting with one another for dominance.

Color saturation—a term for describing purity of color. Colors that appear to be deep and rich are said to be "fully saturated." Emphasis on it is a subjective esthetic choice on the part of the viewer. Underexposing color transparency film slightly or overexposing color negative film will result in more saturation than would normally result if exposure were made at the meter setting. Some films tend to produce more apparent saturation than others because of their higher contrast levels.

Color separation—a method for printing color, usually employed by magazine or book publishers, whereby a color photograph is photographically separated into its primary (or secondary) colors, each of which is printed separately to make the reproduction. It is an expensive but very accurate process. A typical 20 × 25 cm (8″ × 10″) color separation might cost over $150.

Color temperature—a system by which the spectral quality (color) of light is measured. Each source of light has a specific color temperature, measured in degrees Kelvin. The usual range of color temperatures in photography is from 3200 K for studio flood lamps to 5000–6000 K for daylight or electronic flash approximating daylight. Since each color film is formulated to record color accurately only within specific ranges of color temperatures, it is essential that film and light source match. This can be done by either using the film specifically balanced for the light source (e.g., tungsten film for 3200–3700 K tungsten light sources) or by using appropriate color filters. See also **Kelvin.**

Compact camera—a term now in vogue to describe 35 mm SLRs that are appreciably smaller and lighter than previous models. The Olympus OM's, the Canon "A" line, the Nikon FM, the Minolta XD-11, the Pentax ME, and the Konica TC are a few of these new compact SLRs.

Complementary colors—two colors which when added together result in white light.

Composition—the organization of elements within a picture. See also **Mass balance.**

Contrast (film)—limitations in the ability of various films to render a full range of tones between black and white. High-contrast black-and-white film renders only the black and the white. High-contrast color film poses problems, for color cannot be reproduced accurately in high-contrast situations: Light areas tend to wash out toward white, and dark areas go black without much detail or color gradation.

Contrast (scene)—differences in tonal values, referred to as contrast in composition. "High contrast" refers to a scarcity of tones between light and shadow. See also **Lighting ratio.**

Cropping—a term usually associated with darkroom work. It describes the technique of selecting for printing only a portion of the picture projected on the enlarger easel. Composition can be improved by cropping extraneous details from a scene.

Daylight color film—either negative or transparency film balanced to reproduce colors accurately in daylight. Usually balanced for 5500–6000 K, daylight film will also work with electronic flash and blue flashbulbs.

Depth of field—the distance between the nearest objects and the farthest objects that a lens records with equal apparent sharpness. Depth of field is controlled by and varies with the aperture, the subject's distance, and the focal length of the lens.

Diaphragm—in adjustable cameras, a hole of variable size made by a set of metal blades in the form of an iris, mounted either between the glass elements inside a lens or behind the lens. Diaphragms are calibrated in numerical sequence (see *f*-stop) to admit precisely graduated amounts of light. Usually "stopping down" a lens—that is, making the hole smaller—or opening up the lens, is achieved by turning a ring on the lens barrel.

DIN—initials that stand for the West German standards organization, Deutsche Industrie Norm, which set up a measurement standard for film sensitivity. Its ratings are used in most European countries. ASA is the United States equivalent of DIN. See also **ASA.**

Double exposure—exposure of two pictures on the same film frame. Double or, for that matter, multiple exposures have become difficult to achieve in most cameras by mechanisms constructed to guard against more than one exposure being made. Currently, however, cameras with provisions for making intentional multiple exposures are being marketed.

Eighteen-percent (18%) reflectance—an approximate average of the reflectance of a typical daylight scene. Virtually all reflected-light exposure meters (all built-in camera meters) are calibrated to respond to all photographic scenes as if they reflected 18 percent of the light striking them. Photographers should adjust exposures if the scene is appreciably darker or lighter than an average daylight scene, since meters are "idiots" that can do only what they are programed to do.

Electronic flash. See **Strobe.**

Emulsion—a thin layer on film, usually of gelatin containing light-sensitive silver halide crystals. Color film has three individual emulsion layers, each sensitive to a different primary color. These three layers, when exposed by transmitted light, together make up a full-color-range picture or negative.

Ever-ready case—a leather or vinyl case covering only the camera and lens. Many consider it a bother and more trouble than it is worth.

Expose—to subject film to light.

Exposure—the combination of *f*-stop and shutter speed that will subject film to light in such a way as to produce an image. See also **Exposure latitude, Exposure meter.**

Exposure latitude—the range of exposures on either side of the "correct" *f*-stop/shutter-speed combination that will result in acceptable pictures. This range varies by film type. Deliberate exposures at other than the values indicated by an exposure meter can alter the impact of the final picture.

Exposure meter—a device used to determine the correct amount of light needed to produce a negative or transparency that contains the full range of tones and hues present in the original scene.

Extension tubes—tubes attached between the lens and the camera body to make possible closer focusing than would be possible with the lens alone. A drawback is that with an extension tube in place, a lens can only focus within a very narrow range, sometimes measured in inches, and cannot focus at infinity.

Film speed—a designation of a film's sensitivity to light, measured by the ASA and DIN scales (see **ASA, DIN).** Most commonly used color and black-and-white films range from ASA 25 to ASA 400 (DIN 15 to DIN 27). Note that doubling the ASA number increases sensitivity by 100 percent, or one *f*-stop.

Filter factor—a designation of how much light a given filter absorbs. For example: An 80B filter used to balance the color of a 3400 K light source (studio lights) when using daylight film has a filter factor of 4. This means that a correct exposure needs four times the amount of light—an increase of two *f*-stops—to make up for the filter's absorption of light. From our example, it is obvious that to find out how much to increase exposure when using filters, simply divide the filter factor by two. With almost all behind-the-lens meters, this is done automatically for you. See also **Neutral-density filter.**

Flare—a veiling or masking effect that reduces contrast and desaturates color. It is caused mostly by skewed rays of light entering the lens and bouncing off unblackened mechanical components. Lens coatings of various materials and good blackening of lens components minimize flare, as does the use of a lens hood (sunshade). See also **Lens shade.**

Focal length—the distance between the film plane and the optical center of a lens. Confusing to some is the fact that two lenses with identical *physical* length can be of vastly different *focal* lengths because of the construction and design of the particular lenses.

Focal-plane shutter—a mechanism comprised of either one or a pair of curtains which in traveling across the film's focal plane provides a variable slit through which light passes to the film just behind. It eliminates the need for shutters in each interchangeable lens. See also **Leaf shutter.**

Frame—(a) one individual section of film of a designated size: A 35 mm film's frames measure approximately 24 mm × 36 mm (1″ × 1½″); (b) in compositional terms, the process of selecting the elements one wishes to photograph in a camera's viewfinder (see *Cropping*); (c) the boxlike outer construction holding a backing board, a picture with or without mount and/or mat, and (optionally) glass, together with suitable hooks or support for hanging or other display.

***f*-Stop**—a setting on the lens diaphragm. The larger the *f*-stop, or *f*-number, the smaller the diaphragm opening; the smaller the number, the larger the opening. This is because *f*-stop numbers are really fractions arrived at by dividing the effective diameter of the lens into the focal length. Lenses are usually designated by their focal length and largest *f*-stop; therefore, a 50 mm *f*/1.4 lens is one with a focal length of 50 mm and a maximum *f*-stop of *f*/1.4.

Gaffer tape—very handy, strong, cloth-reinforced tape about two inches wide, used to tape lights, scenery, and other items. It is indispensable in the studio and on location.

Grain—suspended crystals of the silver halides that actually make possible the recording of an image on film. All films have grain, which appears as chunks of color or as dark spots. Some grain is more noticeable than other. Big enlargements make grain more noticeable; how noticeable is subjective.

Guide number—a number used to determine the *f*-stop to be used with a specific flash-unit/film combination. In addition, flash units are generally rated by a guide number against a specific film. To find the proper *f*-stop for electronic flash or flashbulb exposure, divide the flash-to-subject distance into the Guide Number (GN). For example: If your flash with ASA 25 film has a GN of 56, and flash-to-subject distance is 10 feet, then $\frac{56}{10} = f/5.6$. Be careful that the guide number you use is the correct one both for the film in the camera and for the flash you are using.

Guide rails—polished rails upon which the film travels in some camera types, such as 35 mm cameras. They are located above and below the shutter opening at the film plane. They should not be touched.

High-key—a type of lighting where most areas of a picture lack significant detail. The overall picture is lighter than an average exposure would be. Used extensively in fashion illustration, high-key lighting can convey a sense of lightness, delicacy, or happiness.

Highlights—the brightest parts of a picture. As a rule, in metering for exposure, slide film should be exposed to retain highlight detail.

Hue—a specific variation of a specific color. See also **Chroma, Shade,** and **Tint.**

Incident light—light falling directly on the subject. Some writers insist incident-light measurement is the only correct way to meter exposures. Many hand-held meters provide for incident-light measurement by pointing the meter toward the camera from the subject position. See also **Reflected light.**

Infrared film—film, either black-and-white or color, that is only sensitive to infrared and not to visible light. Strange and unpredictable results can occur when using these films. They have no ASA ratings.

Inverse-square law—the natural law, discovered by Johannes Keppler, that the intensity of light is inversely proportional to the square of the distance between the subject and the light source. Thus, by *doubling* the distance between the subject and the light, one reduces the light to a *quarter* of its effect. Four times the distance reduces the original illumination to $^1/_{16}$ its original intensity. See also the chapter on composition in *Photography: Composition, Color, Display.*

Kelvin—a means for measuring the quality of light with regard to its spectral (color) properties. Color temperature of light is measured by degrees on the scale named for W. T. Kelvin. See also **Color temperature.**

Latent image—the invisible image contained on exposed but undeveloped film. There is a high probability that latent images change if not developed promptly. This is especially true of color films.

Leaf shutter—a type of shutter found in many cameras, consisting of a series of blades that open or close in a manner similar to that of a lens diaphragm. Its advantage is that it can be synchronized for electronic flash at all shutter speeds; its disadvantage, that it is difficult to manufacture cameras with leaf shutters and interchangeable lenses. See also **Focal-plane shutter.**

Lens cleaning—an equipment-maintenance process that should be carried out gently and only when really needed, since lenses are coated with relatively soft chemical compounds. Never use abrasive materials or fluids. Contrary to some advice, silicon-impregnated cloth is not recommended for cleaning lens surfaces, as it can leave a residue on the glass surfaces that can damage them over a period of time.

Lens shade—a metal or rubber shade or hood attached to the front of a camera lens to keep light that is outside the picture area from entering the lens and thus causing flare, among other things. Caution: Each lens shade is designed to work only with a lens of a specific focal length; be sure the lens-shade/lens combination is compatible. This is critical when using wide-angle lenses. See also **Flare.**

Lighting ratio—a term referring to the ratio of light in the lightest portion of a scene to that in the darkest. If the lightest area is three *f*-stops brighter than the darkest, the lighting ratio would be 3:1. Most modern black-and-white films can handle a wider brightness range than color films; for instance, with a brightness range beyond 8:1 it would be very difficult for color films to render full detail at both ends of the range. See also **Contrast.**

Low-key—a scene in which dark tones are of central importance. Shadowed details are particularly important here, and exposure metering should include them. Low-key lighting is especially effective with masculine subjects or when a brooding or heavy effect is desired.

Macro—a term used in dealing with image magnification expressed in terms of reproduction ratios. Macro range is generally from about half life size to about ten times life size. Thus an object photographed at life size, or 1:1, will appear exactly its own size on the film. A 2.5-cm coin would take up 2.5 cm of the film. (Magnification greater than 10× calls for a microscope and the technique of *photomicrography.*) Special problems occur in making larger-than-life photographs. Of particular concern is flatness of field. Special macro lenses are designed for use with ordinary cameras to reproduce images at high magnification with flat field (no outward or inward curving near the edges). Normal photographic lenses, even those of the so-called close-focus variety, are not designed for critical work in the macro range. The second problem is depth of field or, more precisely, lack of depth of field—the sharp-focus zone is measured in millimetres. This argues against hand-held macro work, because the slightest camera or subject movement can be disastrous.

Mass balance—where a scene is viewed in terms of its basic physical elements and a number of masses become apparent. Good composition dictates that, unless you have a specific reason to ignore it, the most pleasing composition can be achieved by a balancing of masses. A large unimportant mass can distract from the picture's main theme; so some way should be found to subdue its effect. It can be said that mass balance is the composition of a scene so that physical masses work in harmony and reinforce the theme of the picture. See also **Composition.**

M-synchronization—an electrical circuit built into most cameras that allows for a very short delay in time between opening of the shutter and firing of an M-class flashbulb. Since such bulbs burn, it takes a few milliseconds for them to reach maximum intensity, and therefore the delay is built into the system that uses them. Be sure to use proper synchronization if your camera has a selector switch. See also **X-synchronization.**

Multicoating—a process through which multiple layers of chemical compounds are applied in microscopically thin layers to one or more surfaces of a lens. Aimed at increasing light transmission and reducing flare, the process thus improves overall optical performance of lenses.

Negative—an image on film (or paper) in which the tones are reversed and from which a positive image can be printed; also, the film bearing such an image. Negatives can be either black-and-white or color. Any color film whose name ends in the word "color" is a negative film—Fujicolor, Kodacolor, Agfacolor, etc.

Neutral-density filter—a filter that uniformly reduces the amount of light entering a lens, without affecting its quality. For example, using fast film at the beach might demand the use of a neutral-density filter to counteract overexposure. N/D filters, as they are known, are calibrated in series—such as N/D 2 or N/D 4—to indicate how much light they will absorb. See also **Filter factor.**

Normal lens—a lens that "sees" approximately what the eye sees. For 35 mm cameras, lenses between 50 mm and 58 mm are "normal" lenses. For 2¼″ × 2¼″ cameras, lenses in the range of 75–80 mm focal length constitute normal lenses.

Optical distortion—a range of defects in either design or construction of a lens that distorts or degrades the image produced. To some extent, all lenses have degrees of optical distortion, but the better ones are corrected to a point where distortion is eliminated as a practical concern to the photographer.

Overexposure—a condition in which too much light strikes the film. Resulting effects on negatives and slides are opposites: Overexposure in color slides will result in too-light, washed-out-appearing transparencies and loss of detail; in both black-and-white and color negatives, density build-up in shadows can present problems in printing and, if grossly overexposed, prevent printing. See also **Underexposure.**

Panning—a technique whereby the photographer follows along with a moving subject with his camera, in order to arrest motion.

Photomicrography—the technique of using a microscope for making large images of extremely small things. See also **Macro.**

Pincushion distortion—a distortion, apparent at the edges of a picture or negative, in which there is a noticeable concave appearance to vertical lines. This type of distortion plagued early zoom lenses.

Positive—a transparency or print that in effect is an actual picture with correctly distributed tonal values: Dark objects are dark; light ones, light.

Posterization—a technique used with either black-and-white or color materials, whereby a high-contrast negative is made for each main density and/or color an an image and then used singly or together in a composite to produce a final abstract print.

Primary colors—three portions of the spectrum, each representing a third of the visible spectrum, that produce white when combined. The primary colors of light are red, green, and blue. All other colors can be mixed from these.

Rangefinder—a device built into most quality cameras to measure distance from film plane to subject.

Reciprocity failure—loss of accuracy in a film's color rendition. Under normal conditions, photographic film acts in accordance with established tolerances. However, when exposed to very low light levels and, to a lesser extent, to extremely high levels not encountered in everyday picture-taking, film reacts differently. Then film must be exposed for a longer time than a meter indicates because the film is less sensitive to these extremely high and low light levels and the meter does not take this into account. For most films, 1/1000 sec. to 1 sec. presents no problem. Beyond these ranges, up to four *f*-stops more exposure is needed. Consult the film's data sheet for specific instructions.

Reflectance. See **Eighteen percent reflectance.**

Reflected light—light reflected from a photographic subject. Most exposure-metering systems read reflected light. See also **Incident light.**

Reflector—any surface that reflects light. Reflectors can be constructed of cardboard, metal, cloth, or other materials. They can add light to a scene and can increase the amount of light reaching the subject from the principal light source. A good use of simple reflectors is to distribute a bit of the light into the shadow side of an object.

Reflex camera—any camera designed to permit viewing through the lens.

Resolution—a term used to describe the image-forming qualities (resolving power) of a photographic lens. Also termed "sharpness," it is measured in lines per millimetre.

Reversal film, also **transparency film** or **slide film**—film, usually color, that turns into a positive finished picture after processing.

Sensitivity—a measure of any film's ability to record images, given a specific exposure to light.

Shade—a painter's term for the color gradation visible when a pure color alters as it becomes darker (black added). See also **Tint.**

Shutter-priority metering—the system in automatic cameras whereby the user chooses the shutter speed and the camera adjusts to the appropriate lens opening. See also **Automatic camera.**

Side lighting—placement of the main lighting directly to the side of the subject. This produces strong illumination of half the subject and little, if any, of the other half.

Silver halide—a chemical compound that is light-sensitive and effects the production of a latent image on film.

Spectrum—the total range of electromagnetic energy. Only a portion is visible to the human eye; this "visible spectrum" is the range of colors from red to blue that is seen when white light is dispersed into a rainbow by the atmosphere or by a prism.

Strobe, also **electronic flash**—an electronic device that produces a high-intensity, short-duration light of a controlled nature for photographic illumination. See also the chapter on accessories in *Photography: Buying, Choosing, Using.*

Teleconverter—a device fitted between camera body and lens to increase the focal length of the lens. Teleconverters come in 2× and 3× varieties.

Thyristor—an electronic circuit designed to conserve energy in electronic flash units. It permits very fast recycling times—as little as one third of a second.

Tint—a painter's term for a color gradation resulting when a pure color is lightened or desaturated (white added) and the color changes. See also **Shade.**

T-stop—a measure at the film plane of the value of the light actually transmitted through the lens to the film. This can differ greatly from the maximum marked *f*-stop on a given lens.

Underexposure—accidental or deliberate lessening of the light reaching the film. With transparency film, slight underexposure results in more color saturation and higher contrast, an effect preferred by many photographers. Underexposure has the opposite effect on negative film; that is, the negative is lightened and details are washed out, allowing more light to pass through during printing. Resulting prints—whether color or black-and-white—look dark and do not show detail. See also **Overexposure.**

UV filter—one of the most common filters, used both to lessen the effect of ultraviolet rays on color rendition outdoors and to cut through atmospheric haze. Many photographers use it as permanent protection for the lens, since it neither affects exposure metering nor alters hues.

Washed-out color—color that has a bleached or pale (desaturated) look.

X-synchronization—an electrical circuit that permits use of electronic flash. The circuit is designed to fire the flash at the exact instant the shutter opens. See also **M-synchronization.**

Zoom—the technique of changing from one focal length to another to frame or compose a picture properly in the camera's viewfinder; also the short term for "zoom lens." See also the chapter on equipment in *Photography: Buying, Choosing, Using.*

Index